The
Breast Cancer
Prevention
Cookbook

ALSO BY HOPE RICCIOTTI, M.D., AND VINCENT CONNELLY

The Pregnancy Cookbook
The Menopause Cookbook

The
Breast Cancer
Prevention
Cookbook

Hope Ricciotti, M.D.
and
Vincent Connelly

W. W. NORTON & COMPANY
NEW YORK   LONDON

For information about permission to reproduce selections from this book,
write to Permissions, W. W. Norton & Company, Inc., 500 Fifth Avenue,
New York, NY 10110

The text of this book is composed in Berling with the display set in GillSans
with Minion Ornaments and Delectables
Composition by Adrian Kitzinger
Manufacturing by The Maple-Vail Book Manufacturing Group
Book design by Mary A. Wirth
Production manager: Amanda Morrison

LIBRARY OF CONGRESS CATALOGING-IN-PUBLICATION DATA
Ricciotti, Hope.
The breast cancer prevention cookbook / Hope Ricciotti and
Vincent Connelly.
p. cm.
Includes bibliographical references and index.
ISBN 0-393-32153-3 (pbk.)
1. Breast—Cancer Diet therapy—Recipes. 2. Breast—Cancer—
Prevention. I. Connelly, Vincent. II. Title.

RC280.B8 R525 2002
616.99'4490654—dc2   2002069225

W. W. Norton & Company, Inc., 500 Fifth Avenue, New York, N.Y. 10110
www.wwnorton.com

W. W. Norton & Company Ltd., Castle House, 75/76 Wells Street,
London W1T 3QT

1 2 3 4 5 6 7 8 9 0

C O N T E N T S

Many of us live in fear of developing breast cancer. It is constantly in the news and frequently the topic of casual conversations. It is all the more fearsome, because it often seems to strike without warning and appears to be fairly non-selective in its subjects. Breast cancer is the most common cancer diagnosed in women. It accounts for an estimated 16 percent of all cancer deaths and remains the second leading cause of death due to cancer after lung cancer among women. For women ages 20 to 59, breast cancer is the leading cause of cancer mortality.

But you can take some preventive measures that could save your life. These same preventive measures can also protect you from other cancers as well as heart disease, the number one killer of women. There are lifestyle and dietary changes that you can make to minimize your risk and wrest back some level of control against the development of breast cancer.

In addition, you can educate yourself about screening and early detection methods for breast cancer. Finding breast cancer early can make the difference between being cured quickly and easily, and a long and arduous course of therapy. Having taught women preventive health methods for many years, I have seen what a difference it makes when women are knowledgeable about their bodies and the health care system. It can be confusing and frightening, but educating yourself on these preventive measures, as well as being certain to take advantage of all of the screening and early detection procedures available to you, are your best defenses. Being educated about your body makes you an equal partner with your health care provider. Your partnership is the best way to stay healthy and to navigate the health care system to obtain the optimum results.

Breast Cancer,
Health,
and
Nutrition

CHAPTER 1

Assessing Breast Cancer Risk

It is important to understand your own personal risk for breast cancer. However, I want you to read this chapter with the clear understanding that every woman is at risk for developing breast cancer. Simply being female is your greatest risk. Some women are just at higher risk than others. This information can be helpful to you and your health care provider, in that it may motivate you to be vigilant about your diet and lifestyle, and promote good habits in utilizing what the health care system has to offer in screening and early detection of breast cancer. All women, regardless of family history of breast cancer, should take preventive measures.

Assessing breast cancer risk. In counseling and in helping women to make medical decisions, I always try to accurately assess breast cancer risk. For any woman, the average lifetime risk of breast cancer is approximately 12 percent, which translates into one in eight women over a lifetime.

Factors that have been consistently associated with an increased risk of developing breast cancer include age, age at menarche (the age at which you get your first period), age at menopause, whether you have had a child and your age at first birth of a child, and family history of breast cancer. In addition, benign breast diseases (particularly those with hyperplasia and atypical hyperplasia on pathology) and the use of hormone replacement therapy have been associated with increased risk. Despite the recognition of these risk factors, approximately 50 percent of women who develop breast cancer have no identifiable risk factors beyond being female and aging.

Age. Age is a major risk factor for breast cancer. More than 80 percent of breast cancer cases occur in women over 50, and there is a one in eight chance of having breast cancer if a woman lives to 85. The one in eight risk of getting breast cancer gets a great deal of press and causes a great deal of fear. Some of this fear, though, may be overblown. Many perceive there is an uncontrolled epidemic of breast cancer, with some women assuming that one of every eight women will be diagnosed with breast cancer every year. This is not true. The one in eight figure is a lifetime risk. But for any given age, the risk is much smaller than this. For example, by age 30 one woman in 2,525 gets breast cancer. By age 60, one woman in 24 gets breast cancer.

CHANCES OF A WOMAN GETTING BREAST CANCER AS SHE AGES

Age	Incidence of breast cancer
30	1 in 2,525
40	1 in 217
50	1 in 50
60	1 in 24
70	1 in 14
80	1 in 10

Here are the facts:
- at age 40 your odds are one in 217
- at 50 they are one in 50
- in women younger than 30 breast cancer is very rare, accounting for only 1.5 percent of all breast cancer cases.

The incidence of breast cancer in the United States appears to have a bimodal distribution (two humps in the distribution curve). The incidence increases rapidly until age 45, then levels off as women approach menopause. It then increases again at a slower rate. Some researchers have postulated that breast cancer may in fact be two separate diseases: a premenopausal disease influenced by genetic, hormonal, and reproductive factors; and a postmenopausal disease influenced heavily by diet, body habitus, and hormonal factors.

Ethnicity. Native Americans and Asians have lower rates of breast cancer than whites, Hispanics, and African Americans. The mortality rate in African Americans is twice that of whites; the reasons for this appear to be both biologic and economic. African-American women tend to have larger, more aggressive cancers, and they are also less likely to be screened or have access to effective treatments. In Asian countries, the age-specific incidence shows the same bimodal distribution (two humps) as in the United States. The main difference is that postmenopausal breast cancer is far less common in Asian countries than in Western countries. Many have suggested that the Asian diet, rich in phytoestrogens, fruits, and vegetables and lower in fat, provides protection from breast cancer in this population.

Breast cancer rates vary widely, as much as tenfold among populations. The higher rates are in Western countries and the lowest in Asian countries. When a low-risk population migrates to an area of high risk, the low-risk population gradually assumes the higher breast cancer incidence. These facts point to the critical importance of lifestyle factors as a major cause of breast cancer. Such factors include diet, body habitus, hormonal and reproductive history, and family history. In Asian countries where fat makes up less than 20 percent of calories, breast cancer incidence rates are much lower than in Western countries, where fat represents over 40 percent of calories. When citizens of low breast cancer incidence countries move to Western countries, they slowly assume a Western rate of breast cancer as their diet modifies.

Estrogen and breast cancer. Many of the risk factors for breast cancer make sense if you understand the effects of estrogen on your breasts. Because breast tissue is highly sensitive to estrogen, the longer a woman is exposed to estrogen over her lifetime, the higher the risk for breast cancer. Therefore, anything in your life that disrupts the production of estrogen is likely to decrease breast cancer risk, and anything that enhances or maximizes your body's exposure to estrogen is likely to increase breast cancer risk.

Let's look at some of these situations. Women who start their periods early (before age 12) or go through menopause late (after age 55) are at higher risk. This is because your period marks a cycle in which you have ovulated. When you ovulate, the ovary produces estrogen. The more times you ovulate in your life, the more total estrogen to which your breasts are exposed. Thus, having your period early or having menopause occur late means that you have had more ovulations, and therefore more estrogen than average. By the same token, those who never had children, and therefore never had their menstrual cycle interrupted for the nine months of pregnancy, are at higher risk. It also appears that the protective effect is more important when we are younger, since women who have their children after the age of 30 are at higher risk for breast cancer than those who have them before 30.

Pregnancy plays an odd dual role in breast cancer. It appears to increase the risk for up to 15 years following the first birth, particularly in older women. Over the long term, however, most women who have given birth to at least one child have a lower risk than those who have not given birth. Subsequent births do not seem to have any additional impact on risk. Studies have detected an increased risk for breast cancer in women who have had abortions, possibly because high estrogen levels occur in the first trimester when abortions are most often performed (estrogen levels tend not to be high when a natural miscarriage occurs). The increased risk from abortion is most likely to be very small, however.

A small increased risk for breast cancer may be associated with use of oral contraceptives and may last for about 10 years after stopping the pill. This is debatable, however, with many studies not finding this association.

Several studies have reported that breast feeding is associated with a lower risk for cancer in premenopausal women and there is some suggestion that some of the protective effect from breast feeding may last beyond menopause. Studies also indicate that the longer the mother breast feeds, the better. There is, however, still some controversy about whether breast feeding lowers risk.

Postmenopausal hormone replacement therapy for the alleviation of menopausal symptoms and prevention of osteoporosis may increase the risk of developing breast cancer. Several recent studies have shown the risk of developing breast cancer to be 1.5 and 2 times increased in women who have used hormones for greater than 5 to 10 years. The Women's Health Initiative, the largest and only trial that directly compared HRT to placebo, found a slight increased risk after as little as one year. Combined estrogen and progestin treatments confer the highest risk.[1]

Genetic susceptibility. A key factor in assessing risk is genetic susceptibility. Approximately 10 percent of women with breast cancer have a strong family history of the disease, which often appears in young women under the age of 50. In such families, some members may also have developed ovarian cancer as well. It is now known that in 30 to 50 percent of these families, inherited mutations in either the BRCA1 or BRCA2 genes are responsible for the increased risk of developing breast cancer, ovarian cancer, or both. Over 80 distinct mutations in BRCA1 have been characterized in high-risk families. Ashkenazi Jews have a high rate of a specific mutation in BRCA1. If you are concerned about cancer within your family, these are the risk factors for a genetic predisposition: 1. cancer before the age of 55, 2. ovarian cancer or both breast and ovarian cancer in a single family member, and 3. Ashkenazi Jewish ancestry.[2] Only about 0.1 percent of the population carries these abnormal genes, but about 2 percent of all Jewish women of Eastern European descent carry them, making these mutations the most common serious genetic disease in any population group. They account, however, for only 7 percent of breast cancer cases in this population and far fewer in the general population.

If these risk factors exist in your family, you should take measures to protect yourself. Make the lifestyle and dietary changes in this book. And be sure to avail yourself of all of the screening and early detection procedures available. You can fight back.

Assessing your breast cancer risk through genetic testing for these cancer genes requires careful consideration of the pros and cons of testing. You need to be prepared to deal with all the medical, psychological, and social consequences of either a positive, negative, or ambiguous result. The potential risks of genetic testing are primarily psychological, but there is also the potential for genetic discrimination against those testing positive for genetic mutations. If you decide to have genetic testing done to determine if you are a carrier of one of the genes that increases your risk, you should not despair if you turn out to carry one of the high risk genes. Carrying one of the breast cancer gene mutations does not mean that you will definitely develop breast cancer in your lifetime. Estimates of the risk of breast cancer among carriers of BRCA1 or BRCA2 mutations range from 56 to 87 percent.[3] The implications of having the mutated gene but with the absence of a strong family history of the disease are also uncertain. If you do test positive, you will then have the opportunity to decide if prophylactic surgery or preventive medication trials are right for you. This can be a very difficult decision.

BRCA1 and BRCA2 mutations confer similar levels of breast cancer risk. BRCA1 mutations are associated with early-onset breast cancer as well as an increased susceptibility to ovarian cancer. BRCA2 mutations have been shown to contribute to fewer cases of breast cancer among young women than do BRCA1 mutations and do not appear to increase ovarian cancer risk, but do increase men's risk of developing breast cancer.[4]

Studies have also evaluated the opposite phenomenon: What percentage of women who develop breast cancer actually carry one of the breast cancer gene mutations? Studies evaluating the percentage of women with breast cancer who carry the BRCA1 mutation have had varying results. In women who are from families with multiple members with breast and/or ovarian cancer, genetic-linkage studies have suggested that the BRCA1 mutation accounts for approximately half of hereditary cases of breast cancer and about 90 percent of cases of combined breast and ovarian cancer.[5] However, a more recent study evaluating the percentage of BRCA1 mutations among patients with a familial risk factor for cancer found that only 16 percent had detectable BRCA1 mutations.[6] Among women with early onset breast cancer who were not selected because of family history or ethnic origin, the frequency of BRCA1 mutation is 10 percent.[7] Among Ashkenazi Jewish women with early onset breast cancer it is approximately 20 percent.[8]

Benign breast disease. Women who have undergone breast biopsies with results showing proliferative changes—changes in which the cells are benign, but there is a pattern of overgrowth seen under the microscope by the pathologist—have an increased risk of getting breast cancer at a later date. Changes such as ductal or lobular hyperplasia give a woman a 1.5 to 2 times increased risk of ultimately getting breast cancer. Biopsies which show atypical hyperplasia means that in addition to overgrowth, the cells also look slightly abnormal, but not abnormal enough to be called cancer. Not all atypical cells in the body go on to become cancerous. Biopsies which show atypical ductal hyperplasia or atypical lobular hyperplasia incur a three to five times increased risk of getting breast cancer at a later date.

All women should fight back. The message is that all women are at risk and everyone can benefit from preventive measures. A family history of breast cancer puts a woman at risk for the disease, even if these genetic mutations are not detected. If you do not carry the breast cancer gene mutation, you can still develop breast cancer. If you do carry the gene mutation, you can still lower your risk of getting breast cancer. By using preventive methods, you can give yourself a better chance. And these same defensive measures will prevent other cancers and heart disease, while maintaining your general health, longevity, and well-being. What could be better?

NOTES

1. R. K. Ross, A. Paganini-Hill, P. C. Wan, et al. "Effect of hormone replacement therapy on breast cancer risk: estrogen versus estrogen plus progestin." *Journal of the National Cancer Institute* 92:328–32;2000.

2. F. J. Couch, M. L. DeShano, M. A. Blackwood, et al. "BRCA1 mutations in women attending clinics that evaluate the risk of breast cancer." *New England Journal of Medicine* 336:1409–15;1997.

3. D. Ford, D. F. Easton, J. Peto. "Estimates of the gene frequency of BRCA1 and its contribution to breast and ovarian cancer incidence." *American Journal of Human Genetics* 57:1457–62;1995.

4. M. Krainer, S. Silva-Arrieta, M. G. FitzGerald, et al. "Differential contributions of BRCA1 and BRCA2 to early onset breast cancer." *New England Journal of Medicine* 336:1416–21;1997.

5. D. F. Easton, D. T. Bishop, D. Ford, et al. "Genetic linkage analysis in familial breast and ovarian cancer: results from 214 families. The Breast Cancer Linkage Consortium." *American Journal of Human Genetics* 52:678–701;1993.

6. F. J. Couch, M. L. DeShano, M. A. Blackwood, et al. "BRCA1 mutations in women attending clinics that evaluate the risk of breast cancer." *New England Journal of Medicine* 336:1409–15;1997.

7. A. A. Langston, K. E. Malone, J. D. Thompson, et al. "BRCA1 mutations in a population-based sample of young women with breast cancer." *New England Journal of Medicine* 334:137–42;1996.

8. M. G. Fitzgerald, D. J. MacDonald, M. Krainer, et al. "Germ-line BRCA1 mutations in Jewish and non-Jewish women with early onset breast cancer." *New England Journal of Medicine* 334:143–49;1996.

CHAPTER 2

Nutrition and the Prevention of Breast Cancer

Medical ideas of what constitutes a healthy diet are constantly changing and evolving. In the early nineteenth century, nutrition scientists focused on preventing nutrient deficiencies. Diets were developed that provided the recommended intake levels of known essential nutrients and energy. With increasing recognition of the role of diet in preventing chronic diseases, new dietary recommendations and guidelines have been created. Recent U.S. dietary guidelines reflect current beliefs about how nutrients, such as excess fat, or foods, such as fruits and vegetables, relate to our health.[1]

The link between diet and breast cancer remains controversial. Studies have been conflicting, but some of the newer and well-done studies are helping to give us more understanding of the situation. And new and exciting research is ongoing. I'd like to review the findings in order to clarify things for you.

Fat. One of the most extensively studied dietary risk factors for developing breast cancer is fat. In Asian countries, where fat makes up less than 20 percent of calories, breast cancer incidence rates are low. In Western countries, where fat represents over 40 percent of calories, breast cancer incidence rates are much higher. When Asians move to Western countries, their incidence of breast cancer increases as their diet becomes more Westernized. This has led us to believe that the level of fat in the diet may be one of the risk factors for developing breast cancer.

Findings from animal research suggested that saturated fat in the diet might play a role in the development of breast cancer. But studies in humans are conflicting. While earlier studies found this association, more recent and well-controlled studies have not confirmed it. Recent studies show no evidence of an association of saturated fat intake with an increased risk of developing breast cancer. Several major research studies have shown no definitive association with the intake of saturated fat in the diet and the incidence of breast cancer.[2] In addition, there has been no indication that keeping calories from fat to 30 percent or less of your total intake reduces the incidence of breast cancer, as has been suggested in the past.[3] In reviewing the data on thousands of women from six major research studies on women's health (California Seventh-Day Adventists Study; Nurses' Health Study; Canadian Breast Cancer Screening Study; Iowa Women's Studies, New York State Cohort; Dutch Cohort), there was no association with intake of saturated fat and the incidence of breast cancer. When comparing pre- and postmenopausal women, there was no stronger association with older women and fat intake and breast cancer. Finally, there was no indication that keeping calories from fat to 30 percent or less of total calories reduces the incidence of breast cancer, as has been suggested in the past.[4]

There is some question about the reliability of the survey methods used to quantify dietary fat in these studies. The studies rely on women being able to recall their intake, and the amount and type of fat in their diet. This may not adequately represent the real amount or type of fat in the diet. The women surveyed may be more likely to remember obvious sources of saturated fat, such as meats and dairy products, but less likely to remember less visible sources of polyunsaturated fats, such as baked products and snack foods. If unsaturated fat is a contributing factor to cancer risk, this relationship may be harder to document because of this recall problem. There is also some evidence that dietary fat consumption early in life, such as during adolescence, exerts a major influence on breast cancer. Therefore analysis of diets in adult women may not reflect this potentially important time of exposure of the breast to dietary fat. The most likely situation is that both childhood and early adult diets affect the later risk of breast cancer. The type and amount of fat consumed in childhood, adolescence, and early adulthood may be critically important.

Saturated fat in the diet has been consistently, in numerous studies, associated with the risk of developing colorectal cancer. Dietary fat is an important factor associated with many other cancers: prostate, endometrium, and ovary. Dietary fat, particularly saturated fat in the diet, is closely associated with the development of heart disease. Since heart disease is the number one killer of women, it makes sense to decrease your total fat intake, and make the majority of the fat you consume the unsaturated or monounsaturated type (such as olive oil).

There is evidence that caloric restriction in general, rather than a low-fat diet, decreases the risk of breast cancer. Related to this is the fact that physical activity appears to have a protective effect against breast cancer. Caloric restriction may explain why women who exercise have a lower risk of breast cancer, since exercise burns calories.

Obesity and breast cancer risk. There is not a simple relationship between obesity and breast cancer risk. It appears that being obese when you are premenopausal confers a different risk for developing breast cancer than being obese when you are postmenopausal. Premenopausally, high amounts of body fat are associated with decreased breast cancer risk. Postmenopausally, high amounts of body fat are associated with increased breast cancer risk. This is consistent with the notion that exposure of the breast to higher amounts of estrogen and progesterone increase breast cancer risk. Prior to menopause, obesity is associated with an increased frequency of anovulation (menstrual cycles in which an egg is not released) and therefore less production of estrogen and progesterone. After menopause, when ovulation is no longer occurring, the major source of estrogen in the body is now fatty (adipose) tissue. Therefore, postmenopausally, the amount of estrogen produced is directly correlated with body fat. Obesity is therefore associated with decreased breast cancer risk prior to menopause, but increased risk after menopause. Regular exercise may decrease reproductive hormone exposure and breast cancer risk by reducing ovulatory function in the premenopausal period (those who exercise vigorously often ovulate less frequently), and decreasing body fat in the postmenopausal period.

Maintaining a healthy weight. Maintaining a healthy weight is one of the most important ways to prevent disease and maintain well-being. As we age, weight control becomes more difficult, since your metabolism begins to slow. I have no magic prescription for weight maintenance or weight loss. But following the basic guidelines of the Food Guide Pyramid, and keeping the fat content of your diet low are the correct beginnings. Next, the amount of calories you need to consume daily to maintain (or lose) weight depends upon your level of activity. The more active you are, the more you can eat. In my experience, the one factor that assures success in any weight maintenance or weight loss program is regular exercise. The best way to keep your weight under control for a lifetime is maintaining a healthy style of eating every day, not going on fad diets to lose quick weight. Eating from the recipes in this book, which are all relatively low in fat and calories, is a good start.

Olive oil. There is some evidence in the medical literature about the protective effect of olive oil, which is monounsaturated, in reducing risk of breast cancer. Studies of breast cancer in several Mediterranean populations have demonstrated that increased dietary intake of olive oil is associated with a small decreased risk, or no increased risk, of breast cancer, despite a high overall total fat intake from olive oil and other foods combined.[5]

Omega-3 fatty acids. Omega-3 fatty acids are a type of fat found in some fatty fish—salmon, tuna, swordfish, mackerel, anchovies, bluefish, and striped bass. The only significant vegetarian source of omega-3 fatty acids is from flaxseed. There is some evidence that omega-3 fatty acids may decrease breast cancer cell growth. Studies in mice as well as human breast cancer cells in the laboratory have demonstrated a protective effect. In addition, a large human population study showed a significant decrease in deaths from breast cancer as consumption of fish and fish-oil consumption increases.[6] Researchers have proposed that omega-3 fatty acids affect prostaglandins, which in turn modulate the immune response, blood supply, and cell membrane integrity in decreasing breast cancer cell growth.

Omega-3 fatty acids have also been proven to decrease heart disease through their effect as natural blood thinners. Thus, it is a good idea for multiple reasons to increase your intake of these fatty fish, and to learn to cook and bake with flaxseed as a new ingredient in your diet.

The FDA has warned that certain fish in the diet need to be limited due to elevated mercury levels in some species. Nearly all fish contain trace amounts of mercury, but the large predator fish at the top of the food chain have the highest levels. These fish are safe, provided they are eaten infrequently. Limit swordfish, fresh tuna steaks, sushi containing tuna, and King mackerel to no more than once a week. By eating a variety of fish, you can safely enjoy eating them as part of a healthful diet.

Antioxidants. Found in many fruits and vegetables, antioxidants have been shown to have a protective effect against the development of many cancers, including breast cancer.[7] Antioxidants are chemicals that keep other substances from being oxidized. For example, when an apple is left out and turns brown, it is being oxidized. Vitamin C is a natural antioxidant that is used in cooking to prevent changes due to oxidation, such as foods turning brown or rancid. When we sprinkle a cut apple with lemon or lime juice (which contains Vitamin C) to keep it from turning brown, we're preventing oxidation. In the human body, antioxidants have been shown to prevent cells from turning cancerous. Recent medical science supports the finding that antioxidants in the diet may prevent many types of cancer as well as heart disease due to atherosclerosis. Several studies have found that among individuals who have developed breast cancer, those with the lowest risk for death are those with the highest intake of the antioxidants betacarotene and Vitamin C in their diet.[8]

Scientific research has shown that antioxidant vitamins have their greatest protective effect when they are eaten as part of the diet, not as vitamin supplements. Several studies have shown little or no cancer protection effect when they are taken only as vitamin supplements. There is some data that those at high risk for cancer, such as smokers, may benefit from a Vitamin E supplement, which can be difficult to obtain in the diet in sufficient amounts. However, a large study of Vitamin A in the prevention of lung cancer in Finland actually showed an increase in cancer rates in heavy smokers who took large doses of Vitamin A. Taking a multivitamin, folic acid, or some extra Vitamin C is likely not dangerous and may confer some anti-cancer benefit. The beneficial effect of vegetables, fruits, and whole grains may be due to the combined effects of their constituents, including fiber, micronutrients, and phytochemicals. Since antioxidants probably work in conjunction with these elements in fruits, vegetables, or whole grains, it is best to consume the whole fruit and vegetable.

The major antioxidants in the diet which protect against the development of breast cancer are beta-carotene, Vitamin A, Vitamin C, and Vitamin E. The National Research Council currently recommends the consumption of five servings of fresh fruit and vegetables daily. Only 10 percent of the U.S. population actually consumes this amount. Almost any fruit or vegetable will contain antioxidants, and the more variety in your intake of fruits and vegetables, the greater the health benefits. Fruits and vegetables offer many similar nutrients, but vegetables contain a wider assortment of vitamins and minerals than do fruits.

Recent studies ranked blueberries number one in antioxidant activity compared with 40 other fruits and vegetables. Scientists attribute the health benefits of blueberries to anthocyanins (from two Greek words meaning "plant" and "blue") and other phytochemicals (plant-based chemicals) found in blueberries. Anthocyanins are responsible for the intense blue and red pigments of blueberries.[9]

A SERVING OF FRUIT OR VEGETABLES INCLUDES:

1 medium fruit, such as an apple, banana, or orange

½ cup cut-up fruit, such as fruit salad

¼ cup dried fruit, such as raisins, apricots, dates, or prunes

6 ounces fruit or vegetable juice, such as orange or tomato

½ cup raw or cooked vegetables, such as eggplant, broccoli, or carrots

1 cup raw leafy vegetables, such as romaine lettuce or Swiss chard

---

Beta-carotene. Among the 600 or more carotenoids in foods, beta-carotene, lycopene, and lutein are the leaders in reducing the damage to cells in your body from free radicals. Foods high in beta-carotene are generally yellow or orange in color: cantaloupe, carrots, tomatoes, sweet potatoes, and winter squash. Broccoli is also a rich source of beta-carotene. Lycopene, found in high quantities in tomatoes, is one of the most powerful antioxidants. It appears to protect against many cancers, including cancer of the breast, mouth, pharynx, esophagus, stomach, colon, rectum, prostate, and cervix. Lutein is found in broccoli, brussels sprouts, grapefruit, kale, spinach, and watermelon.

Vitamin E. Vitamin E protects the body from cell damage that can lead to cancer, heart disease, and cataracts. Vitamin E works together with other antioxidants, such as Vitamin C, in protecting from many chronic diseases. Vitamin E is found in vegetable oils, wheat germ, whole-grain products, seeds, nuts, and peanut butter. If you are trying to maintain a very low-fat diet, you should be cautious about increasing some of these foods. Speak to your health care provider to see if a Vitamin E supplement may be appropriate for you.

Vitamin C. The most famous antioxidant is Vitamin C, and its touted benefits are well known. Current research has shown that Vitamin C helps lower blood pressure and cholesterol, prevents many cancers, strokes, heart attacks, and diabetes. Foods rich in Vitamin C are fruits (especially citrus fruits such as oranges and grapefruits), green peppers, broccoli, and strawberries.

FOOD SOURCES OF ANTIOXIDANTS

Beta-carotene	Vitamin E	Vitamin C
acorn squash	nuts	cantaloupe
broccoli	peanut butter	grapefruits
butternut squash	vegetable oils	kiwi
brussels sprouts	wheat germ	oranges
cantaloupe	whole grain breads	strawberries
carrots	whole grain cereals	tangerines
grapefruit		
kale		
spaghetti squash		
spinach		
sweet potatoes		
tomatoes		
watermelon		

Vitamin supplements. Several studies have shown no cancer protection from just taking vitamin supplements.[10] It is not totally clear what is missing when one consumes vitamin supplements rather than foods—mostly fruits and vegetables—that are rich in antioxidants. There must be some co-factors present in the foods that are processed away in the development of vitamin supplements. Thus, when you take the purified supplement, you loose the anticancer properties. More and more, we are learning that preventing cancer through diet requires more than just popping a pill.

Alcohol. There is evidence that alcohol consumption increases the risk of developing breast cancer in a linear fashion. This means that the more you drink, the higher your risk of breast cancer. It appears that this effect may be related to the fact that alcohol increases estrogen levels in the body. In general, the incidence of breast cancer begins to rise with an intake of as few as two drinks per day.[11] So it is best to limit your alcohol intake to one drink per day.

NOTES

1. National Research Council: Committee on Diet and Health, Food and Nutrition Board, Commission on Life Sciences. "Diet and Health: Implications for Reducing Chronic Disease Risk." Washington, D.C.: National Academy of Sciences;1989. U.S. Department of Health and Human Services. The Surgeon General's Report on Nutrition and Health. Washington, D.C.: U.S. Government Printing Office;1988. Publication PHS 88–50210. Nutrition and Your Health: Dietary Guidelines for Americans, 4th ed. Washington, D.C.: U.S. Dept of Agriculture and Dept of Health and Human Services;1995. Home and Garden Bulletin No. 232.

2. G. A. Colditz. "Epidemiology of breast cancer. Findings from the nurses' health study." *Cancer* 71:1480–89;1993. P. K. Mills, W. L. Beeson, R. L. Phillips, et al. "Dietary habits and breast cancer incidence among Seventh-Day Adventists." *Cancer* 64:582–90;1989. S. Graham, R. Hellmann, J. Marshall. "Nutritional epidemiology of postmenopausal breast cancer in western New York." *American Journal of Epidemiology* 134:552–66:1991.

3. W. C. Willett, D. J. Hunter. " Prospective studies of diet and breast cancer." *Cancer* 74:1085–89;1994.

4. Ibid.

5. S. Franceschi, A. Favero, A. Decarli, et al. "Intake of macronutrients and risk of breast cancer." *Lancet* 347:1351–56;1996. H. L. Newmark. "Squalene, olive oil, and cancer risk. Review and hypothesis." *Annals of the New York Academy of Science* 889:193–203;1999.

6. C. P. J. Caygill, A. Charlett, M. J. Hill. "Fat, fish, fish oil, and cancer." *British Journal of Cancer* 74:159–164;1996.

7. M. Mezzetti, C. LaVecchia, P. Boyle, et al. "Population attributable risk for breast cancer, diet, nutrition, and physical exercise." *Journal of the National Cancer Institute* 90:389–94;1998. L. Holmberg, E. M. Ohlander, T. Byers. "Diet and breast cancer risk. Results from a population-based, case-control study in Sweden." *Archives of Internal Medicine* 154:1805–11;1994. A. Ronco, E. De Stefani, P. Boffetta, et al. "Vegetables, fruits, and related nutrients and risk of breast cancer: a case-control study in Uruguay." *Nutrition and Cancer* 35:111–19;1999.

8. D. Ingram. "Diet and subsequent survival in women with breast cancer." *British Journal of Cancer* 69:592–95;1994. M. Jain, A. B. Miller, T. To. "Premorbid diet and the prognosis of women with breast cancer." *Journal of the National Cancer Institute* 86:1390–97;1994.

9. W. Kalt, C. F. Forney, A. Martin, et al. "Antioxidant capacity, vitamin C, phenolics and anthocyanins after fresh storage of small fruits." *Journal of Agriculture and Food Chemistry* 47:4638–44;1999.

10. J. H. Weisburger. "Nutritional approach to cancer prevention with emphasis on vitamins, antioxidants, and carotinoids." *American Journal of Clinical Nutrition* 53:226S–237S;1991.

11. S. A. Smith-Warner, D. Spiegelman, S. S. Yaun, et al. "Alcohol and breast cancer in women: a pooled analysis of cohort studies." *Journal of the American Medical Association* 279:535–40;1998.

Phytoestrogens in the Diet and the Prevention of Breast Cancer

Your own body's estrogen plays a key role in the development of breast cancer. For example, we know that the younger you are when you begin having regular periods, the higher your risk of getting breast cancer. The later that you go through menopause, the higher your risk of getting breast cancer. This is because in order to have periods, you have to ovulate. Ovulation is the production of an egg from the ovary. This process results in higher estrogen levels in your body. Once you begin ovulating, your body has higher estrogen levels than you had prior to entering puberty (beginning regular periods). This higher estrogen state lasts until you go through menopause. Once you enter menopause, you stop ovulating, and your estrogen levels drop dramatically.

If you become pregnant before age thirty, your risk decreases. If you have no children, your risk increases. If you exercise more than three times a week in the years before menopause, your risk decreases, likely because the exercise alters your menstrual cycle in a way which decreases your body's levels of estrogen and progesterone. Being overweight increases your risk of breast cancer, because fat tissues produce estrogen. Alcohol consumption, which raises estrogen levels, increases the risk of breast cancer.

There are other examples of how your own body's estrogen affects your risk of developing breast cancer. One study looking at this connection between women's hormones and breast cancer compared groups of women undergoing surgery to remove their ovaries (the organ that produces most of your body's estrogen). Women who had both the uterus and the ovaries removed before age forty had a 75 percent lower incidence of breast cancer than women who had only their uterus removed but kept their ovaries.[1]

Phytoestrogens. Phytoestrogens are compounds found in plants with activity similar to estrogen in the body. The chemical makeup of phytoestrogens resembles your own body's estrogen. Two major categories of phytoestrogens are isoflavones and lignans. Soy is the major source of isoflavones, while flaxseed is the major source of lignans.

The action of phytoestrogens in the body is complex. In some body tissues they act like a weak estrogen. But in other body tissues, such as the breast, they appear to have antiestrogenic properties. Phytoestrogen's affinity for the estrogen receptor (how strong they bind to the receptor) is approximately 35 percent that of estradiol, the estrogen produced from your ovaries. In humans, after consumption of phytoestrogens from plants, complex chemical reactions occur in the gastrointestinal tract, resulting in the formation of compounds with a close similarity in structure to estrogen. After consumption of soy foods or flaxseed, phytoestrogen metabolites can be measured in the urine, plasma, feces, semen, bile, saliva, and breast milk, showing that these compounds are absorbed from the plants and used in the body.

Because of this resemblance to your body's estrogen, phytoestrogens can mimic the action of your natural estrogen on some of your body's tissues and organs. They have been proven to decrease hot flashes,[2] and may have an effect on other symptoms of menopause, including mood disturbances, sleep diffi-culties, fatigue, and vaginal dryness. Evidence from molecular and cellular biology experiments, animal studies, and some human clinical trials suggests that phytoestrogens in the diet may confer health benefits by preventing cardiovascular diseases and cancer.

Phytoestrogens and protection against breast cancer. Phyto-estrogens seem to protect against breast cancer.[3] Japanese women eating a traditional diet rich in soy products have a low incidence of estrogen-dependent cancers, such as breast cancer, compared to Western women. This incidence increases once Asian women westernize their diet.[4] Breast, colon, prostate, endometrial, and ovarian cancers and coronary heart disease all have lower inci-dences in Asia and eastern Europe than in Western countries.[5] Japan has consistently been reported to have the lowest risk of hormone-dependent cancers.[6]

Data from studies with animals have confirmed a protective action against breast cancer.[7] Studies in humans show that women who consume high quantities of soy products and there-fore have greater concentrations of their break-down products in their urine have reduced rates of breast cancer.[8] It appears that the higher the amount of break-down products in the urine, the lower the risk of breast cancer.[9] In 1990, the National Cancer Institute held a workshop to examine the relationship between soy in the diet and cancer prevention. The conclusions of this conference indicated that soy consumption may lower colorec-tal cancer based on epidemiological data, and there was an indi-cation that soy could help prevent breast cancer.

Phytoestrogens as hormone blockers. The mechanism behind this protective effect is not yet fully understood. There are sev-eral theories that are currently being researched that may explain it. It may be that this protective effect relates to the fact that phytoestrogens are a weak estrogen and therefore compete with the body's own natural estrogen, so that the breast is not exposed to as much estrogen in the long run. This effect would likely be important in pregnancy, the premenopausal years, and in adolescence, when estrogen levels are higher. Thus, these plant estrogens in some way block the action of the body's own estrogen on the breast, possibly by occupying the same receptor in the breast that your own natural estrogen usually occupies.

This theory suggests that the protective effect of phytoestrogens on breast cancer risk therefore needs to be started early in life, possibly in the womb. This is important to remember, since many women start consuming soy foods and flaxseed during menopause in order to decrease their menopausal symptoms. However, it appears that to prevent breast cancer through this hormone blocking mechanism, adding soy to the diet should be started much earlier.

Nonhormonal anti-cancer mechanisms of phytoestrogens. The anti-cancer mechanisms of phytoestrogens are also likely to be attributable to metabolic properties that do not involve estrogen receptors. A proposed mechanism for this non-hormonal protective effect of phytoestrogens in the diet is that they have been shown to block an enzyme, tyrosine kinase, that is important in cancer cell growth. Blockage of this enzyme inhibits the growth of cancer cells by decreasing the action of certain cellular growth factors. Other possible explanations include influences on other enzymes, protein synthesis, cell proliferation, angiogenesis, calcium transport, growth factors, lipid oxidation, and cell differentiation.[10,11] Research is actively under way to further elucidate the protective effect of phytoestrogens on breast cancer.

Phytoestrogens during pregnancy. Data has begun to accumulate on the effects of a phytoestrogen-rich diet during pregnancy and a decreased risk of breast cancer later in life in the babies exposed to phytoestrogens in utero. This data, in both animals and humans, indicates that there may be a protective effect of a phytoestrogen-rich diet in pregnancy in preventing breast cancer in babies later in life.

Phytoestrogens have been shown to freely pass from the mother's bloodstream, through the placenta, and into the blood circulation of the fetus. The levels of phytoestrogens in the mother's bloodstream are very similar to those in fetal circulation. Scientists have thus postulated that consuming phytoestrogens during pregnancy may have beneficial effects on the fetus that could decrease the future risk of hormone-dependent cancers in these babies by modulating the amount of estrogen in their in-utero life.

Estrogen exposure in the womb. There is scientific evidence that suggests that high concentrations of phytoestrogens in pregnant women decrease the probability of the future occurrence of breast cancer in their daughters.[12] The theory behind this hypothesis is that phytoestrogens are potential modulators of estrogen action on the body because they act as estrogen antagonists. They bind to the estrogen receptor in the breast, and because they are a much weaker estrogen than estradiol, the body's natural estrogen, the breast is exposed to much less estrogen. This effect is particularly significant in situations when our body's own natural estrogen levels are highest, such as pregnancy. They also may decrease estrogen action by inhibiting several enzymes important in estrogen production and metabolism.

This hypothesis has received support from studies that show a lower risk of breast cancer among daughters of women with preeclampsia or eclampsia during pregnancy. The blood of these women was tested and was found to have low estrogen levels. The offspring of these women were followed and found to have lower rates of breast cancer later in life.[13] The theory is that these babies were exposed to less estrogen, and as adults had lower rates of breast cancer.

Diet in pregnancy and childhood and effects on estrogen levels in the body. Although there does not appear to be a direct correlation between dietary fat in adult women and their risk of breast cancer, there may be an association in children and adolescents. A diet which is high in fat and low in fiber in childhood or during adolescence may increase breast cancer risk by affecting estrogen metabolism. Estrogen levels in childhood and adolescence affect the growth of the mammary glands in the breast and their sensitivity to toxic compounds, which enhances the occurrence of precancerous lesions. There is evidence that phytoestrogens can decrease this risk.

In an experiment, newborn rats were given phytoestrogens in their diet. The rats were less susceptible to carcinogens, took longer to develop a mammary tumor, and had fewer multiple tumors than the rats who had no phytoestrogens in their diet. In the rat mammary tissue on the microscopic level, there was a decrease in the proliferation of mammary cells and less mature development of the ductal cells.[14] This implies a protective effect of phytoestogens in the diet on the growth of mammary tissue in newborns, resulting in structures that are less susceptible to cancer. This may explain why the protective effect of the Asian diet appears to occur early in a girl's life.

Additional support for the theory that a mother's diet in pregnancy affects breast cancer risk in her daughters comes from the Nurses' Health Study at Harvard.[15] Researchers there found a link between birth weight and later risk of breast cancer: the bigger the baby, the greater the risk. A baby's birth weight is largely determined by how much weight a woman gains during pregnancy. Thus, prenatal factors seem to affect later risk of developing breast cancer.

It is therefore possible that a high phytoestrogen diet during pregnancy and childhood may protect our daughters from breast cancer. There is also evidence that phytoestrogens may protect men from prostate cancer. There is no evidence that suggests that eating soy during pregnancy affects the endocrinologic (hormone) status of their offspring in any negative way.

Maximizing the benefits of phytoestrogens in the diet. Phytoestrogens metabolize in the intestine. The action of natural bacteria in the intestine is necessary for their conversion into active forms in the body. Concentrations of phytoestrogens in the body can vary widely between individuals even when a controlled quantity of phytoestrogen is administered. Studies have found that many factors, including dietary fiber and the amount of vegetables and fruit eaten, influence the metabolism of phytoestrogens. Thus, combining phytoestrogen-rich foods with lots of fruits and vegetables will maximize your benefits.

The content of active phytoestrogen from soy products varies dramatically from one crop to another and from one harvest to another. Most important, the active phytoestrogens in different soy products vary substantially, which is attributed to various processing steps. For example, processed soy products, such as soy hot dogs and tofu yogurt, may contain only one-tenth the phytoestrogen content of whole soybeans.[16]

Phytoestrogens from the diet versus from supplements.
I do not recommend obtaining phytoestrogens from supplements such as pills or powders. Phytoestrogen supplements are highly processed, and the effects of this processing on how well the body absorbs them is not clear. Remember that the metabolism of phytoestrogens occurs in the intestine, and the action of natural bacteria in the intestine is necessary for their conversion into active forms in the body. These bacteria are dependent upon other co-factors in the diet, especially fruits and vegetables, to have maximal action. Also, it may be that there are yet unrecognized co-factors in soy foods and flaxseed that could be responsible for the anti-cancer properties and health benefits of phytoestrogens that are processed away in supplements. This is analogous to the fact that antioxidants from vitamin supplements do not appear to be as effective in their anti-cancer properties as eating natural fruits and vegetables that are rich in these substances.

It is also possible that the very high concentrations of phytoestrogens potentially available from supplements could be harmful. There are some supplements in which phytoestrogens are so concentrated that it would be like eating a pound of tofu at a sitting. Too much of a good thing can be dangerous. At this point, there is no data about their safety. I thus do not recommend taking phytoestrogen supplements but rather making changes in your diet to incorporate soy foods and flaxseed.

Food sources of phytoestrogens. There are two major classes of phytoestrogens: isoflavones and lignans. Soy foods are rich in isoflavones, while flaxseed is rich in lignans. In addition, there are small amounts of phytoestrogens (in the form of lignans) in lentils, dried seaweed, wheat, garlic, asparagus, and squash, but the amounts are tiny compared with soy foods and flaxseed. Soy products available in the United States include soy milk, tofu, texturized vegetable protein (TVP), and tempeh.

PHYTOESTROGEN CONTENT FROM LIGNANS[17]		PHYTOESTROGEN CONTENT FROM ISOFLAVONES[17]	
Food	Total (mg/4 oz)	Food	Total (mg/4 oz)
flaxseed meal	77	Roasted soybeans	185
flaxseed flour	60	Texturized vegetable protein	157
lentils	1.8	Soy flour	154
dried seaweed	2.5	Tempeh	128
soybeans	0.9	Tofu	71
wheat	1		
garlic	0.5		
asparagus	0.5		
squash	0.5		

How much soy is the right amount? No one knows the answer to this question. The average Asian woman's diet contains 3 to 4 ounces of soy foods such as tofu a day, yielding 50 to 70 milligrams of isoflavones. If you include soy or flaxseed in one of your meals every day, you will get roughly the same amount. Most of the recipes in this book that contain phytoestrogens have approximately this amount in a serving.

Other Health Benefits of Phytoestrogens

Soy and hot flashes—the evidence. The evidence pointing toward phytoestrogens as a possible dietary alternative for treatment of menopausal symptoms came initially from Asia. Population studies of Japanese women going through menopause indicate that less than 25 percent suffer from hot flashes[18] compared with 85 percent of North American women.[19] Asian populations, such as those in Japan, Taiwan, and Korea, are estimated to consume 20–150 mg/day (with an average of 40 mg/day) of isoflavones, mainly tofu and miso.[20] (2.25 ounces of tofu contains 40 mg of isoflavones.) Although this does not seem like much tofu, it is still a much higher amount than the typical American eats in a day, since Americans often do not consume any soy products.

Several studies have found that dietary phytoestrogens in the form of soy protein significantly decrease vasomotor symptoms such as hot flashes.[21] Several clinical trials have demonstrated a mild but significant improvement in hot flashes with dietary phytoestrogen supplementation (soy products). In one study, menopausal women requesting treatment for hot flashes were given 60 grams (about 2 ounces) of soy protein daily for 12 weeks. Soy was significantly superior to a placebo in reducing the number of hot flashes. By the end of the twelfth week, women taking soy had a 45 percent reduction in their daily hot flashes.[22] In another study, postmenopausal women randomly received either 50 mg of soy isoflavone extract (this is the equivalent of 2¾ ounces of tofu or 11 ounces of soy milk) or a placebo. The soy extract was found to be effective in reducing frequency and severity of flushes when compared to those receiving the placebo. [23]

Soy and heart disease prevention. Studies indicate that consumption of soy protein instead of animal protein (such as beef) decreases serum cholesterol concentrations. Soy is known to lower cholesterol levels by 10 to 20 percent when one eats between 30 and 40 grams (1 to 1½ ounces) daily. A study published in 1995 in the *New England Journal of Medicine* indicates that an average daily consumption of 48 grams (1¾ ounces) of soy protein resulted in a 9.3 percent decrease in total cholesterol; a 12.9 percent decrease in LDL (bad) cholesterol; and a 10.5 percent decrease in triglyceride levels. These reductions are even greater for those with moderate to severe hypercholesterolemia (>250 mg/dl).[24]

The mechanism behind this cholesterol-lowering effect is thought to be an increase in LDL receptors and the inhibition of cholesterol production in the body.[25] This is of particular significance in those with inherited hyperlipidemia (high cholesterol and lipid levels in the blood that can run in families). Independent of this lipid-lowering effect, phytoestrogens seem to decrease the actual development of cholesterol plaques on the cells of the blood vessels.[26] Finally, various studies have suggested that genistein, a breakdown product of isoflavones in the body, is an inhibitor of the enzyme tyrosine kinase. This inhibition results in decreased platelet activity, which ultimately leads to reduced atherosclerosis.[27] More studies are needed to clarify the exact mechanisms by which phytoestrogens affect platelet responses that result in anti-clotting effects.

Cooking with phytoestrogens. Soy and other phytoestrogens are not typically a large part of the average American diet. However, these foods may be incorporated into meals with only minimal changes to more traditional cooking. Soy can be mixed with beef or other meats. Tofu may be marinated and will then take on the flavor of the marinade. Silken tofu, a very creamy form of tofu, can be substituted for dairy products and oil in many recipes, making low-fat and phytoestrogen-rich cream sauces, salad dressings, and desserts.

Some soy products such as vegetarian or soy burgers are made with "soy-protein concentrate," which contains almost no isoflavones. These soy products do not have the phytoestrogen benefits of unprocessed soy products such as tofu and miso. However, if you see "soy-protein isolate" on the label, the isoflavones are largely retained. Tofutti spreads, such as soy cream cheese, are often made with soy-protein isolate. So check the labels carefully if you are eating some of the more "ready-made" soy products.

Breast cancer survivors and phytoestrogens—are they safe? Several animal studies have found that phytoestrogens retard breast cancer development, suggesting that these compounds may have protective effects with regard to estrogen-dependent cancers in animals.[28] In addition, human breast cancer cell lines, which are a way of studying human cells in the laboratory, show that lignans and isoflavones reduce their proliferation.[29] Finally, phytoestrogens have been shown to inhibit enzymes associated with cancer cell proliferation, especially tyrosine kinase.[30] Tyrosine kinase inhibitors have potential as anticancer agents in both the prevention and treatment of cancer.

However, one recent study does show that we should proceed with caution in women with a diagnosis of breast cancer. A one-year study of the effects of a commercial soy protein isolate on breast discharge raised some concern about an increase in cell growth in response to soy. The breast fluid showed increased secretion of overgrown cells, and increased concentrations of estrogen in the discharge. These findings are considered worrisome in terms of breast cancer risk. The study was subject to several limitations, including a high rate of women dropping out of the study, and no control population for comparison. In addition, the soy used was a soy protein isolate, and not the whole foods such as tofu or soy milk. The researchers themselves report their results cautiously as pilot study findings. Thus, further study is warranted.

My advice to women already diagnosed with breast cancer is to consume phytoestrogens only from natural sources in the diet such as soy foods and flaxseed. Do not consume commercially processed sources of phytoestrogens such as pills or powders. These may contain huge doses of phytoestrogens. It is also possible that the anti-cancer properties found in the diet which require dietary co-factors to work are processed away in pills and powders. Finally, in those who are already diagnosed with breast cancer, I would use some caution until more is known, and limit intake to one or two servings of phytoestrogen-containing foods, such as a glass of soy milk and 2–3 ounces of tofu daily. If you are a breast cancer survivor, it is best to check with your doctor to check on the latest research.

NOTES

1. M. Feinleib. "Breast cancer and artificial menopause: a cohort study." *Journal of the National Cancer Institute* 41:315–29;1968.
2. P. Alvertazzi, F. Pansini, G. Bonaccorsi. "The effect of dietary soy supplementation on hot flushes." *Obstetrics and Gynecology* 91:6–11;1998.

3. F. O. Stephens. "The rising incidence of breast cancer in women and prostate cancer in men. Dietary influences: a possible preventive role for nature's sex hormone modifiers—the phytoestrogens (review)." *Oncology Reports* 6:865–70;1999. S. Barnes, T. G. Peterson, L. Goward. "Rationale for the use of genistein-containing soy matrices in chemoprevention trials for breast and prostate cancer." *Journal of Cellular Biochemistry Supplement* 22:181–87;1995.

4. I. Kato, S. Tominaga, T. Kuroishi. "Relationship between westernization of dietary habits and mortality from breast and ovarian cancer in Japan." *Journal of Cancer Research* 78:349–57;1987.

5. D. P. Rose, A. P. Boyer, E. L. Wynder. "International comparison of mortality rates for cancer of the breast, ovary, prostate, and colon, per capita fat consumption." *Cancer* 58:2363–71;1986.

6. D. M. Parkin. "Cancers of the breast, endometrium and ovary: geographical correlations." *European Journal of Cancer Clinical Oncology* 25:1917–25;1989.

7. S. Barnes, C. Grubbs, K. Setchell, J. Carlson. "Soybeans inhibit mammary tumors in models of breast cancer." In: M. Pariza, ed. *Mutagens and carcinogens in the diet.* New York: Wiley-Liss, 239–53;1990. C. A. Lamartiniere, J. B. Moore, N. M. Brown, et al. "Genistein suppresses mammary cancer in rats." *Carcinogenesis* 16:2833–40;1995.

8. H. Aldercreutz, H. Honjo, A. Higashi. "Urinary excretion of lignans and isoflavonoid phytoestrogens in Japanese men and women consuming a traditional Japanese diet." *American Journal of Clinical Nutrition* 54:193–1100;1991.

9. D. Ingram, K. Sanders, M. Kolybaba, D. Lopez. "Case-control study of phyto-estrogens and breast cancer." *Lancet* 350:990–94;1997.

10. H. Adlercreutz, W. Maxur. "Phyto-oestrogens and western diseases." *Annals of Internal Medicine* 29:95–120;1997.

11. D. C. Knight, J. A. Eden. "A review of the clinical effects of phytoestrogens." *Obstetrics and Gynecology* 87:897–904;1996.

12. D. Trichopoulos. "Hypothesis: does breast cancer originate in utero." *Lancet* 335:939–40;1990.

13. A. Ekbom, D. Trichopoulos, H. O. Adami, et al. "Evidence of prenatal influences on breast cancer risk." *Lancet* 340:1015–18; 1992.

14. C. A. Lamartiniere, J. B. Moore, N. M. Brown, et al. "Genistein suppresses mammary cancer in rats." *Carcinogenesis* 16:2833–40;1995.

15. K. B. Michels, D. Trichopoulos, J. M. Robins, et al. "Birthweight as a risk factor for breast cancer." *Lancet* 348:1542–46;1996.

16. H. Wang, P. A. Murphy. "Isoflavone composition of American and Japanese soybeans in Iowa: effects of variety, crop year, and location." *Journal of Agricultural and Food Chemistry* 42:1674–77;1994. H. Wang, P. A. Murphy. "Isoflavone content in commercial soybean foods." *Journal of Agricultural and Food Chemistry* 42:1666–73;1994.

17. J. Blake. "Phytoestrogens: the food of menopause?" *Journal of the Society of Obstetricians and Gynecologists of Canada*. May 1998.
18. M. Lock. *Encounters with aging: Mythologies of menopause in Japan and North America*. Berkeley and Los Angeles: University of California Press, 1993.
19. M. Notelovitz. "Estrogen replacement therapy indications, contraindications, and agent selection." *American Journal of Obstetrics and Gynecology* 161:8–17;1989.
20. A. C. Eldridge, F. Kwolek. "Soybean isoflavones: effect of environment and variety on composition." *Journal of Agriculture and Food Chemistry* 31:394–96, 1983.
21. S. Washburn, G. L. Burke, T. Morgan, et al. "Effect of soy protein supplementation on serum lipoproteins, blood pressure, and menopausal symptoms in perimenopausal women." *Menopause* 6:7–13;1999.
22. P. Albertazzi, F. Pansini, G. Bonaccorsi. "The effect of dietary soy supplementation on hot flushes." *Obstetrics and Gynecology* 91:6–11;1998.
23. S. H. Upmalis, R. Lobo, L. Bradley, et al. "Vasomotor symptom relief by soy isoflavone extract tablets in postmenopausal women: a multicenter, double blind, randomized, placebo-controlled study." *Menopause* 4:236–42;2000.
24. J. W. Anderson, B. M. Johnston, M. E. Newell. "Meta-analysis of the effects of soy protein intake on serum lipids." *New England Journal of Medicine* 333:276–82;1995.
25. C. R. Sirtori, M. R. Lovati, C. Manzoni, et al. "Soy and cholesterol reduction: clinical experience." *Journal of Nutrition* 125:598S–605S;1995.
26. W. E. Raines, R. Ross. "Biology of atherosclerotic plaque formation: Possible role of growth factors in lesion development and the potential impact of soy." *Journal of Nutrition* 125:624–30S;1995.
27. J. N. Wilcox, B. F. Blumenthal. "Thrombotic mechanisms in atherosclerosis: potential impact of soy proteins." *Journal of Nutrition* 125:631–38S;1995.
28. C. A. Lamartiniere, J. B. Moore, N. M. Brown, et al. "Genistein suppresses mammary cancer in rats." *Carcinogenesis* 16:2833–40;1995.
29. F. V. So, N. Gunthrie, A. F. Chambers. "Inhibition of proliferation of estrogen receptor-positive MCF-7 human breast cancer cells by flavonoids in the presence and absence of excess estrogen." *Cancer Letter* 112:127–33;1997. G. Peterson, S. Barnes. "Genistein inhibits both estrogen and growth factor stimulated proliferation of human breast cancer cells." *Cell Growth and Differentiation* 7:1345–51;1996.
30. G. Peterson. "Evaluation of the biochemical targets of genistein in tumor cells." *Journal of Nutrition* 125:784–89S;1995.

CHAPTER 4

General Nutrition Guidelines for Women

A diet that prevents breast cancer also prevents the major causes of ill health and will preserve your well-being, vitality, and longevity. They all go together. Women whose diets include fruits, vegetables, whole grains, low-fat dairy, and lean meats, as recommended by current dietary guidelines, have a lower risk of mortality from all causes. Women who have the highest intake level of recommended foods have a 30 percent lower risk of mortality from all causes compared with those in the lowest level.[1]

It is never too early or too late in life to start eating well. The first thing you need to do is to learn about the basics of good nutrition. My philosophy is that it is always fine to treat yourself on occasion to a sinful dessert or favorite high-fat food. This is only human and will allow you to maintain a sensible diet on a regular basis. Too much self-denial of the foods you love will only lead to long-term regular bad habits when you find it impossible to stick with a spartan diet. Personally, I can't live without sweets and chocolate, so I try to eat well all day, exercise regularly, and then indulge in a few cookies, a little chocolate, or some ice cream in the evening. This prevents major losses of control! And when I eat well-balanced meals all day, I don't have room enough to gorge myself on desserts.

The dietary guidelines. Eating well can preserve your health, prevent disease, and increase your well-being. The most comprehensive advice comes from the Dietary Guidelines for Americans, published jointly by the U.S. Department of Agriculture and the U.S. Department of Health and Human Services. These guidelines were developed to help people obtain the nutrients they need, lead healthier, more active lives, and reduce their risk of certain chronic diseases.

USDA Dietary Guidelines for Americans

- Eat a variety of foods.
- Balance the food you eat with physical activity to maintain or lower your weight.
- Choose a diet with plenty of grains, vegetables, and fruits.
- Choose a diet low in fat, especially saturated fat and cholesterol.
- Choose a diet moderate in sugars.
- Choose a diet moderate in salt and sodium.
- If you drink alcoholic beverages, do so in moderation.

Basic components of the diet. Carbohydrates, protein, and fat are the basic components of your diet. At least half of your calories should come from complex carbohydrates, less than 30 percent of your calories should come from fat, and your protein sources should come from lean meats or vegetables. Your meals should be based upon foods such as pasta, potatoes, grains, and fresh vegetables, with meat or other protein sources serving more as a garnish. The Chinese, among others, have known this for centuries. These basic guidelines are followed in the recipe section of this book. You and your family can enjoy all of the meals in this book together.

Food Guide Pyramid. The U.S. Department of Agriculture Food Guide Pyramid can be used to help you choose healthy foods in the correct proportions. The Food Guide Pyramid is a graphic representation of healthy eating—it replaces the basic four food groups that many of us learned in our youth. It symbolizes a balanced diet that arranges food into five groups to depict their proportion in your diet. For example, the bread, cereal, rice, and pasta group forms the base of the pyramid because most of the food you eat should come from this group. This is in stark contrast to the many popular high fat, high protein, very low carbohydrate diets that are in fashion. I cannot recommend these diets, particularly as a steady way of eating.

The Food Guide Pyramid reinforces three concepts of healthful eating: balance, variety, and moderation. Your diet will be balanced when you eat more foods from the groups toward the base of the Pyramid and fewer from food groups closer to the top. Variety means eating a variety of foods across and within each group in the Pyramid.

The Pyramid suggests a range of recommended daily servings from each food group, for example, 3–5 servings from the vegetable group. The lower number in each group is the recommended range for sedentary adults. The more active you are, the higher the number of servings you should eat from each food group.

Here are some examples of the servings from the different food groups in the Pyramid.

Bread, Cereal, Rice, and Pasta Group
6–11 servings daily
A serving is:
- 1 slice of bread
- ½ bagel or English muffin
- 1 ounce of cold cereal
- ½ cup of cooked cereal, rice, pasta, or grain

Vegetable Group
3–5 servings daily
A serving is:

    1 cup of leafy greens or lettuce
    ½ cup cooked or raw vegetables

Fruit Group
2–4 servings daily
A serving is:
    1 medium apple, orange, pear, peach, or ½ banana
    ½ cup chopped, cooked, or canned fruit
    ¾ cup fruit juice

Milk, Yogurt, and Cheese Group
2–3 servings daily
A serving is:
    1 cup of milk or yogurt
   1½ ounces cheese
    ½ cup part-skim ricotta cheese
    1 cup frozen yogurt

Meat, Poultry, Fish, Dry Beans, Eggs, and Nuts Group
2–3 servings daily
A serving is:
  2–3 ounces beef, poultry, or fish
    ½ cup cooked beans or legumes
    1 egg
    2 tablespoons peanut butter

Carbohydrates. Most of the calories in your diet should come from complex carbohydrates. This may come as a surprise to you since many of the newer fad weight-loss diets emphasize limiting your intake of carbohydrates so that you do not gain too much weight. Many "quick weight loss" diets espouse very low carbohydrate diets. But carbohydrates should make up most of your diet throughout your life, because they are the preferred fuel for your body. Complex carbohydrates are broken down slowly by the body, especially if fiber is also present, providing a constant and steady energy source.

    Carbohydrates come in two forms: simple carbohydrates, which are found in fruits as well as sugar and candy, and complex carbohydrates, which are found in potatoes, vegetables, beans, and whole grains. Foods high in complex carbohydrates are also rich in important vitamins, minerals, and fiber. Fruits, although they contain simple sugars, are also a nutrient- and fiber-packed source of carbohydrates. Other simple carbohydrate foods such as candy and cookies are full of "empty" calories since they generally contain few nutrients (diabetics may need to limit their intake of fruits and other simple carbohydrates).

Protein. The amount of protein recommended is 50 grams per day. This is not a large amount of protein: 10 grams of protein are found in 1 ounce of chicken or ⅓ cup of yogurt. The average American eats much more protein than she needs, on average, from 75 to 110 grams per day. Vegetarians need more protein servings since it all comes from vegetable sources. But a vegetarian diet is perfectly adequate and can be very healthy, since vegetarian sources of protein are often lower in saturated fat.

While you will generally have no problem filling your protein requirement, you should try to obtain protein from low-fat sources. Many people mistakenly believe that protein comes only from animal foods and dairy products, which may also contain undesirable amounts of fat and cholesterol. Yet foods such as grains and vegetables also contain protein.

Tofu and miso are excellent soy-based forms of protein, rich in both phytoestrogens and calcium. Consuming several generous servings of these plant foods each day can help you meet a substantial portion of your protein requirement without increasing your intake of fat or cholesterol.

Some Animal Sources of Protein
Cheese
Eggs
Fish and shellfish
Lean meat
Milk
Poultry
Yogurt

Some Vegetable Sources of Protein
Black beans
Bulgur
Chickpeas
Lentils
Miso
Pinto beans
Quinoa
Rice
Split peas
Tofu
White beans

Fat. Most health organizations, including the FDA, recommend a diet that provides no more than 30 percent of calories from fat for all adults. Some experts recommend keeping fat as low as 20 percent of your daily calories. However, the average American obtains more than 50 percent of her daily calories from fat. While fat in your diet does not appear to increase your risk for breast cancer (see pages 12–13), there is an association between a high-fat diet, high blood cholesterol, and the development of coronary heart disease, which is the number one killer of women.

In order to keep your intake of fat to 30 percent or less of your daily calories, you will need to choose low-fat protein sources, cut back on added oil in cooking and fried foods, eat approximately half of your calories from carbohydrates, and generally be aware of the fat content of the foods you eat. Almost all the recipes in this book derive 30 percent or fewer calories from fat.

Saturated and unsaturated fat. Not all fat is equal. Fat is classified as saturated and unsaturated. It is saturated fat in the diet that has been most closely associated with the development of coronary heart disease. Saturated fat in the diet has been consistently, in numerous studies, associated with the risk of developing colorectal cancer. Dietary fat is an important factor associated with many other cancers: prostate, endometrium, and ovarian. It does not appear, though, that saturated fat is associated with an increased risk of breast cancer, as had been thought in the past (see pages 12–13). In saturated fat, chemical bonds are filled by hydrogen (unsaturated fats have fewer of these bonds occupied by hydrogen). Animal fats, particularly those found in red meat and dairy products, are predominantly saturated, whereas vegetable fats are predominantly unsaturated. Saturated fats include fat from butter, cheese, whole milk, and meat.

It is healthier to make the majority of fat you consume come from unsaturated sources, such as canola, corn, safflower, and sunflower oil. Olive oil is monounsaturated, which has been shown to have a cholesterol-lowering effect, and is also a good choice. There is some evidence that olive oil may lower breast cancer risk. Unsaturated fats are mostly liquid at room temperature (such as oils), while saturated fats are usually solid at room temperature (such as butter).

Hydrogenated fat and trans fatty acids. Other types of fat found in foods as a result of chemical processing are hydrogenated fats and trans fatty acids. Originally manufactured with claims that they were healthier than saturated fats, these types of fats have been found to promote heart disease in a similar fashion as saturated fats.

Some of the chemical bonds in unsaturated fats have hydrogen added in a process known as hydrogenation. This changes the physical state of fat from liquid to solid by changing some unsaturated bonds to saturated ones. Margarine is an example of a fat that has been hydrogenated in order to convert it from a liquid to a solid. In a similar process in trans fatty acids, the position of the hydrogen bond is changed from its natural position (known as *cis*) to an unnatural position (known as *trans*).

Products containing hydrogenated fats and trans fatty acids, especially margarine, were heavily promoted as being healthier than foods containing saturated fat. It was thought that they did not raise blood cholesterol in the same manner that saturated fats did. However, such claims were never substantiated. Concerns have arisen because consumption of these hydrogenated vegetable fats and trans fatty acids has tracked closely in time with a rise in coronary heart disease. Trans fatty acids have been found to raise bad cholesterol to a similar degree as saturated fats; they also decrease the good cholesterol. Both of these factors increase the risk of heart disease.

The composition of dietary fat, rather than simply the quantity in your diet, is also of importance. Some recent studies have shown that replacing saturated fats, hydrogenated fats, and trans fatty acids with monounsaturated (such as olive oil) and unsaturated fats is more effective in preventing coronary heart disease in women than reducing overall fat intake. To be prudent, it is probably best to do both: Reduce your overall fat intake to less than 30 percent of your daily calories and eat mostly unsaturated fat or olive oil.

Omega-3 fatty acids. One other type of fat is omega-3 fatty acids. Omega-3 fatty acids have been shown to have multiple health benefits. These fats are from fish, especially fatty fish such as salmon, swordfish, bluefish, mackerel, tuna, and wild striped bass. The only vegetarian source of omega-3 fatty acids is in flaxseed. These fats have been found to decrease the risk of coronary heart disease and thrombotic stroke, and have also been associated with a decreased risk of breast cancer recurrence in those already diagnosed and treated for breast cancer (see page 15). It is thought that they function as natural blood thinners, allowing the blood to flow more freely by not clogging the coronary arteries of the heart. You should therefore try to increase your intake of these types of fish in your diet.

Cholesterol and lipoproteins. A high blood-cholesterol level (200 milligrams or more) is a well-established risk factor for coronary heart disease. Cholesterol, which is not a fat but a member of a chemical family called lipids, is very important in the body, forming the basic structure of many hormones, including estrogen.

Lipoproteins are complexes that carry fat in the bloodstream through the body. These complexes come in two major varieties: high-density lipoproteins (HDLs) and low-density lipoproteins (LDLs). Research has shown that high levels of HDLs (sometimes called the "good cholesterol"), which carry cholesterol to the liver for processing, are associated with a lower risk of heart disease. In contrast, high levels of LDLs (sometimes called the "bad cholesterol") are associated with a higher risk of heart disease. A high cholesterol diet has been shown to raise HDLs, and lower LDLs, both of which are risk factors for developing heart disease. High levels of cholesterol in the blood, primarily cholesterol attached to LDL, is linked to an increased risk for coronary heart disease and heart attacks.

Blood cholesterol levels. Most health care providers advise trying to keep one's blood cholesterol less than 200 milligrams. Although cholesterol comes from your diet, it is also produced in the liver. Liver synthesis of cholesterol happens independent of dietary intake, but it is increased by the ingestion of saturated fats in the diet. To a degree, one's blood cholesterol level is inherited, but diet can strongly affect it. The effect dietary cholesterol has on blood cholesterol varies from person to person. For some, the amount of cholesterol in the diet has only a small effect on the level of cholesterol in the blood. But for others, especially people who already have high levels of blood cholesterol, dietary cholesterol can raise blood cholesterol levels even further.

Diet and cholesterol. Your body makes most of the cholesterol circulating in your blood from the saturated fat you eat and to a lesser degree from the cholesterol in the food that you consume. Thus the two ways to keep your blood cholesterol low through dietary changes are to minimize your intake of foods high in saturated fats and cholesterol. Foods which are high in cholesterol are not necessarily high in fat or saturated fat and vice versa. Vegetable oils, for example, are 100 percent fat but do not contain any cholesterol.

The best way to lower the overall fat, saturated fat, and cholesterol in your diet is to eat plenty of fruit, vegetables, and grains. In their natural form, most of these foods have little or no fat and are all cholesterol free. Certain foods are high in cholesterol and should be consumed in moderation: beef, bacon, butter, cheese, eggs, and whole milk.

A word about cholesterol in fish and shellfish: In general, fish and shellfish are low in fat and cholesterol when compared to beef, chicken, and dairy products. Although shellfish have a reputation for being high in cholesterol, this is not completely accurate. Shrimp, with about 150 milligrams of cholesterol in 3½ ounces, are now considered an acceptable alternative to red meat by the American Heart Association. Even lobster, which many on cholesterol-limited diets have been forbidden, has only 70 to 95 milligrams of cholesterol per 3½ ounces. Compare an egg with about 200 milligrams of cholesterol or 3½ ounces of hamburger with 100 mg. The key here is moderation.

Foods High in Cholesterol
Beef
Bacon
Butter
Cheese
Eggs
Whole milk

BETTER SOURCES OF FAT

Unsaturated fats	Monounsaturated fats	Omega-3 fatty acids
Canola oil	Olive oil	Bluefish
Corn oil		Mackerel
Sunflower oil		Salmon
Safflower oil		Swordfish
		Tuna
		Wild striped bass

FATS TO TRY TO AVOID

Saturated fat	Hydrogenated fat	Cholesterol
Butter	Coconut oil	Beef
Beef	Margarine	Egg yolk
Cheese	Palm oil	Liver
Whole milk		

Vitamins, minerals, and antioxidants. Vitamin and mineral deficiencies are relatively uncommon in the United States. Most of us obtain enough vitamins and minerals from a well-balanced diet so that we do not need extra vitamins. The benefits of taking vitamin supplements in amounts that exceed the recommended daily allowances remain uncertain.

Antioxidants include Vitamin C, beta-carotene (which is

converted to Vitamin A in the body), and Vitamin E. Research on the anti-cancer properties of antioxidants appears promising. Studies have found that only when antioxidants are eaten in their natural state in the form of fruits and vegetables, not when they are processed into vitamin supplements, do they exert their protective effect against a variety of cancers. Thus, your best defense is to be sure to eat a wide variety of both fruits and vegetables every day.

Calcium. Calcium is an important nutrient for women and deserves special mention. Calcium requirements vary with the stage of the lifecycle: 800 mg daily for premenopausal women, 1500 mg daily for menopausal women (1,000 mg daily for those taking hormone replacement therapy), and 1200 mg daily for pregnant women. Unfortunately, on average, women aged 50–65 are getting less than 700 mg daily.

Calcium is vital to the maintenance of strong bones. Calcium is also involved on the cellular level in diverse body functions: the beating of your heart, controlling your blood pressure, and even in the prevention of premenstrual syndrome. Numerous studies have now confirmed that calcium aids in the prevention of colon cancer.

Understanding the regulation of calcium in the body will help you to understand why calcium in the diet is so important. Bones consist of a matrix of collagen containing calcium and phosphate. The most significant function of bone is actually not as a supporting structure but rather its role as a calcium reservoir for many body functions. Calcium is an essential element for all cell functions. Your heart requires calcium to beat, your muscles require calcium to function, and your nervous system requires calcium to transmit messages. We must eat calcium-rich foods to supply these needs, and a reserve supply of calcium is stored in bones. For normal cellular activity, blood calcium levels must be maintained in a very tight range. The reservoir of calcium in the skeleton is critical in allowing a steady supply of calcium for cellular functions at a moment's notice.

Achieving the recommended daily amounts of calcium is not difficult for people whose diets are rich in dairy products.

Drinking three or four glasses of skim milk a day, for example, will get you close to your daily requirement through milk alone. But other sources of calcium, as well as calcium supplements, can provide a non-dairy source.

Food is nearly always a better source of calcium than supplements, if for no other reason than food provides more nutritional benefits than a supplement, and less risk of side effects. Dairy products are a well-known and rich source of calcium. In addition, tofu and certain vegetables are excellent non-dairy sources of calcium.

If you find it difficult to meet your daily calcium requirement from your diet, calcium supplements can fill the needs. Calcium supplements are sold over the counter and come in many forms. It does not make much difference which type you choose in order to meet your daily requirement of calcium—calcium supplements in many forms are absorbed in a similar fashion by the body.

Maximizing calcium absorption. Calcium is best absorbed with meals, because the acid load of the meal provides enhanced absorption. Calcium is better absorbed when the diet is rich in fruits and vegetables. Some substances can hinder the absorption of calcium, including oxalic acid (found in spinach and Swiss chard) and phytic acid (found in tea and the outer layers of whole grains). These substances form insoluble compounds with calcium, binding it in such a way that it cannot be absorbed from the intestine. Therefore, you may not absorb as much calcium in foods containing these substances. High phosphate drinks (such as soda, in which phosphate is used as a preservative) impair the absorption of calcium. Dietary calcium is enhanced by Vitamin D. In general, only the impaired elderly and others who get minimal exposure to sunlight need to supplement Vitamin D. But it is not generally necessary for all women to take Vitamin D supplements. Being outside as little as 30 minutes a day in the sun will give your body ample amounts of this vitamin.

Many forms of calcium supplements are available: calcium carbonate, calcium citrate, calcium chloride, calcium acetate, calcium gluconate, and others. The more soluble salts, such as calcium citrate, are better absorbed. However, they are expensive.

Calcium carbonate is less expensive, and adequately absorbed, so is often recommended as a compromise.

SOURCES OF CALCIUM

Food	Quantity	Calcium (mg)
DAIRY PRODUCTS		
Blue cheese	1 ounce	183
Ice cream, soft vanilla	1 cup	236
Mozzarella	1 ounce	147
Milk, whole	1 cup	291
Milk, skim	1 cup	302
Parmesan	1 ounce	336
Ricotta, part skim	½ cup	337
Romano	1 ounce	330
Yogurt, frozen	½ cup	147
Yogurt, nonfat	1 cup	415
BEANS AND LEGUMES		
Black beans	½ cup cooked	30
Chickpeas	½ cup cooked	45
Soybeans	½ cup cooked	131
Soybeans, dry roasted	½ cup	232
Soy milk	1 cup	46
Tempeh	2 ounce	47
Tofu	2 ounce	154
VEGETABLES AND FRUITS		
Bok choy	1 cup	116
Broccoli, cooked	1 cup	132
Collard greens	1 cup	357
Dandelion greens	1 cup	147
Fortified juices	1 cup	300
Kale	1 cup	206
Mustard greens	1 cup	193
Romaine lettuce	1 cup	37
Sea vegetables (wakame)	¼ cup dry	67

Spinach	1 cup	56
Swiss chard	1 cup	128
Turnip greens	1 cup	252
NUTS AND SEEDS		
Almonds	2 tbs.	42
Pine nuts	1 ounce	38
Sesame seeds	2 tsp.	218
Tahini	2 tbs.	139

Dairy products. Milk is one of the best dietary sources of calcium for two reasons: the lactose (milk sugar) that occurs naturally in milk and the Vitamin D added to it enhance calcium absorption through the intestine. This maximizes the amount of calcium your body obtains from each glass you drink. Because whole milk is also high in fat, I recommend that most women drink skim milk, which retains all of the calcium content and almost none of the fat. I would choose skim over low-fat (2%) milk, unless you really dislike the taste of skim milk. Even low-fat milk (2%) has a fair amount of saturated fat, and if you can get used to drinking skim milk, it is an excellent low-fat, high calcium protein source. Most individuals find that once they switch to skim milk, after a few weeks they do not miss the flavor of whole or low-fat milk. In addition, choose non-fat over low-fat or whole milk yogurt, as it is very similar in taste and texture, yet much healthier.

NUTRITION COMPARISON OF WHOLE, LOW-FAT, AND SKIM MILK

1 cup	Fat (grams)	Calcium (mg)	Calories
whole milk	8.14	291	150
low-fat milk (2%)	4.78	297	121
skim milk	0.44	302	86

Eating well can be a pleasure. Dining with friends and family is an important part of our culture as a way of being social and celebrating. Take pleasure in choosing beautiful fresh ripe tomatoes, juicy peaches, and the freshest fish. Eating in this manner is fulfilling yet healthy. When you choose such delicious foods, you'll never miss the sinful ones. It is all a matter of taste and conditioning. You and your family will love eating this way.

NOTE

1. A. K. Kant, A. Schatzkin, B. I. Graubard, et al. "A prospective study of diet quality and mortality in women." *Journal of the American Medical Association* 283:2109–115;2000.

CHAPTER 5

Exercise and the Prevention of Breast Cancer

Studies have shown that individuals who exercise regularly or are physically active on a regular basis, either through exercise or occupational activity, have decreased rates of cancer. In addition, exercise will help you maintain or lose weight, and will enhance your self-esteem and sense of well-being.

Several mechanisms by which exercise can decrease the risk of cancer have been proposed—enhanced immunity, decreased oxygen free radicals, and general enhanced health behavior. It appears that risk from almost all types of cancer is lowered to some degree by regular exercise. However, some cancers, such as breast cancer, colorectal cancer, and prostate cancer have been more extensively studied and proven with regard to this preventive effect.

The immune system and cancer prevention. One theory is that physical activity decreases cancer through a common mechanism. The body's natural immune system consists of cells called monocytes, macrophages, and natural killer cells. They are thought to be the primary line of defense on the cellular level in the body that fights against the development and spread of cancer.[1] Studies have shown that endurance-trained athletes at rest have enhanced natural killer cell activity compared with sedentary individuals. It is thought that this enhanced natural immunity increases resistance to the development of all types of cancer.[2]

Decreased free radicals and cancer prevention. Free radicals are reactive chemical compounds that are naturally produced in the body during the metabolism of food. They are also produced in connection with exposure to air pollution, smoke, and sunlight. Free radicals can cause cells to mutate and induce the proliferation of tumor cells. Exercise actually increases the production of free radicals. However, the body has an extensive free radical scavenger and antioxidant defense system that appears to be enhanced by exercise. So the exercising individual produces more free radicals, but then the revved up defense system of free radical scavenging works so well that the antioxidant defenses in the body work more efficiently than in sedentary individuals.[3]

Exercise promotes other behaviors. People who exercise are also more likely to engage in other health promoting behaviors. Those who exercise are much less likely to smoke, be overweight, or to eat a poor quality diet. Therefore, exercise tends to enhance other health behaviors that reduce cancer development.

Physical activity and breast cancer risk reduction. A specific association of decreased breast cancer risk with regular physical activity was first suggested by a study in 1985 that reported a significantly greater prevalence of breast cancer in women who were not involved with athletics in college compared with athletes. The study looked at the incidence of breast cancer in a group of women 56 years after graduation.[4] Many studies since that time have shown a significantly decreased risk of breast cancer associated with increased physical activity levels.[5] The earlier you begin exercising, the better off you are. One study found that women who exercised vigorously once a day between the ages of 14 and 22 had a 50 percent reduction in breast cancer later in life.[6]

Vigorous exercise and decreased breast cancer risk. The greatest risk reduction for breast cancer is in women who exercise very vigorously. The protective effect appears to come out only after you reach a certain level of energetic exercise.[7] One study found that only women who engaged in high intensity exercise at least three hours per week had a significantly reduced breast cancer rate.[8] Another study found the greatest risk reduction in women who exercised at least 4 hours per week.[9] Running, swimming, or biking at 65 percent of your maximum heart rate (220 minus your age) for 30 minutes six days per week are examples of this level of exercise.

The mechanism of decreased breast cancer risk in women who exercise is thought to be related to the effects of exercise on the menstrual cycle and lowered hormone production. Exercise decreases the number of ovulatory menstrual cycles and shortens the luteal phase (second half) of the menstrual cycle, the phase that follows ovulation in which estrogen levels are higher.[10] Early puberty is associated with more rapid onset of regular ovulatory cycles and an increased risk of breast cancer. Exercise around the time of puberty delays menarche, the beginning of regular periods. It has been estimate that for every year that menarche is delayed, breast cancer risk is reduced by 5 to 15 percent.

Body fat and breast cancer risk. Regular exercise is associated with decreased body fat, but the relationship between body fat and breast cancer risk is not quite that simple. Premenopausally, body fat is associated with a decreased breast cancer risk, but a worse prognosis if you are diagnosed with breast cancer. This is because obesity is associated with an increased frequency of anovulatory cycles—menstrual cycles in which no egg is produced and therefore estrogen levels are not as high. However, being overweight or obese puts you at greater risk for heart disease and can never be recommended. Postmenopausally, higher body fat levels increase the risk for breast cancer. This is because fatty tissue (adipose tissue) produces estrogen and is the major source of estrogen in the body after menopause. It is important to remember that exercise decreases breast cancer risk overall, whether you are premenopausal or postmenopausal. Premenopausally it decreases risk by reducing ovulatory function and postmenopausally by decreasing body fat.

Types of exercise. Even a small increase in your activity level can have a large effect on your overall health. You should get a total of 30 minutes of moderate exercise every day. Any type of activity counts toward this total, you do not necessarily need to join a gym or become an athlete. Such daily activities as yard work, gardening, walking upstairs, walking during lunchtime, and heavy cleaning all are beneficial. Walking, jogging, swimming, playing tennis, and weight training are excellent physical activities during your entire life span. Staying fit and active will help you control your weight, increase your feelings of well-being, and help you sleep better. Remember, you can start out walking around the block and build up to longer, enjoyable walks or more physically strenuous exercise.

NOTES

1. J. A. Woods, J. M. Davis. "Exercise, monocytes/macrophage function, and cancer." *Medical Science Sports Exercise* 26:147–57;1994.
2. I. M. Lee. "Exercise and physical health: cancer and immune function." *Research Quarterly Exercise and Sports* 66:286–91;1995. R. J. Shepard, P. N. Shek. "Cancer, immune function, and physical activity." *Canadian Journal of Applied Physiology* 20:1–25;1995.
3. R. D. Robertson, R. J. Maughan, G. C. Duthie, et al. "Increased blood antioxidant systems of runners in response to training load." *Clinical Science* 80:611–18;1991.
4. R. E. Frisch, G. Wyshak, N. L. Albright, et al. "Lower prevalence of breast cancer and cancers of the reproductive system among former college athletes compared to nonathletes." *British Journal of Cancer* 52:885–91;1985.
5. L. Bernstein, B. E. Henderson, R. Hanisch, et al. "Physical exercise and

reduced risk of breast cancer in young women." *Journal of the National Cancer Institute* 86:1403–08;1994. C. M. Friedenreich, T. E. Roham. "Physical activity and risk of breast cancer." *European Journal Cancer Prevention* 4:145–51;1995.

6. R. Mittendarf, M. P. Longnecker, et al. "Strenuous physical activity in young adulthood and risk of breast cancer." *Cancer Causes and Control* 6:347–53;1995.

7. H. Y. Hu, C. Nagata, et al. "Association of body mass index, physical activity, and reproductive histories with breast cancer: a case-control study in Gifu, Japan." *Breast Cancer Research and Treatment* 43:65–72;1997.

8. A. McTiernan, J. L. Stanford, N. S. Weiss, et al. "Occurrence of breast cancer in relation to recreational exercise in women age 50–64 years." *Epidemiology* 7:598–604;1996.

9. I. Thune, T. Breen, E. Lund, et al. "Physical activity and the risk of breast cancer." *New England Journal of Medicine* 336:1269–75;1997.

10. M. D. Holmes, W. C. Willett. "Can breast cancer be prevented by dietary and lifestyle changes?" *Annals of Internal Medicine* 27:429–30;1995.

Hormone Replacement Therapy and Breast Cancer Risk

Hormone replacement therapy.** Hormone replacement therapy (HRT) is a medical intervention in which a woman takes medication containing estrogen and progesterone to replace what her body is no longer producing at menopause. It is usually given to treat the symptoms of menopause—hot flashes, sleep disturbances, mood lability, and vaginal dryness. It can also be used to prevent and treat osteoporosis. In the past, HRT was frequently used to lower cholesterol and improve lipid profiles, but newer studies are not finding this as useful in the prevention of heart disease as once was thought.

Taking estrogen alone (called unopposed estrogen) can cause the lining of the uterus to build up, increasing your chances of getting endometrial cancer (cancer of the lining of the uterus). In order to protect from this, progesterone is also given when hormone replacement therapy is prescribed. Progesterone functions in the body to keep the uterine lining from building up. In fact, women who take both estrogen and progesterone have a decreased incidence of endometrial cancer compared to those who do not take HRT at all. However, progesterone can decrease somewhat the health benefits of estrogen. Because its only purpose is to decrease the risk of endometrial cancer, women who have had a hysterectomy need not take it.

Symptoms of menopause. Hot flashes are the most common symptom of menopause. They can occur well before the cessation of menses, and usually increase in frequency and intensity as menopause approaches. Menopausal symptoms vary widely among individuals and cultures. Symptoms may include hot flashes, night sweats, sleeplessness, irritability, fatigue, depression, anxiety, mood swings, backache, joint and muscle pains, new facial hair, vaginal dryness, pain with intercourse, and urinary frequency. While usually not a serious threat to health, these symptoms may negatively affect women's quality of life. All of these symptoms are related to the loss of estrogen in their bodies. The hot flashes and night sweats can cause sleep disturbances, making women moody, irritable, and fatigued.

Hormone replacement therapy for menopausal symptoms. HRT is an effective therapy for these problems. In fact, HRT is by far the most effective therapy for menopausal symptoms. The duration of therapy for the treatment of menopausal symptoms varies, but can range between a few months and a few years. In general, the younger the woman, or the more abrupt the onset of the menopause, the worse these symptoms tend to be. These menopausal symptoms will go away on their own after a few months to a few years, with or without the use of HRT.

Hormone replacement therapy and osteoporosis. Hormone replacement therapy is effective in the prevention and treatment of osteoporosis. Fractures from osteoporosis can have devastating effects on health and quality of life in older women. HRT stabilizes bone mineral density, and studies suggest that fracture risk is reduced between 30 and 50 percent for women taking HRT long term (more than five years).[1] Estrogen is one of the drugs approved by the Food and Drug Administration for the prevention of osteoporosis.

Risk factors for developing osteoporosis include women with low body weight, Caucasian and Asian women, smokers, and a family history of osteoporosis. All women, regardless of risk, may benefit from diet and exercise to prevent osteoporosis. This includes weight-bearing exercise (walking, running, aerobics, weight training) and adequate calcium intake in the diet or in supplements. Current calcium recommendations are 1500 mg/day for menopausal women not taking HRT and 1,000 mg/day for women taking HRT.

Hormone replacement therapy and heart disease. Heart disease is the most common cause of death among post-menopausal women. Until recently, it was thought that hormone replacement therapy was an effective strategy for reducing the risk of heart disease in women after menopause. Estrogen causes the liver to produce more of the good cholesterol HDL and less of the bad cholesterol LDL. Estrogen also inhibits the formation of artery-clogging plaques in the coronary arteries. It was thought that this improved lipid profile and protective effect on the heart in women taking hormone replacement therapy would decrease their risk of developing coronary heart disease.[2]

However, in the Heart and Estrogen Replacement Study (HERS), there was no reduction in cardiovascular heart disease events in women taking hormone replacement therapy despite the beneficial changes in LDL and HDL levels.[3] This study is one of the largest and one of the most well-done studies to date on hormone replacement therapy and protection from heart disease. In this study, there was not any decrease in coronary heart disease risk by using continuous combined hormone replacement therapy. Its dramatic findings have reversed our thinking about prescribing hormone replacement therapy solely for the prevention of heart disease and have caused many clinicians, myself included, to stop prescribing hormone replacement therapy for the prevention of heart disease until further data is collected.

There may even be an increased risk of heart attacks in the first year after starting hormone replacement therapy. In the

HERS study there was a trend toward an increase in non-fatal heart attacks as well as deaths in the first year among women taking hormone replacement therapy. There was a trend toward decreased mortality from heart disease in the hormone replacement therapy–treated group from the second to fourth years of the study.[4] Until this debate is clarified, it may be prudent to lower heart-disease risk through such proven treatments as diet, exercise, smoking cessation, and lipid-lowering drugs.

Hormone replacement therapy and Alzheimer's disease. A number of studies have suggested that women who take HRT may be at lower risk of developing Alzheimer's disease.[5] Supporting this possibility are studies in which women with Alzheimer's disease have demonstrated cognitive improvements after having received estrogen.[6] Despite these exciting developments, many questions remain to be answered, and HRT should not be considered a proven method for preventing Alzheimer's disease.

Side effects of hormone replacement therapy. Side effects from HRT occur and persist in approximately 10 percent of women. The most frequent symptoms are bloating, nausea, mood changes, and breast tenderness. Women prone to migraines may find that HRT precipitates the headaches. These side effects can be debilitating. Occasionally, changing the dosage of HRT or switching to different formulations can be helpful.

What to consider when deciding for or against HRT. A number of factors should be considered when deciding whether hormone replacement therapy is right for you. There are a wide variety of symptoms and disease processes that are helped by hormone replacement therapy. If you are suffering from severe hot flashes and are moody and irritable from them, hormone replacement therapy is the most effective form of therapy. Taken for a short period of time, hormone replacement therapy may slightly increase your risk of breast cancer. If you have mild menopausal symptoms, and are wanting to potentially prevent diseases that run in your family such as osteoporosis or

Alzheimer's disease, hormone replacement therapy can be a good "one stop shopping" treatment. If, however, you are looking for a more specific treatment for osteoporosis or heart disease, then perhaps a more targeted therapy is a better choice.

Finally, there are women for whom HRT is contraindicated for medical reasons. Women with a previous history of breast cancer, a blood-clotting disorder, or undiagnosed vaginal bleeding should not take hormone replacement therapy. Cigarette smoking is not a contraindication to hormone replacement therapy use, but it is a good idea for your overall health to stop before treatment starts.

Hormone Replacement Therapy and Breast Cancer

The truth about breast cancer risk. The fear of an increased risk of breast cancer is perhaps the principal reason women choose not to use hormone replacement therapy. And this fear is not unfounded. Reliable data on the effects of long-term hormone replacement therapy on the risk of developing breast cancer have demonstrated an increased risk in women taking these drugs. A number of studies have indicated an increased risk for breast cancer of 15 to 30 percent over baseline risk in postmenopausal women taking hormone replacement therapy (HRT). The Nurses' Health Study, following nurses taking hormone replacement therapy for 16 years, is one of the best studies to date.[7] During that time period, 69,000 postmenopausal women were followed long-term and their risk of developing breast cancer along with their use of hormones was evaluated. It was found that women who used hormones long term (10 or more years) were 1 ½ times as likely to develop breast cancer than those who did not take hormones.

By virtue of the large number of women studied, and the careful analysis by investigators, this study has great credibility and the increased risk of breast cancer found here is quite significant. For women with a strong family history of breast cancer, such as two first-degree relatives (mother or sister) or a mother who died of breast cancer at a premenopausal age, there may be an even higher risk. The Women's Health Initiative, a study of 16,000 women, is the largest and only trial that has compared women taking HRT to women taking a placebo. The data indicate that approximately 8 more women will develop breast cancer after one year of taking hormones than women taking placeboes. While this is only a small increase in breast cancer risk, it is still significant. Based on this data, it makes sense to limit the amount of time you take hormones to diminish menopausal symptoms.

Progestin in hormone replacement therapy and breast cancer risk. Early reports had suggested that using progestin in hormone replacement formulations might reduce the risk of breast cancer. However, recent data has refuted this claim. Reliable long-term studies now report that progestin plus estrogen may actually pose a greater risk for breast cancer than estrogen alone.[8] This makes intuitive sense, since many breast tumors have both estrogen and progesterone receptors. This means that both estrogen and progesterone can make them grow through different receptors, and therefore the effect could be additive with both estrogen and progesterone.

Short-term hormone replacement therapy and breast cancer risk. Short-term use of hormones, such as for the treatment of menopausal symptoms, which generally does not exceed five years and frequently can be utilized for only a year or two, does not appear to increase your risk of breast cancer. This is good news for women who are suffering from severe menopausal symptoms and have not been able to obtain relief from other sources.

Women with breast cancer and use of hormone replacement therapy. Women who have already been diagnosed with breast cancer should generally avoid hormone replacement therapy. Since these tumors are often estrogen responsive, the estrogen in hormone replacement therapy has the potential to activate any microscopic remaining tumor that might exist in your body. The one exception to this may be in a new form of estrogen, the estering, which is a treatment for vaginal dryness related to menopause have found relief with this treatment. And several studies have confirmed its relative safety in women previously diagnosed with breast cancer. You should, of course, check with your physician to see if this treatment is appropriate for you.

Alternatives to hormone replacement therapy for menopausal symptom reduction. For women with a personal history of breast cancer, or for those with a strong family history who have reservations about even short-term therapy, there are some alternatives to hormone replacement therapy for the treatment of menopausal symptoms.

Dietary phytoestrogens. There is data that supports that diets rich in phytoestrogen-containing foods reduce the incidence of menopausal hot flashes. The most important phytoestrogens found in the human diet are from isoflavones derived mainly from soy foods and lignans, found in flaxseed. Women in Western countries have approximately an 80 percent incidence of hot flashes, whereas Asian women living in China (where there is a high consumption of soy foods) have an incidence of only 20 percent.[9] Randomized controlled trials have shown that hot flashes are reduced in women who consume soy or isoflavones as compared with control subjects.[10] And since data indicate that women ingesting high amounts of phytoestrogens, particularly in the form of isoflavones in soy products, have less breast and uterine cancer, as well as cardiovascular disease, than those eating Western diets, there appear to be no risks.[11]

Behavioral changes to decrease hot flashes. Women who cannot take hormone replacement therapy can also try some behavioral changes to reduce hot flashes. Moderate exercise and the avoidance of potential hot-flash triggers—caffeine, spicy foods, alcohol, and warm rooms—can help. Exercise promotes deeper sleep and stimulates production of brain endorphins that help decrease negative thoughts and depressed feelings. Many women notice they are having fewer hot flashes when they exercise regularly. A moderate exercise regimen of 30 minutes each day of aerobic exercise, such as walking or swimming, has the greatest effect on your overall health in addition to your hot flashes. Some women notice fewer hot flashes when they meditate, do yoga, relax with a massage, or take a leisurely bath. Dressing in layers can help, since you can feel cold one minute and warm the next. Or you can ask those with whom you share an office to wear a sweater while you blast the air conditioner!

Serotonin reuptake inhibitors. Serotonin reuptake inhibitors are medications that increase the level of serotonin in the brain. They are an effective treatment for depression. Preliminary data shows great promise for these drugs in the treatment of hot flashes. Hot flashes are less frequent and less severe in women taking venlofexine (brand name effexor) from 37 to 61 percent decreased. Decreased libido (sex drive) can be a problem with this class of medications in the higher doses used to treat depression. However, in the low doses required to decrease hot flashes, sex drive does not appear to be affected. There are many formulations of serotonin reuptake inhibitors available, but venlofexine is the only one currently studied for the treatment of hot flashes.

Clonidine. One final alternative to hormone replacement therapy for the treatment of hot flashes is a medication called clonidine. Clonidine was originally marketed as a treatment for high blood pressure. Clonidine stimulates receptors in the brain that can decrease hot flashes in some women. Studies have shown that treatment with Clonidine results in significant decreases in the incidence of hot flashes when compared with a placebo.[12] When compared to estrogens, however, women taking clonidine had a significant decrease in hot flashes over baseline, but this effect was inferior to estrogen therapy.[13] In women with normal blood pressure, there were no significant decreases in blood pressures in any of the clonidine treatment groups. The most frequent side effects in the clonidine treatment groups were dry mouth and fatigue.

Raloxifene—a new estrogen. Raloxifene is the newest addition to women's choice of menopausal therapies. It should be noted, however, that raloxifene is not a treatment for menopausal symptoms. In fact, most women find hot flashes worsen when taking raloxifene. Therefore, this drug should only be taken when one is well past menopause, when hot flashes and other menopausal symptoms are no longer an issue.

Raloxifene is a synthetic preparation made in the laboratory of a type of estrogen that acts on some parts of the body but not on others—and is therefore termed a *selective estrogen receptor modulator.* For example, raloxifene is active on bones and lipids and has been shown to prevent osteoporosis in a similar fashion as traditional hormone replacement therapy. However, studies have been going on in this country for only up to three years, so it is not as well proven. It is not active on the vaginal tissues, so it will not improve vaginal dryness. Thus, for long-term health benefits, raloxifene is a promising alternative to HRT. However, for the short-term discomforts of menopause—hot flashes, resulting sleep disturbances, and vaginal dryness—raloxifene does not help. Long-term studies are under way to determine whether selective estrogen receptor modulators have beneficial effects on heart disease.

Importantly, raloxifene is not active on the breast, so it has the additional benefit of not increasing a woman's risk of breast cancer. In fact, there is some preliminary evidence that it may even decrease a woman's breast cancer risk. It may become a regular treatment for chemoprevention of breast cancer (see pages 79–80).

Hormone replacement therapy—an individual choice. Hormone replacement therapy for short-term treatment, less than five years, for menopausal symptoms does not appear to increase the risk of breast cancer. Long-term use, 10 years or more, does appear to significantly increase risk. The right choice for you should depend upon your own symptoms, while taking into consideration your family history of breast cancer. And there are alternatives to hormone replacement therapy that work for menopausal symptoms for those who do not wish to take hormones, or those for whom hormones are contraindicated, such as women who have already been diagnosed with breast cancer. You should educate yourself about these issues, then speak to your doctor or heath care provider about what choice is right for you. There is no one right way for everyone.

NOTES

1. J. A. Cauley, D. G. Seeley, K. Ensrud, et al. "Estrogen replacement therapy and fractures in older women: Study of Osteoporotic Fractures Research Group." *Annals of Internal Medicine* 122:9–16;1995.

2. M. J. Stampfer, W. C. Willett, G. A. Colditz, et al. "A prospective study of postmenopausal estrogen therapy and coronary heart disease." *New England Journal of Medicine* 313:1044;1985.

3. S. Hully, D. Grady, T. Bush, et al. "Randomized trial of estrogen plus progestin for secondary prevention of coronary heart disease in postmenopausal women. Heart and Estrogen/Progestin Replacement Study (HERS) Research Group." *Journal of the American Medical Association* 280:605–13;1998.

4. S. Hully, D. Grady, T. Bush, et al. for the Heart and Estrogen/Progestin Replacement Study (HERS) Research Group. "Randomized trial of estrogen plus progestin for secondary prevention of coronary heart disease in postmenopausal women." *Journal of the American Medical Association* 269:3015–23;1993. S. Hully, D. Grady, T. Bush, et al. "Randomized trial of estrogen plus progestin for secondary prevention of coronary heart disease in postmenopausal women. Heart and Estrogen/Progestin Replacement Study (HERS) Research Group." *Journal of the American Medical Association* 280:605–13;1998.

5. M. X. Tang, D. Jacobs, Y. Stern, et al. "Effect of oestrogen during menopause on risk and age at onset of Alzheimer's disease." *Lancet* 348:429–32;1996.

6. V. W. Henderson, A. Paganini-Hill, C. K. Emanuel, et al. "Estrogen replacement therapy in older women: comparisons between Alzheimer's disease cases and nondemented control subjects." *Archives of Neurology* 51:896–900;1994.

7. G. A. Colditz, E. D. Hankinson, D. J. Hunter, et al. "Use of estrogens and progestins and the risk of breast cancer in postmenopausal women." *New England Journal of Medicine* 332:1589–93;1995.

8. C. Schairer, J. Lubin, R. Troisi, et al. "Menopausal estrogen and estrogen-progestin replacement therapy and breast cancer risk." *Journal of the American Medical Association* 283:485–91;2000.

9. G. W. K. Tang. "The climacteric of Chinese factory workers." *Maturitas* 19:177–82;1994.

10. S. Washburn, G. L. Burke, T. Morgan, et al. "Effect of soy protein supple-

mentation on serum lipoproteins, blood pressure, and menopausal symptoms in perimenopausal women." *Menopause* 6:7–13;1999. P. Albertazzi, F. Pansini, G. Bonaccorsi, et al. "The effect of dietary soy supplementation on hot flushes." *Obstetrics and Gynecology* 91:6–11;1998. D. C. Knight, J. B. Howes, J. A. Eden. "The effect of Promensil, an isoflavone extract, on menopausal symptoms." *Climacteric* 2:79–84;1999. L. Murkies, C. Lombard, B. J. G. Strauss, et al. "Dietary flour supplementation decreases postmenopausal hot flushes: effect of soy and wheat." *Maturitas* 21:189–95;1995. A. Brzezinski, H. Adlercreutz, R. Shaoul, et al. "Short-term effects of phytoestrogen-rich diet on postmenopausal women." *Menopause* 4:89–94;1997. D. Upmalis, R. Lobo, L. Bradley. "Evaluation of the safety and efficacy of an oral soy extract in the treatment of vasomotor symptoms in menopausal women" (abstract 30). *Menopause* 6:327;1999.

11. L. W. Lissin, J. P. Cooke. "Phytoestrogens and cardiovascular health." *Journal of the American College of Cardiology* 35:1405–10;2000.
12. R. F. Edington, J. P. Changnon, W. M. Steinberg. "Clonidine for Menopausal Flushing." *Canadian Medical Association Journal* 123:23–06;1980.
13. W. Barr. "Problems related to postmenopausal women." *South African Medical Journal* 49:437–39;1975.

CHAPTER 7

Screening and Early
Detection of Breast Cancer

Until now, we have been discussing the measures that you can take to prevent breast cancer. But even those who eat well, avoid alcohol, and exercise regularly can still develop breast cancer. Your next best defense is through screening methods for the early detection of breast cancer, so that you can receive the most effective treatment possible. Effective cancer-screening methods detect disease before the development of symptoms, and thereby have a favorable impact on your life. Luckily, breast cancer is one of the cancers for which effective screening methods exist.

Time of detection of breast cancer and survival rates. Detecting breast cancer early on is associated with a better prognosis. In breast cancer, women diagnosed with small tumors (1.0 cm or less) have an 80 to 90 percent 20-year disease-free survival, whereas women with tumors measuring 1.1 to 2.0 cm have a 70 to 80 percent 20-year disease-free survival. Women with axillary (armpit) lymph node involvement have a worse prognosis compared with those without (86 percent versus 66 percent 20-year survival). The likelihood of positive lymph nodes is directly related to the size of the primary tumor. Not only is earlier-stage disease associated with a more favorable prognosis, but also treatment options available are more effective and less difficult to tolerate compared with those for later-stage disease. Don't let fear prevent you from getting the care you need. Early detection of breast cancer can save your life.

Methods for early detection. The three tests used in the early detection of breast cancer are breast self-examination, clinical breast examination, and mammography. These tests, while widely accepted and performed, have varying levels of effectiveness in the early detection of breast cancer. I'd like to explain the strengths and limitations of each of these techniques, so that you can take advantage of them while at the same time understanding their limitations so that you are not falsely reassured and caught unaware.

Breast self-examination. Most cases of breast cancer are discovered by women doing self-examinations, not by their doctors. A breast self-exam is a monthly exam that you can do yourself to check for breast cancer. When you do a breast self-examination, you check for lumps, thickening, dimples in the breast, or discharge from the nipple. When breast cancer is found early and treated, the chances for a cure are better. Every woman should do regular breast self-examinations.

What is the best time to examine my breasts? I usually recommend that you examine your breasts once a month at the end of your period. This is because your period will serve as a monthly reminder, and it is also a time when your breasts usually aren't tender or swollen. If you have already been through menopause or have had a hysterectomy, check your breasts on the first day of every month or whenever you can best remember to do it monthly.

How do I do a breast self-exam? A breast self-exam consists of the following five steps:

Step 1: Examine your breasts in the shower. Your hands move more easily over wet skin. With your fingers flat, move gently over the entire area of each breast, checking for any lump, hard knot, or thickening. If you do it monthly, you will get used to what is normal for you and it will be easy to detect changes.

Step 2: Look at your breasts while standing in front of a mirror. Look at them first with your hands at your sides, then with your hands raised over your head, then with your hands pressed firmly on your hips so that your chest muscles are flexed. Look for lumps, new differences in size and shape, and swelling or dimpling of the skin. Most women have a small amount of asymmetry between their breasts that is normal.

Step 3: Examine your breasts with your fingers while sitting or standing. Slowly and methodically press on a breast with the fingers of the opposite hand. With your fingers flat, work in a circular or spiral direction, beginning at the nipple and moving gradually outward.

Step 4: Lie down and repeat step 3. Use your right hand to examine your left breast, as in step 3, then use your left hand to examine your right breast. Feel for any lumps or thickening, especially those that cannot be felt in the same area in the other breast.

Step 5: Squeeze the nipple of each breast gently between your thumb and index finger. Report any discharge or fluid to your doctor.

If you find a lump, dimple, or discharge during your breast self-exam, see your health care provider. Don't be frightened. Most lumps are not cancerous, but only your health care provider can make the diagnosis. And remember, even if it is breast cancer, finding it early can make a big difference.

Breast self-examination effectiveness. Although breast self-examination has been advocated in the United States for more than 35 years, there does exist some conflict about its effectiveness as a screening method. One study found that breast self-examination was associated with a decrease in advanced cancer, suggesting that there may have been some benefit in detecting breast cancer before it became advanced.[1] A large randomized trial of breast self-examination done in China involving over 260,000 women with five years of follow-up showed no difference in mortality due to breast cancer and no significant difference in stage or size of cancer detected. There was, however, a trend toward decreasing size of tumor in women older than 50 performing breast self-examination.[2] In 1996, the US Preventive Services Task Force stated that there was "insufficient evidence to recommend for or against teaching breast self-exam in the periodic health examination."[3] The National Cancer Institute, the American Cancer Society, and the American College of Obstetrician Gynecologists recommend monthly breast self-examinations.

I continue to teach breast self-examinations. There is data in the medical literature, as I have just mentioned, that indicates that it does prevent breast cancer from becoming too advanced before it is detected. In addition, I feel it is important for women to understand their bodies and have some measure of control over examining oneself. It is, however, important to understand that breast self-examination is only one small part of the whole picture of breast health and it definitely has its limitations. A normal breast-self examination in the face of an abnormal mammogram, for example, certainly warrants further investigation. If your doctor feels a lump that you do not, this warrants investigation. It is also a frequent occurrence that you feel something abnormal and your doctor does not. These "false positives" are the major downside of breast self-examination. They create worry and anxiety, since the true "abnormals" are luckily few and far between.

Clinical breast examination. A clinical breast examination is an examination of your breasts done by a health care provider, usually annually. Recent scientific data shows that combining clinical breast examination with mammography is consistently better in detecting breast cancer early than mammography alone.[4] The National Cancer Institute, the American Cancer Society, and the American College of Obstetrician Gynecologists recommend yearly clinical breast examinations starting at age 40.

Mammograms. A mammogram is a low-dose X-ray that examines breast tissue. Screening mammography is useful for detecting breast cancer at an early stage. A mammogram can detect some types of cancer before you or your health care provider can feel a lump. Mammography was first used in the late 1800s in the differential diagnosis of breast masses in symptomatic women. It was not until the mid 1900s that mammography was used to detect pre-clinical disease.[5]

What to expect with a mammogram. A mammogram is done in your health care provider's office or in an X-ray clinic. You will be asked to take off your shirt, bra, and jewelry. Be sure your underarms and chest are clean. Don't put any deodorants, powders, or perfumes on your underarms or chest on the day your mammogram is to be done. These products can make it difficult to interpret the test results correctly. The technician will use a large machine to take X-rays of each breast. The mammogram appointment takes only a few minutes and is normally not painful. However, you will feel some pressure when your breasts are pressed between two plates for the X-rays, and your breasts may ache for a short time afterward. Each X-ray position requires just a few seconds.

Benefits of mammograms. Since mammograms were introduced, there have been eight major randomized controlled trials of breast cancer screening enrolling nearly 500,000 women in the United States, Canada, and Europe. Analyses of these trials have shown that for women aged 50–69 breast cancer mortality is decreased by about 30 percent.[6] Initial reports did not show a benefit of breast cancer screening for women aged 40–49 years. More recently, a 1997 analysis that included data from a follow-up time of 12 years showed a statistically significant mortality reduction of 18 percent.[7] Still, researchers debate screening this younger population because of false positive results, small absolute benefits, and poor cost-effectiveness.[8] Mammography in women 65 and older shows a higher positive predictive value and higher cancer detection rates when compared to younger women.[9] In addition, the incidence of breast cancer rises steeply with age.[10]

Schedule for mammogram screening. If you are 40 to 49 years old, I recommend that you have a mammogram every 1 to 2 years, depending on your personal and family history (this is controversial, as mentioned above). At age 50 and after, you should have one every year. Comparing mammograms from year to year helps detect early cancer. For those with a close family member (mother, sister, daughter) with the disease, annual mammograms can begin 10 years earlier than the age at which the relative was diagnosed.

Mammography helps find breast cancer at an early stage. The mammogram allows the detection of some types of breast cancer 1 to 2 years before you or your health care provider would be able to feel it. There is a better chance of curing the cancer if it is found at an early stage. There are no known significant risks from having mammograms according to the recommended screening schedule.

Mammogram screening schedule for women aged 40 to 49. The major area of controversy in terms of how frequently mammograms should be done is in women aged 40–49. This is because is it not totally clear if mammograms improve outcomes in this age group. In 1997, the National Institutes of Health, along with the National Cancer Institute, convened a consensus development conference to consider additional follow-up data from the trials which showed a benefit in women aged 40–49. They declined to recommend routine screening in women aged 40–49 and instead advised that each woman should decide for herself whether to undergo mammography. The American Cancer Society and the American College of Obstetrician Gynecologists recommend screening by mammography every 1–2 years in women aged 40–49 and yearly after 50. Most groups agree that women with a strong family history of breast cancer should be screened annually in their forties. I follow the American College of Obstetrician Gynecologists in my advice for screening frequency, recommending annual screening for women in their forties.

Why not screen women under 40? The reason that mammograms are not done in even younger women is that young women have denser breasts compared to older women. This means that their breast tissue contains a significant amount of fibrous connective tissue and less fatty tissue. On a mammogram, fibrous tissue is visualized as dense, and appears bright white, compared with normal breast ducts and lobules. This increased density, unless it is associated with microcalcifications, can obscure tumors and makes the test much less useful. In addition to young age and a low body mass index, several factors have been associated with increased breast density. The second half of the menstrual cycle (the luteal phase) is associated with an increase in breast density, making this a suboptimal time to screen.

In addition to this technical limitation, breast cancers are luckily few and far between in young women. Thus, screening younger women has not been proven to be cost-effective or to improve outcomes in these women. There are also a great many "false positives," meaning breast abnormalities are found that after biopsy are determined to be benign. This creates a great deal of worry and pain and suffering for little or no benefit in outcomes.

Mammograms for evaluation of breast abnormalities. In addition to screening women with no evidence of disease, mammograms are also used to evaluate lumps you or your health care provider have found in a physical exam. They can help determine which lumps are cancerous and which are benign. Once a breast lump is found, a mammogram can add information that can be helpful in deciding the next step, such as whether a biopsy is needed. Significant findings on a mammogram consist of alterations in the density of breast tissue, calcifications (especially microcalcifications, which are tiny specks of calcium frequently associated with malignancy), thickening of the skin, fibrous streaks, and nipple changes. Some of these mammography patterns may suggest early carcinoma and warrant further evaluation.

All suspicious lumps should be biopsied or removed, even when the lump appears noncancerous (benign) on a mammogram. Mammograms can be extremely helpful in the early diagnosis of breast cancer, even in the very early stages before a breast cancer can be felt. But the reverse is not always true: A negative mammogram in the face of a persistent breast lump does not always mean the absence of cancer. Some cancers do not show up on a mammogram, and can only be diagnosed definitively by breast biopsy. Mammograms can also be used to show breast surgeons where a lump is located in the breast before surgery or biopsy is done to remove it, especially if it cannot be felt by physical examination.

Ultrasound in the evaluation of breast lumps. Occasionally, your health care provider may recommend an ultrasound of the affected area in the breast as the next step. This is usually to determine if the lump is a breast cyst. If the ultrasound of the breast containing the mass identifies a cyst or variations in normal breast architecture that account for the lump, this is generally good news, since breast cysts are usually benign. Cysts may be aspirated both for diagnosis and therapy for painful lesions. Needle aspiration of cysts can be performed in an office setting, and local anesthesia is usually not necessary. When cyst aspiration is performed, the fluid may be discarded if the fluid is clear (transparent and not bloody) and the mass disappears. Cytological evaluation, a microscopic examination of the cells in the cyst fluid in order to detect abnormal appearing cells, may be performed if there are worrisome characteristics of the lump present, or if you have high risk factors for breast cancer. Malignancy in breast cysts is rare, with only 0.1–1 percent of breast fluid aspirations showing evidence of malignancy.[11]

Unlike mammography, ultrasound cannot identify microcalcifications, which can be hallmarks of early breast cancer. Frequently, you might have both an ultrasound and a mammogram of your breast so that these signs are not missed.

Nipple aspirate fluid for early detection of breast disease.
A new technique that shows great promise in the early detection of breast disease involves evaluation of nipple aspirate fluid. The female breast secretes and absorbs fluid constantly even in the resting state.[12] These processes occur in the ductal system of the breast. The fluid is, therefore, in intimate contact with the lining that gives rise to the majority of breast cancers.[13] Interest has increased in this breast ductal fluid as a type of "Pap smear" to screen for breast cancer.[14]

Fluid can be aspirated from the nipple by a suction device. This fluid is not the same as the fluid obtained from aspiration of breast cysts. Nipple aspirate fluid is collected by the use of a transparent cup placed over the nipple and negative pressure applied by means of a syringe attached to the cup by a plastic tube. The resulting fluid is collected from the surface of the nipple. This method has been widely used in an outpatient setting and is safe, reliable, and well tolerated by women.[15]

Nipple aspirate fluid is biochemically complex, containing a variety of proteins, lipids, carbohydrates, hormones, and other substances. There are a variety of hormonal influences on the breast, and the hormonal microenvironment of the nipple aspirate fluid may be relevant to disease processes within the breast because of the potential effect of these hormones on this lining.

Interest has centered on the cytology of the ductal lining cells present in nipple aspirate fluid. In an early series reporting on the cytology of nipple aspirate fluid, when there were suspicions of carcinoma, a diagnosis of cancer was confirmed in 66 percent of these women. Of note, 7 of these women were diagnosed by aspirated cytology alone, having had normal mammography and clinical examinations.[16]

There is evidence of a strong association with nipple fluid aspirate cells showing abnormalities and the presence of hyperplasia or cancer in the breast.[17] If the aspirated fluid shows abnormal cells, even in the presence of a normal physical examination and mammogram, further investigation is warranted. Those with a first degree relative as well as abnormal cells are at the highest risk for the development of breast cancer.[18] While the presence of normal cells in the nipple fluid is reassuring, this alone is not enough. One should still continue mammograms and breast examinations.

In a series auditing the use of nipple discharge cellular examination, 7 out of 15 breast cancers from 338 patients were correctly identified. It was concluded that examination of such fluid was a useful adjunct to other diagnostic methods, but that it was not safe to rely on it as the sole method of investigation of nipple discharge. Additional information that may be obtained from nipple aspiration cellular examination includes DNA analysis and hormone receptors status.

Similar to a Pap smear, breast cytology obtained by nipple aspirate sampling can detect abnormalities on the cellular level that are associated with the earliest stages of malignancies and potentially can reduce the mortality from breast cancer. There is hope that breast cytology could become as effective for the prevention of breast cancer as the Pap smear is for cervical cancer.

Be diligent about breast cancer screening. The bottom line in all of this is that screening and early detection of breast cancer works. Finding breast cancer early means your treatment is easier and your chance of cure higher. I urge you to do breast self-exams, have yearly physicals, and maintain appropriate mammogram screening. Do not let your fear of breast cancer get in the way of good health care. Breast cancer is curable if found early, so be diligent in your efforts.

NOTES

1. P. A. Newcomb, N. S. Weiss, B. E. Sorer, et al. "Breast self-examination in relation to the occurrence of advanced breast cancer." *Journal of the National Cancer Institute* 83:260–65;1991.
2. D. B. Thomas, D. L. Gao, S. G. Self, et al. "Randomized trial of breast self-examination in Shanghai: methodology and preliminary results." *Journal of the National Cancer Institute* 89:355–65;1997.

3. *Guide to Clinical Preventative Services: Report of the U.S. Preventive Services Task Force.* Baltimore: Williams & Wilkins 1996.

4. C. J. Baines. "Reflections on breast self-examination." *Journal of the National Cancer Institute* 89:339–40;1997. M. B. Barton, R. Harris, S. W. Fletcher. "Does this patient have breast cancer? The screening clinical breast examination: should it be done? How?" *Journal of the American Medical Association* 282:1270–80;1999.

5. B. E. Sirovich, H. C. Sox Jr. "Breast Cancer Screening." *Surgical Clinics of North America* 79:961–90;1999.

6. S. W. Fletcher, W. Black, R. Harris, et al. "Report of the International Workshop on Screening for Breast Cancer." *Journal of the National Cancer Institute* 85:1644–56;1993. B. E. Sirovich, H. C. Sox Jr. "Breast Cancer Screening." *Surgical Clinics of North America* 79:961–90;1999. *Guide to Clinical Preventive Services: Report of the U.S. Preventive Services Task Force.* Baltimore: Williams & Wilkins 1996. K. Kerlikowske, D. Grady, S. M. Rubin, et al. "Efficacy of screening mammography. A meta-analysis." *Journal of the American Medical Association* 273:149–54;1995.

7. R. E. Hendrick, R. A. Smith, J. H. Rutledge III, et al. "Benefit of screening mammography in women aged 40–49: a new meta-analysis of randomized controlled trials." *Journal of the National Cancer Institute Monographs* 22:87–92;1997.

8. B. E. Sirovich, H. C. Sox Jr. "Breast Cancer Screening." *Surgical Clinics of North America* 79:961–90;1999. K. Kerlikowske, D. Grady, S. M. Rubin, et al. "Efficacy of screening mammography. A meta-analysis." *Journal of the American Medical Association* 273:149–54;1995. NIH Consensus Statement 1997.

9. R. M. Faulk, E. A. Sickles, R. A. Sollitto, et al. "Clinical efficacy of mammographic screening in the elderly." *Radiology* 194:193–97;1995.

10. B. E. Sirovich, H. C. Sox Jr. "Breast Cancer Screening." *Surgical Clinics of North America* 79:961–90;1999.

11. B. Fisher, J. P. Constantino, D. L. Wickerham, et al. "Tamoxifen for prevention of breast cancer: report of the National Surgical Adjuvant Breast and Bowel Project P-1 study." *Journal of the National Cancer Institute* 90:1371–88;1988.

12. N. L. Petrakis. "Physiologic, biochemical, and cytologic aspects of nipple aspirate fluid." *Breast Cancer Research and Treatment* 8:7–19;1986.

13. E. L. Winder, P. Hill. "Prolactin, oestogen and lipids in breast fluid." *Lancet* 11:840–42;1977.

14. S. Masood. "The missing link: a 'pap smear' for early breast cancer detection and prevention." *The Breast Journal* 5:1–2;1999.

15. E. B. King, K. L. Chew, N. L. Petrakis, et al. "Nipple aspirate cytology for the study of breast cancer precursors." *Journal of the National Cancer Institute* 71:1115–21;1983.

16. O. W. Sartorius, H. S. Smith, P. Morris, et al. "Cytologic evaluation of breast

fluid in the detection of breast disease." *Journal of the National Cancer Institute* 59:1073–80;1977.

17. E. B. King, K. L. Chew, N. L. Petrakis, et al. "Nipple aspirate cytology for the study of breast cancer precursors." *Journal of the National Cancer Institute* 71:1115–21;1983.

18. M. R. Wrensch, N. L. Petrakis, E. B. King, et al. "Breast cancer incidence in women with abnormal cytology in nipple aspirates of breast fluid." *American Journal of Epidemiology* 135:130–41;1992.

CHAPTER 8

Chemoprevention for Breast Cancer

A new and promising area in the prevention of breast cancer is called chemoprevention. Chemoprevention involves taking drugs in order to prevent the development of breast cancer. Recent new data has shown that chemoprevention for breast cancer is possible, offering new options for women at increased risk for breast cancer. In the past, women at high risk for breast cancer had only close surveillance for early detection of breast cancer and prophylactic mastectomy to decrease their risk of getting breast cancer as options for breast cancer prevention.

Prophylactic mastectomies and oophorectomies. Women at high risk for breast cancer have some surgical options. Preventive (prophylactic) mastectomies (breast removal) or oophorectomies (ovary removal) certainly can significantly reduce, but not eliminate, the risks of breast and ovarian cancers in women in high-risk categories. Simply having the genes BRCA1 or BRCA2, or a strong family history, however, does not guarantee that these cancers will occur. And these types of surgeries can significantly impair the quality of life, have major consequences for one's body image, and have their own surgical complication rates.

And there still are no guarantees. Undergoing a mastectomy or oophorectomy does not completely eliminate the risk of breast or ovarian cancers since some cells may remain that can activate the disease later on. Nevertheless, studies indicate that prophylactic mastectomy reduces the incidence in women at high risk for breast cancer by 90 percent. It is still impossible to determine whether a specific woman with genetic susceptibility will actually get breast cancer, so it is a very hard choice.

Chemoprevention of breast cancer. Currently, two drugs, tamoxifen and raloxifene, have shown great promise in the chemoprevention of breast cancer as the first alternative to pro-phylactic mastectomy in decades of treatment. These drugs are a type of hormone therapy for the prevention of breast cancer. The body's own estrogen can cause cells in the breast to duplicate and potentially to become cancerous. This hormone therapy works by blocking estrogen from causing cells in the breast to duplicate.

Tamoxifen. You have probably heard of tamoxifen, which has been used for years to treat breast cancer. Tamoxifen acts as an estrogen antagonist in the breast, where it binds to receptors, and prevents your own body's much stronger estrogen from binding there. Tamoxifen, the first anti-estrogen available for the treatment of breast cancer, has been in clinical use for the last thirty years. Tamoxifen is usually given to those women with early breast cancer that is hormone receptor-positive. It is used for five years after surgery. Combining tamoxifen with chemotherapy appears to be more effective than tamoxifen alone in preventing tumor recurrence in postmenopausal women with estrogen-positive tumors following lumpectomy. It may also improve outcomes in this group of women whose cancer has spread to the lymph nodes. Studies are under way to determine its protection along with its risks when taken for periods of five years and more.

In addition to its anti-estrogen benefits in the treatment of breast cancer, tamoxifen has been shown to have favorable effects on serum lipids and bone mineral density. However, endometrial cancer is increased in women taking tamoxifen, and it carries an increased risk of stroke, pulmonary embolism, and deep-vein thrombosis.

Tamoxifen in the prevention of breast cancer. Tamoxifen is now being used and studied for the prevention of breast cancer. The results of the first large-scale breast cancer prevention trial, the *Breast Cancer Prevention Trial*, were recently reported.[1] This trial found that women who were given tamoxifen who had a high risk of developing breast cancer had a 49 percent reduction in the development of invasive breast cancer. Tamoxifen has been approved by the US Food and Drug Administration (FDA) to try to reduce breast cancer incidence in high-risk women. The FDA noted that tamoxifen does not eliminate breast cancer risk in these women.

Raloxifene in the prevention of breast cancer. Raloxifene is a newer option for breast cancer prevention. Raloxifene is a *selective estrogen receptor modulator* (SERM). This means that it binds to estrogen receptors in some tissues, such as the breast, with no stimulating effect. In other tissues, such as the bones, it has an estrogen-like effect. Raloxifene (brand name Evista) was originally marketed as an alternative to hormone replacement therapy for the prevention of osteoporosis. Raloxifene appears to prevent fractures almost as well as traditional hormone replacement therapy. Unlike tamoxifen, raloxifene is a complete estrogen antagonist in the uterus and does not stimulate the endometrium, whereas tamoxifen stimulates endometrial proliferation. This difference between the selective estrogen receptor modulator profiles of tamoxifen and raloxifene is perhaps the most important difference between the two. Raloxifene has been shown to prevent bone loss, reduce serum cholesterol, and provide anti-cancer effects on the breast. Best of all, raloxifene does not appear to increase the risk of breast cancer. Side effects include hot flashes and leg cramps. Serious side effects are rare, but an increase in blood clotting has been reported.

That raloxifene did not stimulate the breast, along with the fact that raloxifene is structurally related to tamoxifen caught doctors' attention in terms of raloxifene's potential role in the chemoprevention of breast cancer. So researchers are looking closely at raloxifene to see if there might be a protective effect on the breast. The results of the Breast Cancer Prevention Trial are the basis for a second-generation prevention study initiated in 1999: the STAR trial (Study of Tamoxifen and Raloxifene) in the prevention of breast cancer. Like tamoxifen, raloxifene was originally developed for the treatment of breast cancer. Between 1982 and 1986 a series of clinical studies exploring the use of raloxifene were undertaken. The results of the STAR trial will shed light on the preventive effects of raloxifene on the development of breast cancer. We will wait with great excitement for the results of this study.

Retinoids. Retinoids are a form of Vitamin A. They are being studied for their role in protection against breast cancer in high-risk patients and recurrence in those who have been treated for breast cancer. In general, results have been disappointing. One such drug, fenretinide, may offer some protection against a second breast cancer incidence in premenopausal women, but not in postmenopausal women. Unlike tamoxifen and similar agents, retinoids may actually increase the risk for osteoporosis.

Hope for the future. Breast cancer research is moving at lightning speed. As newer and more effective drugs for chemoprevention are developed, we will likely see chemoprevention replace surgical methods for preventing breast cancer. This provides hope not only for those with known genetic mutations or family histories that put them at high risk for developing breast cancer but for all women. With a one in eight lifetime risk of getting breast cancer, everyone needs to be vigilant about breast health. Now, instead of sitting back and wondering if you will be next, you can fight back with the strong arm of modern science combined with a good diet and exercise routine that will keep you healthy for life.

NOTE

1. B. Fisher, J. P. Constantino, D. L. Wickerham, et al. "Tamoxifen for prevention of breast cancer: report of the National Surgical Adjuvant Breast and Bowel Project P-1 Study." *Journal of the National Cancer Institute* 90:1371–88;1998.

Recipes

CHAPTER 9

Smoothies

Smoothies are the quickest and easiest way to incorporate a variety of breast cancer fighting nutrients into your diet. They make an ideal snack or a quick breakfast and are a real treat on a steamy day. With a high-quality blender, ripe fruit, silken tofu, or a flavored soy yogurt, you can prepare tasty and nutritious drinks in a matter of minutes. The drinks are rich in phytoestrogens from the soy and contain abundant amounts of antioxidants from the fruits and fruit juices.

The wide variety of frozen fruit in today's markets makes smoothies convenient to prepare. If you want to save money and use the ripest and sweetest fruit in your drinks, purchase or pick fruits that are in season, wrap them tightly in individual portions, and freeze. Even bananas that may seem past their prime can be frozen. Peel and slice them in half before placing them in your freezer. Also, when using all frozen fruit in a smoothie, eliminate the ice cubes.

Whether you like berries or bananas, mangoes or kiwis, a

sweet or tart flavor, we are sure you will be able to find a frozen drink in this section that you will enjoy. Hopefully, after seeing how simple these drinks are to prepare and how delicious they taste, you will be inspired to create your own delectable concoctions.

All of the recipes in this chapter call for a blender; others call for a food processor. You may be wondering which appliance performs best and perhaps which you should choose if you wish to purchase only one.

During the 1980s, food processors were staples in both home and restaurant kitchens. They could perform multiple tasks, from making bread and pastry doughs to chopping nuts and making bread crumbs. Blenders, with their weak motors, were pushed to the back of the cabinet. During the past several years, though, blenders have staged a remarkable comeback. Manufacturers have spruced up their machines with new motors and larger carafes; they are now able to make frozen drinks and pureed sauces and vegetables significantly better than their predecessors.

A food processor's strength is with dry ingredients. With its various blades, it can slice, dice, shred, and knead. A blender's strong point is with wet ingredients. It purees liquids, emulsifying them into an incredible lightness. A vegetable puree or a frozen drink will be smooth when made in a food processor, but it will be practically buoyant when made in a blender. This difference occurs because a blender has two additional blades and a smaller cutting area than a food processor. Most important, however, is that the blades of a high-quality blender move much faster than those of a food processor. It is important to note that there are still old-style blenders available with multiple speeds and poor motors that have a difficult time pureeing even a single carrot.

So what is our choice if we had to choose only one? We would choose a high-quality blender over a food processor—simply because many of the tasks a food processor does well, we can do manually (though not as quickly). A great blender is indispensable.

🌿 Apricot and Mango Smoothie

Mangoes are an ingredient often used in smoothies. They blend wonderfully with other ingredients and add a natural sweetness. They are also an excellent source of beta-carotene and Vitamin C. This drink is one of our favorites.

Tip: *Frozen mango chunks can often be found in the freezer section of a supermarket. If you can't locate them, peel, seed, and cube a fresh mango. Wrap it tightly and freeze for 24 hours.*

PREPARATION:
5 MINUTES

YIELD:
2 10-OUNCE
SERVINGS

1 large banana
1 mango, peeled and cubed
½ cup orange juice
8 ounces apricot-mango soy yogurt
2 ice cubes

1. Place the banana, mango, orange juice, and yogurt in a blender.
2. Blend the ingredients until they are smooth. Drop the ice cubes into the container and blend the drink for 30 seconds more.
3. Pour the smoothie into 2 glasses and serve immediately.

MANGOES

A ripe mango is best peeled and eaten like any other fresh fruit. In the kitchen, though, a mango finds its way into both sweet and savory dishes. Because of their incredible sweetness, the most obvious use for mangoes is in a dessert or smoothie. However, their assertive and complex flavor makes them very versatile. They pair well in dishes that contain chilies, garlic, ginger, citrus, and a variety of herbs. When combined with tomatoes and black beans, they make a delectable salsa. When tossed with seared scallops, lime, and cilantro, they make a memorable seafood dish.

When buying fresh mangoes, look for smooth-skinned fruits that are blemish-free. Also, mangoes do not need to be orange or red to be ripe; greenish-tinged ones can be ripe as well. As when choosing melons, choose mangoes that smell fruity. Unripe mangoes can be ripened at room temperature. Once ripe, they should be refrigerated. Mangoes, like all deep orange–fleshed fruits and vegetables, are very rich sources of beta-carotene.

❧ Kiwi and Mango Smoothie

PREPARATION:
5 MINUTES

YIELD:
2 10-OUNCE
SERVINGS

Kiwis are not a fruit often found in smoothies. They need to be combined with sweeter-tasting ingredients that enhance their mild flavor without overpowering their taste. In this recipe mangoes and apple juice provide the sweetness and silken tofu adds the texture. The result is a not-too-sweet, refreshing, and antioxidant-rich beverage.

2 kiwi fruits, peeled and quartered
1 mango, peeled and cubed
1½ cups apple juice
5 ounces silken tofu
2 ice cubes

1. Place the kiwis, mango, apple juice, and tofu in a blender.
2. Blend the ingredients until they are smooth. Drop the ice cubes into the container and blend the drink for 30 seconds more.
3. Pour the smoothie into 2 glasses and serve immediately.

SILKEN TOFU

Phytoestrogen-rich silken tofu is the tofu to use when you are "hiding" tofu in recipes. It is much softer than firm tofu and has a creamy consistency. When it is pureed in a blender or food processor, it can be used in place of cream in soups and sauces. It makes silky dressings and smooth-textured frozen drinks, luscious puddings, and dense cheesecakes. It adds a wonderful consistency to dips and spreads and makes surprisingly rich mashed potatoes. Silken tofu is available in the refrigerated sections of most markets in firm and soft varieties. They can be used interchangeably in your favorite recipes. Silken tofu is usually packed in 12.3-ounce aseptically sealed containers or 1-pound blocks packed in plastic containers.

❧ Mango and Strawberry Smoothie

Since super-sweet mangoes are such a rich source of beta-carotene, we use them in many of our smoothies. In this recipe a mango is paired with Vitamin C-rich strawberries and orange juice to create an ideal on-the-go breakfast or snack.

    Tip: *Frozen strawberries are widely available, but the quality tends to vary. We like to purchase or pick fresh ones when they are in season and freeze them for future use.*

PREPARATION:
5 MINUTES

YIELD:
2 10-OUNCE
SERVINGS

1 mango, peeled and cubed
1 cup frozen strawberries
1 cup orange juice
5 ounces silken tofu
8 ounces soy strawberry yogurt

1. Place the mango, strawberries, orange juice, tofu, and yogurt in a blender.
2. Blend the ingredients until they are smooth.
3. Pour the smoothie into 2 glasses and serve immediately.

❧ Lemon and Mango Smoothie

When we first tested this recipe, we used silken tofu and fresh lemon juice but found the drink too sour. When we substituted soy lemon yogurt for the tofu and lemon juice, the balance between sweet and tart was perfect. The drink is rich in breast cancer preventing phytoestrogens and beta-carotene.

PREPARATION:
5 MINUTES

YIELD:
2 8-OUNCE
SERVINGS

1 mango, peeled and cubed
1 banana
8 ounces soy lemon yogurt
½ cup orange juice
4 ice cubes

1. Place the mango, banana, yogurt, and orange juice in a blender.

2. Blend the ingredients until smooth. Drop the ice cubes into the container and blend the drink for 30 seconds more.
3. Pour the smoothie into 2 glasses and serve immediately.

⚘ Carrot-Mango Blast

PREPARATION:
10 MINUTES

YIELD:
2 8-OUNCE
SERVINGS

Although carrots are not often used in smoothies, when they are cooked, cooled, and pureed, they provide a wonderful sweetness and texture to a frozen drink. Both the mango and carrots are very rich sources of beta-carotene.

½ cup water
2 carrots, scraped and sliced
1 mango, peeled and cubed
8 ounces vanilla soy yogurt
½ cup orange juice
4 ice cubes

1. Prepare an ice bath.
2. Bring the water to a boil in a small saucepan. Add the carrots. Cook until tender, approximately 5 minutes. Drain them in a strainer. Place the strainer into the ice bath. Allow the carrots to cool for a moment.
3. Combine the mango, yogurt, orange juice, and carrots in a blender. Blend the ingredients until smooth.
4. Drop the ice cubes into the container and blend the drink for 30 seconds more.
5. Pour the smoothie into 2 glasses and serve immediately.

🌿 Banilla-Blueberry Smoothie

Bananas and blueberries are a common smoothie combination. By adding vanilla yogurt and a touch of vanilla extract we have created a more interesting drink with a pronounced vanilla flavor. Blueberries are an excellent source of fiber and antioxidants.

PREPARATION:
5 MINUTES

YIELD:
2 10-OUNCE
SERVINGS

1 large banana
1 cup frozen blueberries
½ cup orange juice
8 ounces vanilla soy yogurt
½ teaspoon vanilla extract
2 ice cubes

1. Place the banana, blueberries, orange juice, yogurt, and vanilla extract in a blender.
2. Blend the ingredients until smooth. Drop the ice cubes into the container and blend the drink for 30 seconds more.
3. Pour the smoothie into 2 glasses and serve immediately.

BLUEBERRIES

Cultivated blueberries are grown all over the world, but wild blueberries are one of the few fruits that are native to North America. Except for a few areas in New Hampshire and Massachusetts, they thrive only in northeast Maine. The season is short, stretching from early August until about the middle of September. Wild and cultivated blueberries are interchangeable in cooking but wild blueberries taste better. They are significantly smaller than the cultivated variety, have a deeper blue color, and a more concentrated flavor.

Blueberries, wild or cultivated, fresh or frozen, are one of the most versatile fruits. They can be the star ingredient in cakes, pies, syrups, and muffins as well as vinegars, salads, and savory sauces.

Besides their wonderful versatility and great taste, blueberries are prized for their incredible nutritional value. Recent studies indicate that blueberries, both wild and cultivated, rank highest among forty other common fruits and vegetables regarding antioxidant activity. That is, they have the ability to neutralize free radicals. Free radicals are the prime suspects that researchers believe cause cancer and heart disease.

Whether you are fortunate enough to pick and indulge in fresh wild blueberries during their brief appearance or purchase cultivated or frozen berries, the flavor and nutrition of this delectable fruit should not be missed.

🐾 Cantaloupe-Berry Smoothie

PREPARATION:
5 MINUTES

YIELD:
2 10-OUNCE
SERVINGS

In our work The Pregnancy Cookbook, *Cantaloupe-Banana Shake was a recipe that many people found interesting. Since smoothies were just becoming popular, it was a timely recipe. Here is an updated version. It is still quick and easy. But now, since it contains tofu and berries, it is more nutritious. Cantaloupe, like all deep orange–fleshed fruits and vegetables, is a great source of beta-carotene. Blueberries, strawberries, and orange juice provide abundant amounts of Vitamin C.*

1 cup cantaloupe chunks
1 small banana
½ cup strawberries
½ cup blueberries
4 ounces silken tofu
1 cup orange juice
2 ice cubes

1. Place the cantaloupe, banana, strawberries, blueberries, tofu, and orange juice in a blender.
2. Blend the ingredients until smooth. Drop the ice cubes into the container and blend the drink for 30 seconds more.
3. Pour the smoothie into 2 glasses and serve immediately.

✤ Peach and Raspberry Smoothie

This is the drink we like to make during summer when peaches and raspberries are at their sweetest and freshest. Peaches, like all deep orange–fleshed fruits and vegetables, are rich in beta-carotene. Raspberries are an excellent source of Vitamin C.

PREPARATION:
10 MINUTES

YIELD:
1 12-OUNCE
SERVING

⅔ cup peach juice or orange juice
2 medium peaches, pitted and sliced
½ cup fresh or frozen raspberries
1 medium banana
3 ice cubes

1. Place the peach juice or orange juice, peach slices, raspberries, and banana in a blender.
2. Blend the ingredients until smooth. Drop the ice cubes into the container and blend the drink for 30 seconds more.
3. Pour the smoothie into a glass and serve immediately.

🍃 Tropical Delight

PREPARATION:
5 MINUTES

YIELD:
2 10-OUNCE
SERVINGS

When we come across sweet and reasonably priced pineapples, we always purchase a few. We skin, core, and cube the flesh of all of them. We enjoy some of the pineapple fresh, but most of it we freeze in several small packages to use in smoothies. In this recipe we combine the pineapple with orange sherbet for a taste of the Islands. Vanilla soy yogurt adds creaminess and phytoestrogens. Pineapples are an excellent source of Vitamin C.

  2 cups frozen pineapple chunks
  ½ pint orange sherbet
  4 ounces vanilla soy yogurt
  1 cup pineapple juice

1. Place the pineapple chunks, orange sherbet, yogurt, and pineapple juice in a blender.
2. Blend the ingredients until smooth.
3. Divide the smoothie between 2 glasses and serve immediately.

❧ The Maine Connection

Wild Maine blueberries, the antioxidant superstars, are the primary ingredient in this creamy concoction. Of course, if you can't locate wild blueberries, you can still make a great smoothie with cultivated ones.

PREPARATION:
5 MINUTES

YIELD:
2 12-OUNCE
SERVINGS

2 cups frozen wild Maine blueberries or 2 cups frozen cultivated blueberries
½ pint nonfat vanilla frozen yogurt
4 ounces silken tofu
1 cup apple juice

1. Place the blueberries, frozen yogurt, tofu, and apple juice in a blender.
2. Blend the ingredients until smooth.
3. Divide the smoothie between 2 glasses and serve immediately.

❧ Peach-Cantaloupe Smoothie

With two of the richest fruit sources of beta-carotene and fabulous taste and texture, this smoothie is sure to be one that you will want to add to your repertoire.

PREPARATION:
5 MINUTES

YIELD:
2 10-OUNCE
SERVINGS

2 cups peeled frozen peach chunks
1 cup frozen cantaloupe chunks
1½ cups orange juice
4 ounces silken tofu

1. Place the peach chunks, cantaloupe chunks, orange juice, and tofu in a blender.
2. Blend the ingredients until smooth.
3. Divide the smoothie between 2 glasses and serve immediately.

CHAPTER 10

Soups

There are few things more satisfying or nutritious on a cool evening than a steaming bowl of soul-warming soup. A soup is the perfect meal to prepare when you want to include many of the breast cancer fighting ingredients in your diet that are rich in antioxidants, phytoestrogens, fiber, and folic acid. Winter squash, dried peas and beans, sweet potatoes, carrots, greens, tofu, miso, tomatoes, soy milk, and corn can all be used in various combinations with an array of seasonings to create wonderful soups.

We like to serve many of our soups as main courses. Along with a variety of vegetables, if they contain beans, grains, or tofu, they are essentially one-pot dishes that need little else to accompany them to create a satisfying and nutritious meal. A hunk of crusty bread or a quesadilla and a green salad are great accompaniments to a soup meal.

Soups are an opportunity for an imaginative cook to allow her creative juices to flow. They are also a good way for a novice cook to begin experimenting with different combinations of herbs, spices, grains, and vegetables to discover those that work best together. The skills that one acquires by being able to create a delectable soup will allow you to make any stew, braised meal, or sauce. In fact, if you glance through the recipes in this book, you will notice that many of the techniques used in soup cookery are also used to make pasta, fish, meat, poultry, and casserole meals.

A great soup requires little more than quality ingredients and a sound understanding of several basic techniques. All of our soups are broth based. Their liquid is water or stock; they contain no cream or milk. First, it should be mentioned that although a flavorful stock is important in making tasty soup, it is not essential. Plain water or water in which potatoes or other vegetables have been cooked will suffice. Technique is much more important.

We almost always start our soups with a few cloves of sliced garlic cooked in a tablespoon of olive oil until they begin to soften. Onions or leeks are added next, along with a sprinkling of salt. Salt added at this juncture is important. It helps to draw the moisture out of the onion causing it to sweat and soften. This is where the flavor begins to develop. Next, carrots, celery, and other root vegetables are added along with another sprinkling of salt. The vegetables are cooked over medium-low heat in a covered pot until they begin to soften.

Dried herbs or spices are added next. By adding them before any liquid, and cooking them for a minute or two, they will have time to lose their edge and intensify in flavor. Fresh herbs should be added just before the soup is served.

At this point the soup already has plenty of flavor and the liquid can be added. Add the water or stock and bring the soup to a boil. Tomatoes and cooked beans or dried peas can now be added. The soup is simmered until the vegetables are tender. If you are going to add pasta, rice, or grains, they should be cooked beforehand and added during the last 5 minutes of simmering. Since they tend to absorb liquid, be certain not to add an excessive amount.

If you want to give your soup a creamy texture, pureed silken or soft tofu added during the last few minutes will do the trick. It will magically give your soup a silky-smooth consistency. Another method to alter the consistency of a soup is to puree half the soup. This will give it a creamy texture and make it heartier. Winter squash and potato-based soups turn out especially well when pureed.

The final step is to season the soup with sea salt and a few grinds of fresh black pepper. This final seasoning is critical. It rounds out and intensifies the flavor of the soup. Your goal should be to serve the soup so that it needs no additional seasoning at the table.

In addition to these techniques, a good pot is essential to making a successful soup. We like to use a large enameled cast-iron Dutch oven with a tight-fitting lid. In fact, this type of pot is one of the best and most versatile cooking vessels one can own. We have 2-, 5-, and 7-quart Dutch ovens; they are the busiest pots in our kitchen. You can do everything from cooking pasta and rice to braising meat and stir-frying vegetables in a Dutch oven.

Whether your pleasure is a light broth-based soup such as Tomato and Corn Soup, a creamy soup such as Butternut Squash and Tofu Soup with Fried Leeks, a hearty dried pea soup such as "Creamy" Lentil and Tofu Soup with Garlicky Chard and Tomatoes, or a more traditional soup such as Corn Chowder, you will discover that to create a delectable soup, you do not need fancy equipment or esoteric ingredients—just a bit of time and a great imagination.

❧ Chickpea, Potato, and Chard Soup with Saffron

In vegetarian Indian cooking, chickpeas and potatoes are the base to a hearty, curry-flavored stew. In Spanish cuisine, they are the main ingredients in a vegetarian paella. We have used them in a wonderful saffron-infused soup that is laced with Swiss chard. The chard provides great color contrast and just the right amount of earthiness. The soup is rich in beta-carotene, Vitamin C, and folic acid.

PREPARATION:
15 MINUTES

COOKING:
1 HOUR

YIELD:
4 MAIN-COURSE
SERVINGS

2 tablespoons olive oil
4 cloves garlic, peeled and sliced
1 onion, peeled and diced
　Sea salt to taste
2 medium carrots, scraped and diced
2 stalks celery, diced
2 medium Yukon Gold potatoes, cubed
1 16-ounce can chickpeas, drained and rinsed
8 cups water
½ teaspoon saffron
½ pound chard, leaves and stems rinsed, trimmed, and chopped
8 ounces cooked broad egg noodles
　Black pepper to taste

1. Heat the olive oil in a Dutch oven over medium heat. When it is hot, add the garlic to the pot. Cook the garlic for 30 seconds.
2. Add the onion and sprinkle with sea salt. Cook the onion until it begins to soften, stirring often. Add the carrots, celery, and potatoes to the pot.
3. Reduce the heat to low and cover the pot. Cook the vegetables for 10 minutes, stirring often.
4. Add the chickpeas and water to the pot. Raise the heat to high and bring the soup to a boil.
5. Place the saffron in a small bowl. Crush it with your fingers. Remove ¼ cup of the soup and pour it into the bowl. Allow

the saffron to steep for 10 minutes. Add the saffron liquid to the soup. Reduce the heat and simmer the soup for 35 minutes.

6. Raise the heat to high. Add the chard to the soup. Cook the soup until the chard is tender, approximately 5 minutes.
7. Add the noodles to the soup. Season the soup with sea salt and black pepper.
8. Ladle the soup into 4 large bowls and serve at once.

SWISS CHARD

A member of the beet family, chard is one of our favorite vegetables. We love it for its nutrition, flavor, and versatility in the kitchen. The most widely available varieties are red and green chard. Farmers' markets and specialty grocers often carry a sweeter-tasting chard marketed as Bright Lights with pink, purple, yellow, and orange stems. When choosing chard, choose bunches with uncut leaves and unbruised stems. Chard is rich in iron and calcium and is an excellent source of the antioxidants beta-carotene and Vitamin C.

In the kitchen, a bunch of chard can be treated as two separate vegetables. The leaves can be cooked like spinach and the stems like bok choy. If you are going to use both the leaves and stems in one preparation as we often do, separate them and cook the stems for 3 minutes before adding the leaves. Cook the leaves only until they are wilted and tender, approximately 5 minutes more.

Chard's sweet and earthy flavor adapts well to a variety of seasonings. Olive oil, garlic, lemon, sesame, soy nuts, and pine nuts all work well with chard. Whether you serve Swiss chard as a side dish, stir it into a soup or stew, or use it as the main ingredient in a pasta meal, its taste and nutrition can't be beat.

🌿 "Creamy" Navy Bean, Broccoli Rabe, and Tomato Soup

The creaminess of this soup is not from dairy products but from a combination of pureed silken tofu and navy beans. The soup not only tastes great but is a nutritional powerhouse as well. It provides abundant amounts of calcium, phytoestrogens, beta-carotene, Vitamin C, and fiber.

Tips: *Broccoli rabe's peppery flavor provides an interesting flavor contrast to the mellow-sweet taste of the soup. If you don't care for its sharp taste, spinach or chard are fine substitutes.*

BEAN SOAKING:
12 HOURS

PREPARATION:
25 MINUTES

COOKING:
1 ½ HOURS

YIELD:
4 MAIN-COURSE SERVINGS

12 ounces navy beans, sorted and rinsed
8 cups water
1 15-ounce can whole tomatoes, chopped
Sea salt to taste
Black pepper to taste
1 tablespoon olive oil
4 cloves garlic, peeled and thinly sliced
1 onion, peeled and diced
3 medium carrots, scraped and diced
2 ribs celery, diced
2 teaspoons dried basil
12 ounces silken tofu
½ pound broccoli rabe, trimmed, rinsed, and chopped
4 ounces cooked small pasta

1. The night before preparing the soup, place the beans in a large bowl and cover with water. The following day, drain the water from the beans and discard it. Transfer the beans to a large Dutch oven.
2. Add the 8 cups of water to the pot and cover it. Bring the beans to a boil. Reduce the heat and simmer the beans until they are tender, approximately 1 hour. Add the tomatoes to the pot. Season the mixture with sea salt and black pepper.

3. While the beans are cooking, heat the olive oil in a large skillet over low heat. When the oil is hot, add the garlic. Cook until soft and fragrant. Raise the heat slightly and add the onion. Sprinkle with sea salt. Cook the onion until it begins to soften.

4. Add the carrots, celery, and basil to the skillet. Cover the skillet and cook for 10 minutes, stirring occasionally. Set aside.

5. Transfer 4 cups of the bean mixture to a blender or the work bowl of a food processor fitted with the metal blade. Add the tofu and puree.

6. Bring the remaining beans and liquid in the Dutch oven to a boil. Transfer the vegetables in the skillet to the Dutch oven. Reduce the heat and simmer until tender, approximately 15 minutes.

7. Raise the heat to high. Add the broccoli rabe to the soup and simmer for 5 minutes.

8. Add the pasta to the soup.

9. Stir the puree into the soup. Season the soup with sea salt and black pepper.

10. Ladle the soup into 4 large bowls and serve at once.

BROCCOLI RABE

Although it resembles a thin stalk of broccoli, broccoli rabe has a completely different taste. When you first bite into it, you will detect an earthy and grassy flavor. During the next several seconds, a mild peppery flavor will rattle your taste buds.

Although broccoli rabe is the most common name for this unique vegetable, it is occasionally labeled rape, rapini, rabe, or raab. When choosing broccoli rabe, select bunches with firm and straight stems and deep green leaves and flowers. Avoid those with yellowing leaves and flowers. Generally, the younger the rabe, the thinner its stems and the sweeter it will be. More mature rabe has thicker stems and more of an edge to its taste that can mellow by an extended time in the pan.

To prepare broccoli rabe for cooking, first rinse it under cold running water. Then trim approximately 1 inch from the stems. If the stems are very thick, they should be peeled. Coarsely chop the stems and leaves.

Like all members of the Brassica family, broccoli rabe can be used in a variety of dishes. Perhaps its most common pairing is with sweet sausage and pasta. The sweetness of the sausage tempers the sharpness of the rabe. It can also be used as a topping for pizza or stirred into soups and casseroles. It can be braised with raisins or cooked in olive oil and garlic to create wonderful side dishes. Once you acquire a taste for broccoli rabe, it can be addictive.

🌿 Curried Chickpea and Spinach Soup

A puree of cooked chickpeas and silken tofu provide the creaminess in this Indian-inspired soup. The soup is filling, intensely flavored, and a great source of phytoestrogens, calcium, and the antioxidants beta-carotene and Vitamin C.

PREPARATION:
15 MINUTES

COOKING:
45 MINUTES

YIELD:
4 MAIN-COURSE
SERVINGS

1 tablespoon canola oil
4 cloves garlic, peeled and sliced
1 onion, peeled and diced
  Sea salt to taste
2 carrots, scraped and diced
2 ribs celery, diced
1 sweet potato, peeled and cubed
2 teaspoons curry powder
2 15-ounce cans chickpeas, drained and rinsed
6 cups water
1 pound silken tofu
  Black pepper to taste
  Fresh parsley for garnish

1. Heat the oil in a Dutch oven over low heat. When the oil is hot, add the garlic. Cook the garlic until soft and fragrant.
2. Add the onion and sprinkle with sea salt. Cook the onion until it begins to soften, stirring occasionally.
3. Raise the heat to medium. Add the carrots, celery, sweet potato, and curry powder to the pot. Cover the pot and cook for 5 minutes, stirring occasionally.
4. Raise the heat to high. Add 1 can of the chickpeas and the water. Bring the soup to a boil. Reduce the heat and simmer for 20 minutes.
5. While the soup is simmering, combine the remaining can of chickpeas and the tofu in a blender or food processor fitted with a metal blade and puree.
6. Stir the puree into the soup. Simmer the soup for 5 minutes more.
7. Season the soup with sea salt and black pepper. Ladle the soup into 4 large bowls and garnish with parsley.

PARSLEY

The two varieties of parsley most commonly available are flat leaf (Italian) and curly leaf. Besides the obvious difference in appearance, there is a significant difference in taste. Flat-leaf parsley is the one to choose for all of your cooking needs. It has an intense herb flavor. When it is added at the end of cooking, it provides a burst of freshness. With its frilly leaves, curly leaf parsley makes an attractive garnish but adds minimal flavor.

🐾 Corn Chowder

With an abundance of cream, butter, and bacon fat, a traditional corn chowder is a nutritional nightmare. We have created a much more healthful version that is rich in phytoestrogens and folic acid. A combination of turkey and tempeh bacon gives the chowder a wonderful smoky flavor without the carcinogens and fat of traditional bacon. A puree of silken tofu and corn provides a silky texture and an intense corn taste.

Tip: *When fresh corn is in season, substitute it for the frozen.*

PREPARATION:
15 MINUTES

COOKING:
30 MINUTES

YIELD:
4 MAIN-COURSE
SERVINGS

  1 teaspoon canola oil
  2 ounces turkey bacon, minced
  1 onion, peeled and diced
     Sea salt to taste
  3 ounces tempeh bacon, diced
  1 teaspoon dried thyme
  2 medium Yukon gold potatoes, scrubbed and cubed
  6 cups water
  6 cups frozen sweet corn
12 ounces silken tofu
     Black pepper to taste

1. Heat the oil in a Dutch oven over medium heat. When the oil is hot, add the turkey bacon. Cook until crisp. Add the onion and sprinkle with sea salt. Cook the onion until it is soft. Add the tempeh bacon and cook for 2 minutes more.

2. Add the thyme and potatoes. Cook the potatoes for 2 minutes.
3. Raise the heat to high. Add the water. Bring the liquid to a boil. Reduce the heat and simmer the potatoes until tender, approximately 12 minutes.
4. While the potatoes are simmering, combine 2 cups of corn and the silken tofu in the work bowl of a food processor fitted with a metal blade. Add 2 cups of the simmering potato liquid to the work bowl and puree.
5. Reduce the heat to low in the Dutch oven. Add the remaining corn to the pot. Stir in the corn-tofu puree. Gently heat the soup to serving temperature, stirring occasionally.
6. Season the soup with sea salt and black pepper. Ladle the soup into 4 large bowls and serve at once.

❧ White Bean, Bacon, and Corn Soup

BEAN SOAKING:
12 HOURS

PREPARATION:
15 MINUTES

COOKING:
1 ³/₄ HOURS

YIELD:
4 MAIN-COURSE
SERVINGS

Whether they are combined with tomato and basil to make a bed for fish, used as the base for a hearty pasta meal, or as the main ingredients in a soup, smoky bacon and earthy-sweet beans and corn are a wonderful combination. This soup is a great source of calcium, fiber, folic acid, and phytoestrogens.

Tip: Since we like to plan another meal based on white beans several days later, when we prepare this soup, we cook a full pound of beans. For the additional 4 ounces of beans, add 2 cups of water. After the beans are cooked, remove 3 cups along with their cooking water for the later meal.

12 ounces navy beans
 7 cups water
 1 tablespoon olive oil
 2 ounces turkey bacon, diced
 3 cloves garlic, peeled and sliced
 1 onion, peeled and diced
   Sea salt to taste

  3 carrots, scraped and diced
  2 ribs celery, peeled and diced
  4 ounces tempeh bacon, sliced
12 ounces silken tofu
  1 cup frozen corn
     Black pepper to taste
⅓ cup flat-leaf (Italian) parsley, chopped

1. The night before preparing the soup, rinse and sort the beans. Place them in a large Dutch oven and cover with water. Soak for 12 hours.
2. The following day, drain and discard the soaking water. Return the beans to the pot. Add 6 cups of the water. Cover the pot and bring the beans to a boil. Reduce the heat and simmer the beans until tender, approximately 1¼ hours.
3. While the beans are simmering, heat the olive oil in another Dutch oven over medium heat. Add the turkey bacon to the pot and render it until crisp.
4. Reduce the heat to low. Add the garlic to the pot. Cook the garlic until soft and fragrant. Add the onion and sprinkle with sea salt. Cook the onion until it begins to soften.
5. Add the carrots and celery. Cover the pot and cook the vegetables for 10 minutes, stirring occasionally. Add the tempeh bacon.
6. Raise the heat to high. Add the remaining cup of water to the vegetables. Bring the vegetables to a boil. Reduce the heat and simmer the vegetables until tender, approximately 10 minutes.
7. When the beans are tender, transfer 2 cups to the work bowl of a food processor fitted with the metal blade. Add the tofu and puree.
8. Transfer the puree to the bean pot. Transfer the vegetables to the bean pot. Add the corn. Simmer the soup for 10 minutes, stirring occasionally. Season the soup with sea salt and black pepper.
9. Ladle the soup into 4 large bowls and sprinkle with parsley.

🐦 Seitan and Vegetable Chile

PREPARATION:
15 MINUTES

COOKING:
1 1/4 HOURS

YIELD:
4 MAIN-COURSE
SERVINGS

We all have our favorite chile recipes. Some versions contain meat and others are vegetarian. In this recipe we have replaced the meat with seitan. The result is a hearty and unique-textured chile that is sure to please everyone.

We prefer our chile on the mild side so all of the flavors have a chance to shine. The combination of a fresh jalapeño pepper and dried chipotle peppers (dried and smoked jalapeños) provides not only heat but also a wonderful smoky flavor. The dish is a great source of Vitamin C, beta-carotene, fiber, and folic acid.

2 chipotle peppers
1/4 cup boiling water
2 tablespoons olive oil
4 cloves garlic, peeled and sliced
1 onion, peeled and diced
 Sea salt to taste
1 red bell pepper, sliced
1 jalapeño pepper, seeded and minced
2 small carrots, scraped and sliced
1 zucchini squash, sliced
1 1/2 teaspoons chili powder
1 1/2 teaspoons ground cumin
1 teaspoon oregano
1 pound chicken-style seitan, drained, liquid reserved
1 15-ounce can black beans, drained and rinsed
1 15-ounce can red kidney beans, drained and rinsed
1 28-ounce can whole tomatoes in juice, chopped
 Black pepper to taste
4 ounces Cheddar cheese, grated

1. Place the chipotle peppers in a bowl. Pour the water onto them. Allow to soften for 20 minutes. Remove from the water. Remove the stems and seeds and discard them. Chop the peppers. Set them aside. Reserve the soaking water.

2. While the peppers are softening, heat the olive oil in an ovenproof Dutch oven over medium heat. When the oil is hot, add the garlic. Cook the garlic for 30 seconds. Add the onion and sprinkle with sea salt. Cook the onion until it begins to soften.

3. Add the red and jalapeño peppers. Cook for 2 minutes. Add the carrots, zucchini, chili powder, cumin, and oregano. Reduce the heat to low and cover the pot. Cook for 10 minutes, stirring occasionally.

4. Raise the heat to high. Coarsely chop the seitan. Add it to the pot along with the liquid from its container. Add the two varieties of beans, and the chipotles and their soaking water to the pot. Bring the liquid to a boil.

5. Add the tomatoes and return the chile to a boil. Reduce the heat to low, cover the pot, and simmer the chile for 40 minutes, stirring occasionally.

6. Heat the broiler.

7. Uncover the pot and cook the chile for 10 minutes more, stirring occasionally. Season the chile with sea salt and black pepper.

8. Scatter the cheese on the chile and place the pot under the broiler. Cook the chile until the cheese bubbles and begins to brown. Spoon the chile into bowls and serve at once.

SEITAN

Seitan (wheat gluten) is the spongy material remaining after the starch in a flour dough has been removed. It is a common ingredient in Chinese vegetarian cookery. Its mild flavor and chewy texture make it a versatile food. It can be steamed, stir-fried, or braised. It is an ideal substitute for meat in your favorite chile, stew, or soup.

It is generally found alongside tofu and other soy products in the refrigerated section of a market. It is packaged in 1-pound containers and is often available in chicken, beef, and pork flavors.

ᴥᴥ Roasted Garlic Soup

PREPARATION:
15 MINUTES

COOKING:
40 MINUTES

YIELD:
4 MAIN-COURSE
SERVINGS

There are several methods to thicken a soup. The most common way is with a roux (a combination of melted butter or oil and flour). Used less frequently but more healthful are pureed potatoes or pureed beans. Even less common but probably the most interesting and economical is thickening a soup with day-old crusty bread. We have used this technique with the addition of silken tofu in our heady roasted garlic soup. It is comfort food at its best. The aroma alone drifting through your kitchen is reason enough to make this soup a regular cool weather meal. The soup is rich in phytoestrogens and Vitamin C.

Tip: *To save time on the day you plan to prepare the soup, roast the garlic a day in advance. If you are like us, you will want to roast several extra heads. The sweet flesh is great spread on bread and stirred into soups and pasta dishes.*

⅓ cup flat-leaf (Italian) parsley, chopped
3 plum tomatoes, cored and diced
Sea salt to taste
2 tablespoons olive oil
1 onion, peeled and diced
6 cups water, vegetable stock, or chicken stock
5–6 cups day-old bread cubes, cut from a crusty loaf
12 ounces silken tofu
3 heads roasted garlic, flesh removed and skin discarded (see box)
Black pepper to taste

1. To prepare the garnish, combine the parsley and tomatoes in a small bowl. Season with sea salt. Set the bowl aside while you prepare the soup.
2. Heat the olive oil in a Dutch oven over low heat. Add the onion and sprinkle with sea salt. Cook the onion until soft, stirring occasionally.
3. Raise the heat to high. Add the water or stock. Bring the liquid to a boil. Reduce the heat and simmer for 10 minutes.

4. Raise the heat to high. Stir the bread cubes into the pot. Bring the soup to a boil. Reduce the heat and simmer for 20 minutes, stirring occasionally.

5. Transfer approximately half of the soup to the work bowl of a food processor fitted with a metal blade. Add the tofu and roasted garlic to the work bowl and puree. Transfer the puree to the pot. Stir the soup thoroughly. Simmer the soup for 10 minutes more.

6. Season the soup with sea salt and black pepper. Divide the soup among 4 large bowls. Garnish with the parsley-tomato mixture and serve at once.

ROASTED GARLIC

Cook the garlic in a slow oven to allow the sugar to carmelize and the flavors to intensify.

   3 heads of garlic
      Olive oil
      Sea salt to taste
      Black pepper to taste
   ½ cup water

1. Heat the oven to 275°F.
2. Prepare the garlic heads by removing any loose skin and cutting ¼ inch off the top (nonstem side) of each head to expose the raw garlic cloves. Place the garlic in a baking dish, drizzle the bulbs with the olive oil, and sprinkle with sea salt and black pepper. Pour the water onto the bottom of the dish.
3. Bake the garlic for 1½ hours, or until the inner cloves are very soft.
4. Remove the garlic from the oven and allow the heads to cool. Press the soft garlic out of the loose skin.

❧ Sausage, Tofu, Artichoke Heart, and Tomato Soup

PREPARATION:
10 MINUTES

COOKING:
45 MINUTES

YIELD:
4 MAIN-COURSE
SERVINGS

We tasted this soup, without the tofu, at the beautiful Public Market in Portland, Maine. With the addition of tofu, it is a perfect breast cancer preventing meal. The tomatoes and artichoke hearts provide healthy doses of beta-carotene and Vitamin C and the tofu plenty of phytoestrogens.

Tip: *This soup can be prepared a day in advance. This is not only convenient but gives all the flavors an opportunity to develop and marry.*

    2 tablespoons olive oil
   12 ounces sweet turkey or chicken sausage, crumbled
    5 cloves garlic, peeled and sliced
    1 onion, peeled and diced
       Sea salt to taste
    2 carrots, scraped and diced
    1 rib celery, diced
   12 ounces firm tofu, crumbled
    6 artichoke hearts, quartered
    1 28-ounce can whole tomatoes in juice, chopped
    4 cups water
       Black pepper to taste

1. Heat the olive oil in a Dutch oven over medium-high heat. Add the sausage. Cook until golden, stirring often. Transfer to a plate.
2. Pour off all but 1 tablespoon of the accumulated drippings from the pot. Reduce the heat to low. Add the garlic. Cook the garlic until soft and fragrant.
3. Add the onion and sprinkle with sea salt. Cook the onion until it begins to soften, stirring occasionally. Add the carrots and celery. Return the sausage to the pot. Cover the pot and cook for 10 minutes, stirring occasionally.
4. Raise the heat to high. Add the tofu, artichoke hearts, tomatoes, and water. Bring the soup to a boil. Reduce the heat and simmer for 30 minutes.

5. Season the soup with sea salt and black pepper. Divide the soup among 4 large bowls and serve at once.

❧ Tomato and Corn Soup

We love creating recipes using two of the best summer vegetables: corn and tomatoes. This soup, with a corn stock as the base, is a real winner. With so few ingredients, be certain the corn is "just-picked" and the tomatoes are very ripe. The soup is very rich in folic acid and Vitamin C.

Tip: *We debated whether to add silken tofu to the soup to enhance its nutrition and texture; we decided not to. If you choose to do so, add 8 ounces of silken tofu to the blender when you puree the corn.*

PREPARATION:
10 MINUTES

COOKING:
40 MINUTES

YIELD:
4 MAIN-COURSE
SERVINGS

1   tablespoon olive oil
3   cloves garlic, peeled and thinly sliced
1   onion, peeled and diced
    Sea salt to taste
5   ears corn (approximately 6 cups), kernels removed and cobs reserved
6   cups water
4   ripe tomatoes, cored and diced
½   cup fresh basil, snipped
    Black pepper to taste

1. Heat the olive oil in a Dutch oven over medium heat. Add the garlic and cook for 30 seconds. Add the onion and sprinkle with sea salt. Cook the onion until soft.
2. Add the corn. Cook the corn for 5 minutes, stirring occasionally. Raise the heat to high. Add the water. Break the corncobs in half. Add them to the pot. Bring the soup to a boil. Reduce the heat. Simmer for 20 minutes.
3. Remove the corncobs from the soup and discard them.
4. Transfer half the soup to a blender or the work bowl of a food processor fitted with the metal blade. Puree the soup. Return

it to the pot. Add the tomatoes and simmer the soup for 5 minutes more.

5. Remove the pot from the heat. Stir in the basil. Season the soup with sea salt and black pepper. Divide the soup among 4 large bowls and serve at once.

🐝 Roasted Eggplant, Corn, Tomato, and Tofu Soup

PREPARATION:
30 MINUTES

COOKING:
35 MINUTES

YIELD:
6 MAIN-COURSE
SERVINGS

When you think of the main ingredients in this soup—eggplant, corn, and tomato—you may imagine a light dish. However, by roasting and pureeing the eggplant, we have created a thick and filling soup that is a meal in itself. The addition of cubed tofu adds texture and absorbs the wonderful sweetness of the eggplant and corn. The soup is a great source of phytoestrogens, folic acid, and Vitamin C.

2 large eggplants
1 tablespoon olive oil
3 cloves garlic, peeled and sliced
1 onion, peeled and diced
   Sea salt to taste
3 ears fresh corn, kernels removed, cobs reserved
5 cups water
3 ripe tomatoes, cored and diced
1 pound firm tofu, cubed
⅓ cup cilantro, chopped
4 scallions, thinly sliced
   Black pepper to taste

1. Heat the oven to 425°F.
2. Place the eggplants in the oven. Roast them until they are very soft, approximately 30 minutes. Remove them from the oven and allow to cool.

3. Meanwhile, heat the olive oil in a large Dutch oven over medium heat. Add the garlic and cook for 30 seconds. Add the onion and sprinkle with sea salt. Cook the onion until it is soft.

4. Add the corn. Cook the corn for 5 minutes, stirring occasionally. Raise the heat to high.

5. Add the water and corncobs. Bring the soup to a boil. Reduce the heat and simmer the soup for 20 minutes.

6. Grasp one of the eggplants by its stem. Peel and discard the skin. Cut in half. Remove the seeds and discard them. Cut off and discard the stem. Transfer the flesh to a blender or a food processor fitted with the metal blade. Repeat the procedure with the other eggplant.

7. Add half of the soup to the blender or food processor and puree. Return puree to the pot. Stir in the tomatoes and tofu. Simmer the soup for 10 minutes more.

8. Add the cilantro and scallions. If necessary, thin the soup with water. Season with sea salt and black pepper. Divide the soup among 6 bowls and serve at once.

🎝🎝 Butternut Squash and Tofu Soup with Fried Leeks

Butternut squash is a nutritious and versatile vegetable. One cup contains 5 milligrams of beta-carotene, more than any other winter squash. Butternut squash can be grilled, roasted, or pan fried. It can be boiled and mashed and substituted for canned pumpkin in breads, muffins, and pies. When pureed with silken tofu, it makes a delectable and creamy soup rich in beta-carotene and phytoestrogens.

PREPARATION:
15 MINUTES

COOKING:
40 MINUTES

YIELD:
4 MAIN-COURSE
SERVINGS

1 tablespoon canola oil
  1-inch piece gingerroot, peeled and chopped
1 onion, peeled and diced
  Sea salt to taste
1 teaspoon cumin
½ teaspoon ground coriander
1 medium butternut squash, peeled, seeded, and diced
3 cups water
12 ounces silken tofu
  Black pepper to taste
1 tablespoon olive oil
3 medium leeks, trimmed, washed, and thinly sliced

1. Heat the canola oil in a Dutch oven over medium-low heat. Add the ginger and onion. Sprinkle with sea salt. Cook the onion until it is soft, stirring occasionally.
2. Add the cumin and coriander. Cook for another minute.
3. Add the squash. Cover the pot and cook the squash until it begins to soften, stirring occasionally, approximately 10 minutes.
4. Raise the heat to high. Add the water. Bring the water to a boil. Reduce the heat. Simmer the squash until it is very tender, approximately 20 minutes. Crumble the tofu into the pot.
5. Transfer the soup to a blender or food processor fitted with the metal blade. It may be necessary to do this in 2 batches. Puree the soup.

6. Return the soup to the pot. Season with sea salt and black pepper.
7. Heat the olive oil in a large skillet over high heat. When the oil is hot, add the leeks. Sprinkle with sea salt. Cook the leeks until they are soft and golden, stirring constantly, approximately 3 minutes.
8. Ladle the soup into 4 large bowls. Garnish with the leeks and serve at once.

LEEKS

During early fall, after tomatoes have passed their peak and corn no longer hails from local farms, it is time for the autumn harvest. One of the gems of the fall crop is the leek. Unfortunately, leeks are often overlooked in favor of harsher tasting onions, shallots, and garlic.

Leeks, which resemble thick scallions (green onions), are very versatile; they have many more uses than just in vichyssoise. They can be thinly sliced and used to flavor soups, stews, and stocks. If they are thin, they can be trimmed and braised, broiled, or grilled and drizzled with olive oil and served as an accompaniment. They can also be thinly sliced and cooked in a bit of olive oil over high heat until soft and lightly browned. They can then be used as a bed for fish, poultry, beef, or tofu or used to garnish a soup or salad.

When preparing leeks for cooking, it is important to thoroughly wash them. Since they grow partially underground, they tend to be gritty and sandy. To clean them, first slice off the hairy root end at the point where it meets the white of the leek. Then slice off the green tops about 4 inches above where the green begins. Cut the leek in half lengthwise. Wash the leek, one-half at a time, under running water, spreading the layers with your fingers to remove the dirt.

❧ "Creamy" Lentil and Tofu Soup with Garlicky Chard and Tomatoes

PREPARATION:
15 MINUTES

COOKING:
1 HOUR

YIELD:
6 MAIN-COURSE
SERVINGS

During the colder seasons, our tastes change; we like to prepare heartier soups. Dried peas or beans are the ideal starting point. They are wonderfully nutritious and, when simmered in water or stock, create a delectable broth. In addition to the peas or beans, a couple of different slow-cooked root vegetables and a quick garnish are all that are needed to create a great soup.

This simple lentil soup tastes creamy because of a puree of part of the lentils with soft tofu. A garnish of chard and tomatoes adds great texture and complements the earthy flavor of the lentils. The soup provides plenty of breast cancer fighting phytoestrogens, beta-carotene, and Vitamin C.

Tips: *If you can't locate French lentils, regular brown ones can be substituted. Also, the soup can be prepared earlier in the day and gently reheated. When reheating, it may be necessary to add a bit of water. Prepare the garnish just before serving.*

SOUP
- 2 cups French lentils, rinsed
- 6 cups water
- 2 bay leaves
- 12 ounces soft tofu
- 1 tablespoon olive oil
- 4 cloves garlic, peeled and thinly sliced
- 1 onion, peeled and diced
  Sea salt to taste
- 2 medium carrots, scraped and diced
- 2 ribs celery, diced
  Black pepper to taste

CHARD AND TOMATO GARNISH
- 1 tablespoon olive oil
- 5 cloves garlic
- 12 ounces chard, trimmed, washed, drained, and chopped
- 3 medium tomatoes, cored and diced
  Sea salt to taste
  Black pepper to taste

1. Place the lentils in a medium-sized Dutch oven. Add 4 cups of the water and bay leaves. Cover the pot and bring the lentils to a boil. Reduce the heat. Simmer the lentils until tender, approximately 45 minutes.

2. Remove and discard the bay leaves. Transfer one-half of the lentils to a blender or the work bowl of a food processor fitted with the metal blade. Add the tofu and puree. Return the puree to the Dutch oven. Stir together the puree and whole lentils. Set the mixture aside for a moment.

3. Heat the olive oil in another Dutch oven over medium heat. When the oil is hot, add the garlic. Cook for 30 seconds. Add the onion and sprinkle with sea salt. Cook the onion until it is soft, stirring occasionally.

4. Add the carrots and celery. Cover the pot and cook the ingredients until they begin to soften, stirring occasionally, approximately 10 minutes.

5. Stir in the remaining 2 cups of water. Bring the soup to a boil. Reduce the heat and simmer the mixture for 10 minutes, stirring occasionally.

6. Add the lentil and tofu puree. Season the soup with sea salt and black pepper.

7. While the soup is simmering, prepare the chard and tomato garnish. Heat the olive oil in a wok over medium heat. Add the garlic and cook for 30 seconds.

8. Raise the heat to high. Add the chard. Cook the chard until it wilts, stirring constantly. Cover the wok and cook the chard until tender, approximately 8 minutes, stirring occasionally. Add the tomatoes. Cook the ingredients for 2 minutes more. Remove the pan from the heat. Season the chard with sea salt and black pepper.

9. Divide the soup among 4 large bowls. Garnish with the chard mixture and serve at once.

🦋 "Creamy" Tomato and Cheddar Soup

PREPARATION:
15 MINUTES

COOKING:
30 MINUTES

YIELD:
6 SIDE-DISH
SERVINGS

A soup can be thickened with potatoes, bread, pureed beans, or a roux. A roux is a combination of butter or oil and flour. It enhances a thin liquid by giving it more body and a silky texture.

Tomato and Cheddar soup sounds like kids' food. This version, though, contains three excellent sources of breast cancer fighting phytoestrogens: soy milk, tofu, and edamame. Tomatoes are an excellent source of Vitamin C and beta-carotene.

    1 28-ounce can whole tomatoes in juice
    8 ounces silken tofu
    2 tablespoons olive oil
    4 cloves garlic, peeled and sliced
    1 onion, peeled and diced
       Sea salt to taste
    2 carrots, scraped and diced
    2 ribs celery, diced
    2 tablespoons unbleached all-purpose flour
 1½ cups soy milk
 1½ cups frozen and blanched edamame
    3 ounces sharp Cheddar cheese, grated or sliced
       Black pepper to taste
   ⅓ cup flat-leaf (Italian) parsley, chopped

1. Combine the tomatoes and tofu in a blender or the work bowl of a food processor fitted with the metal blade and puree. Set the mixture aside for a moment.
2. Heat the olive oil in a Dutch oven over low heat. When the oil is hot, add the garlic. Cook until soft and fragrant. Add the onion and sprinkle with sea salt. Cook the onion until it begins to soften.
3. Add the carrots and celery. Cover the pot. Cook the vegetables until they begin to soften, stirring occasionally, approximately 10 minutes.

4. Stir in the flour to make the roux. Cook the roux for 3 minutes, stirring often.
5. Whisk in the soy milk. Add the reserved tomato-tofu mixture. Bring the soup to a boil. Reduce the heat. Add the edamame and simmer the soup for 15 minutes, stirring occasionally.
6. Stir in the cheese, an ounce at a time. Simmer the soup for another 3 minutes.
7. Season with sea salt and black pepper. Divide the soup among 6 bowls. Garnish with parsley and serve at once.

EDAMAME

Fresh soy beans, called edamame in Japanese and mao dou in Chinese, have long been a staple in Asian cuisine. Enter a Japanese restaurant and you will find them served as a snack still in their pods. Diners remove the beans from their pods and pop them into their mouths.

In America, until recently, soybeans were grown primarily for animal feed. Now, however, with the health benefits of all forms of soy being well touted, the humble soybean is becoming increasingly popular in our restaurants and home kitchens. They are rich in protein, fiber, Vitamin C and, most important, they are great sources of breast cancer preventing phytoestrogens.

In the kitchen, edamame add great texture and an earthy and slightly sweet-salty flavor to any dish. They can be added to soups, stews, and casseroles. They can also be stir-fried or pureed and used as a sandwich spread.

During the warmer months, edamame are available fresh at specialty and farmers' markets. During the remainder of the year, we use the frozen variety. Frozen edamame are available in the pods or shelled. The pod variety has to be blanched and peeled. The shelled variety needs only to be blanched. We prefer the shelled ones for their convenience and short (5 minutes) cooking time.

✺ Potato and Kale Soup with Chorizo

PREPARATION:
15 MINUTES

COOKING:
45 MINUTES

YIELD:
4 MAIN-COURSE
SERVINGS

Chorizo, that wonderfully spicy pork sausage, is usually off limits to people careful about their diet. Fortunately, several companies now produce chorizo made with turkey or chicken instead of pork. It has that same intense flavor but is significantly leaner. When it is seared to a delectable crispness, it makes an ideal garnish for our potato and kale soup. Pureed soft tofu and soy milk give this soup a creamy consistency and make it rich in phytoestrogens. Kale is a great source of beta-carotene and calcium.

Tip: *The kale most often found in markets is ornamental kale. It makes an attractive garnish but it is strongly flavored. Red Russian, Dutch kale, or Dinosaur kale are sweeter tasting and more tender.*

2 tablespoons olive oil
6 ounces chicken chorizo, sliced
3 cloves garlic, peeled and sliced
1 onion, peeled and diced
  Sea salt to taste
2 Russet potatoes, peeled and quartered
12 ounces Red Russian or similar nonornamental kale, trimmed, chopped, washed, and drained
6 cups water or chicken stock
12 ounces soft tofu
2 cups soy milk
  Black pepper to taste

1. Heat 1 tablespoon of the olive oil in a Dutch oven over high heat. When the oil is hot, add the chorizo. Sear until golden. Transfer to a plate.
2. Reduce the heat to low. Add the garlic and cook it for 30 seconds. Add the onion and sprinkle with sea salt. Cook the onion until soft.
3. Add the potatoes and kale. Cover the pot. Cook for 10 minutes.
4. Raise the heat to high. Add the water or stock. Bring the soup to a boil. Reduce the heat. Simmer the soup until the potatoes and kale are tender, approximately 20 minutes.

5. Transfer the soup to a work bowl of a food processor with a metal blade. Add the tofu and puree. Return it to the pot.
6. Gently heat the soup. Add the soy milk.
7. Season the soup with sea salt and black pepper. Divide the soup among 4 bowls. Garnish with the chorizo.

✿ Spiced Butternut Squash and Tomato Soup

Butternut squash and tomatoes are two of the richest sources of beta-carotene. When pureed with soft tofu, they also make a deceptively rich and satisfying soup. A hint of ginger and cumin are the perfect seasonings.

PREPARATION:
15 MINUTES

COOKING:
30 MINUTES

YIELD:
4 MAIN-COURSE
SERVINGS

SOUP
1 tablespoon canola oil
1-inch piece gingerroot, peeled and chopped
1 large leek, trimmed, cleaned, and sliced
Sea salt to taste
¾ teaspoon cumin
¼ teaspoon nutmeg
1 medium butternut squash, peeled, seeded, and cubed
1 28-ounce can whole tomatoes in juice, drained and chopped
5 cups water
8 ounces soft tofu, crumbled
Black pepper to taste

GARNISH
½ cup slivered almonds
Sea salt to taste
2 cloves garlic, peeled
⅓ cup flat-leaf (Italian) parsley, chopped

1. Heat the canola oil in a Dutch oven over low heat. Add the ginger and cook until soft and fragrant. Add the leek and sprinkle it with sea salt. Cook the leek until soft.

2. Add the cumin, nutmeg, and squash. Cook for 2 minutes.
3. Raise the heat to high. Add the tomatoes and water. Bring the soup to a boil. Reduce the heat. Simmer until the squash is tender, approximately 20 minutes.
4. Add the tofu.
5. Transfer the soup to a blender or food processor fitted with the metal blade. Puree the soup. Return it to the pot. Season with sea salt and black pepper. Keep the soup warm while you prepare the garnish.
6. Place the almonds in a small skillet over low heat. Sprinkle with sea salt. Toast them until they are golden, shaking the pan occasionally, approximately 10 minutes.
7. While the nuts are toasting, combine the garlic and parsley on a cutting board. Chop together finely to make a *persillade*.
8. Divide the soup among 4 bowls. Garnish with the nuts and *persillade*.

CHAPTER 11

Salads

The best salads are those that combine produce at its ripest and freshest with top-quality dressings. Salads can be as simple and light as mesclun greens tossed with fruity olive oil and sea salt or as creative and hearty as one prepared with soba noodles, vegetables, tofu, and sesame seeds. Salads are a perfect opportunity to showcase many of the foods that contain large amounts of breast cancer fighting nutrients.

Mangoes are one of the fruits richest in beta-carotene. We take advantage of their versatility and use them in several salads. Their wonderful sweetness contrasts beautifully with the earthy greens, tart dressing, and nutty sesame seeds in the unique Romaine and Red Leaf Salad with Mango, Peanuts, and Sesame.

Tofu is a great source of phytoestrogens and a great way to introduce soy into one's diet. When combined with bold-flavored ingredients and pureed, silken tofu creates a delectable and nutritious salad dressing. Try our Romaine Salad with Orange-Soy

Tofu, Edamame, and Mango. You will be pleasantly surprised just how delectable and versatile tofu truly is.

Sweet potatoes, bell peppers, tomatoes, and carrots are the richest sources of Vitamin C and beta-carotene. They get top billing in our Roasted Sweet Potato and Tofu Salad with Curry, Roasted Sweet Pepper and Tomato Salad, Tomato and Fresh Mozzarella Stacks, and Ellie's Chilled Carrot Salad with Cilantro and Garlic.

Omega-3 fatty acids are most abundant in oily-fleshed fish, which conveniently includes canned tuna. Don't just settle for a tuna sandwich or for flaking canned tuna into a salad. Spend a bit more time in the kitchen and indulge in our Chilled Pasta with Tuna, Tomatoes, Olives, and Capers.

Hearty noodle salads are an excellent way to include several breast cancer preventing foods in one dish. Whole Wheat Shells with Bok Choy, Broccoli, Cashews, and Miso contains plenty of beta-carotene, phytoestrogens, calcium, fiber, and vitamins C and E.

Whether you prefer a simple salad to accompany a meal, a substantial main-course salad, or simply want to take advantage of the best produce the season has to offer, these salads will not only please your taste buds but will also fuel your body with a great deal of breast cancer preventing nutrients.

🐿 Roasted Asparagus and Mesclun Salad with Pine Nuts and Lemon

Roasted asparagus is a great addition to the common mesclun salad. It adds a smoky flavor and a unique texture. The pine nuts add crunch and a sweet flavor contrast to the tart dressing. The asparagus and greens are rich in beta-carotene, and pine nuts are an excellent source of Vitamin E.

PREPARATION:
10 MINUTES

COOKING:
10 MINUTES

YIELD:
4 SIDE-DISH
SERVINGS

1 pound asparagus, tough stems snapped off and discarded
3 tablespoons olive oil
Sea salt to taste
Black pepper to taste
¼ cup pine nuts
2 tablespoons fresh lemon juice
1 teaspoon Dijon mustard
4 cups mesclun
4 tablespoons Asiago cheese, grated

1. Heat the oven to 400°F. Place the asparagus on a baking tray. Drizzle with 1 tablespoon of the olive oil. Season with sea salt and black pepper. Place the tray in the oven and roast the asparagus until tender, approximately 10 minutes. Transfer to a plate. Place in the refrigerator to cool.
2. While the asparagus are roasting, place the pine nuts in a small skillet over low heat. Sprinkle with sea salt. Toast them until they are golden, shaking the pan occasionally, approximately 5 minutes. Set them aside for a moment.
3. To prepare the dressing, whisk together the remaining 2 tablespoons of olive oil, the lemon juice, and mustard. Set the dressing aside for a moment.
4. Place the mesclun in a salad bowl. Add the cooled asparagus and pine nuts to the bowl. Whisk the dressing and pour into the bowl.
5. Toss the salad. Garnish with the Asiago cheese and serve at once.

❧ Romaine and Red Leaf Salad with Mango, Peanuts, and Sesame

PREPARATION:
10 MINUTES

COOKING:
10 MINUTES

YIELD:
4 SIDE-DISH
SERVINGS

When we tire of a simple salad dressed with balsamic vinegar and olive oil, this is what we prepare. This salad combines the earthy flavors of the greens with the sweetness of the mango and tanginess of the dressing. The peanuts and sesame seeds provide just the right textural contrast. The greens and mango are a great source of beta-carotene and the peanuts and sesame seeds provide Vitamin E.

2 tablespoons unhulled sesame seeds
2 tablespoons sesame oil
2 tablespoons cider vinegar
2 tablespoons tamari
1 teaspoon Dijon mustard
1 tablespoon sugar
1 medium head red leaf lettuce, trimmed, torn, washed, and spun dry
1 medium head romaine lettuce, trimmed, torn, washed, and spun dry
Sea salt to taste
1 ripe mango, peeled, pitted, and cubed
¼ cup unsalted peanuts, chopped

1. Place the sesame seeds in a small skillet over low heat. Toast them until they are golden, tossing occasionally, approximately 10 minutes. Remove the pan from the heat.
2. While the sesame seeds are toasting, prepare the dressing by whisking together the sesame oil, vinegar, tamari, mustard, and sugar.
3. Place the red leaf and romaine in a large salad bowl. Sprinkle the greens with sea salt. Pour the dressing onto the greens. Toss the greens.
4. Garnish the greens with the mango, peanuts, and sesame seeds.
5. Divide the salad among 4 plates and serve at once.

❧ Romaine Salad with Orange-Soy Tofu, Edamame, and Mango

When the weather turns hot and we don't feel like heating the house any further by cooking, we often prepare a main-course salad for dinner. By adding lean beef, chicken breast, or as we have done here, tofu, you can transform a simple green salad into a healthful and substantial dinner. With edamame, mango, tomatoes, and sesame seeds, this salad provides an abundance of phytoestrogens, beta-carotene, and vitamins C and E.

   Tip: *This recipe makes approximately twice the amount of dressing you will need to dress the salad. The extra can be kept tightly sealed in your refrigerator for 3 days. It is also the base of the sauce in our Chile-Crusted Sea Scallops with Mango and Bell Peppers (page 285).*

PREPARATION:
10 MINUTES

COOKING:
5 MINUTES

YIELD:
4 MAIN-COURSE
SERVINGS

2 cups water
2 cups frozen shelled and blanched edamame
4 tablespoons unhulled sesame seeds
1 mango, peeled, pitted, and chopped
4 ounces silken tofu, drained
2 tablespoons rice wine vinegar
1 tablespoon canola oil
1 pound extra-firm tofu
  Sea salt to taste
  Black pepper to taste
2 tablespoons orange juice
2 tablespoons tamari
1 tablespoon sugar
2 medium heads romaine lettuce, trimmed, torn, washed, and spun dry
½ pint cherry tomatoes, halved

1. Bring the water to a boil in a small saucepan. Add the edamame. Cook the edamame until tender, approximately 5 minutes. Drain and set aside for a moment.
2. While the edamame are cooking, place the sesame seeds in a small skillet over low heat. Toast them until they are

golden, stirring occasionally, approximately 5 minutes. Set them aside for a moment.

3. To prepare the dressing, combine the mango, silken tofu, and rice wine vinegar in a blender and puree. Transfer the dressing to a bowl.

4. To prepare the extra-firm tofu, heat the canola oil in a wok over medium-high heat. Place the tofu on a kitchen towel. With the heal of your hand, gently press on the tofu to remove excess moisture. Cube the tofu and sprinkle it with sea salt and black pepper.

5. When the oil is hot, carefully place the tofu into the wok. Sear it until golden, tossing occasionally. Add the orange juice, tamari, and sugar. Cook the tofu for 2 minutes more. Transfer to a plate. Set aside for a moment.

6. Place the lettuce in a large salad bowl. Pour one-half of the dressing onto the lettuce. Toss the ingredients. Garnish the salad with the edamame, tomatoes, tofu, and sesame seeds. Divide the salad among 4 large plates and serve at once.

TOFU

Tofu or bean curd comes from soy milk. It is made by adding nigari (a compound from seawater), calcium sulfate, and vinegar to soy milk. The excess moisture is removed and the remaining curds are pressed into blocks.

Tofu is bland-tasting and requires creativity and bold flavors to make it into something special. Tofu acts like a sponge in absorbing flavors during cooking. It turns out especially well when paired with full-flavored seasonings, such as herbs, spices, vinegars, citrus, garlic, and onions.

Tofu is available in several forms. Firm and extra-firm tofu work well as a meat replacement in stir-fries, stews, meatballs, sandwiches, and egg dishes. It can also be crumbled and seasoned with onions, garlic, Romano cheese, and parsley and substituted for ricotta cheese in your favorite lasagna or stuffed shells recipe. Soft tofu and Japanese-style silken tofu are the types that provide the cook with the most opportunities to be creative. They are the varieties to use when you are "hiding" tofu in recipes. When pureed in a blender or food processor, they can be used in place of cream in soups and sauces and oil in salad dressings. They are also the types to use in desserts. They make wonderful puddings, fruit whips, and cheesecakes. If you are going to make a pudding or fruit whip a day in advance, use soft tofu rather than silken tofu. Silken tofu gets its smooth texture from a high moisture content. It tends to separate if it sits too long. Soft tofu will produce a dessert with a denser texture.

❦ Roasted Sweet Potato and Tofu Salad with Curry

This sweet potato salad is a creative alternative to a traditional mayonnaise-based white potato salad. The sweetness of the apples, onions, and potatoes pairs well with the bold flavor of the curry. Although it is a wonderful side dish, we often serve it as a main course with rustic bread and a crisp green salad. Sweet potatoes are one of the richest sources of beta-carotene. Tofu is a great source of phytoestrogens and the pumpkin seeds are rich in Vitamin E.

Tip: If you don't have a roasting tray large enough to accommodate the tofu and vegetables, use two smaller ones. To be certain everything cooks evenly, it may be necessary to rotate the trays once during cooking.

PREPARATION:
10 MINUTES

COOKING:
45 MINUTES

YIELD:
6 SIDE-DISH
SERVINGS

4 tablespoons canola oil
2 Granny Smith apples, cored and cubed
Sea salt to taste
1 pound extra-firm tofu
4 medium sweet potatoes, peeled and cubed
2 red onions, peeled and sliced
2 tablespoons curry powder
3 tablespoons brown sugar
1-inch piece gingerroot, peeled and finely chopped
2 tablespoons orange juice concentrate
3 tablespoons water
Black pepper to taste
½ cup roasted pumpkin seeds

1. Heat 1 tablespoon of the canola oil in a skillet over low heat. Add the apples. Sprinkle with sea salt. Cook them until they are soft and carmelized, stirring occasionally, approximately 25 minutes. Transfer the apples to a large serving bowl.
2. While the apples are cooking, heat the oven to 425°F. Place the tofu on a kitchen towel. With the heal of your hand, gently press on the tofu to remove the excess moisture. Cube the tofu. Transfer it to a heavy and large roasting tray.
3. Place the potatoes and onions on the tray. Drizzle with 2

tablespoons of the canola oil. Sprinkle with sea salt, 1 table-spoon of the curry powder, and brown sugar.

4. With your hands, toss the ingredients thoroughly. Place the tray in the oven. Roast the ingredients until the potatoes are tender and just beginning to carmelize, stirring occasionally, approximately 45 minutes.

5. Remove the tray from the oven. With the back side of a spatula loosen the ingredients. Transfer to the serving bowl.

6. While the apples and potatoes are cooking, heat the remaining tablespoon of oil in a small skillet over low heat. Add the ginger, cooking until soft and fragrant. Add the remaining tablespoon of curry powder. Cook the ingredients for 1 minute. Add the orange juice concentrate and water. Cook the ingredients for 1 minute more.

7. Pour the sauce onto the vegetables and tofu in the serving bowl. Toss the salad thoroughly. Season with sea salt and black pepper. Garnish with the pumpkin seeds. Serve hot or at room temperature.

❧ Whole Wheat Shells with Bok Choy, Broccoli, Cashews, and Miso

On warm summer days, when we know we are going to be out all day and won't feel like cooking when we arrive home, we prepare this pasta salad before we leave. When we arrive home, we put together a simple green salad such as Romaine and Red Leaf Salad with Mango, Peanuts, and Sesame (page 128) and we have a great meal with little fuss. This Asian-inspired pasta salad is rich in beta-carotene, Vitamin E, phytoestrogens, and fiber.

PREPARATION:
10 MINUTES

COOKING:
20 MINUTES

YIELD:
6 MAIN-COURSE
SERVINGS

1   cup hot water
1   tablespoon dark miso
3   tablespoons orange juice concentrate
3   tablespoons tamari
2   tablespoons brown sugar
    Sea salt to taste
1   pound whole wheat pasta shells
1   pound broccoli, trimmed and sliced into large florets
2   tablespoons canola oil
1   pound extra-firm tofu
2   tablespoons sesame seeds
    1-inch piece gingerroot, peeled and finely chopped
3   cloves garlic, peeled and finely chopped
1   red bell pepper, cored and diced
1   pound bok choy, trimmed, stems and leaves chopped
    and separated
⅓   cup unsalted cashews, chopped

1. To prepare the sauce, whisk together the hot water, miso, orange juice concentrate, tamari, and brown sugar. Set the sauce aside for a moment.
2. Bring a large pot of water to a boil. Add sea salt to the water followed by the pasta. After the pasta has been cooking for 5 minutes, add the broccoli to the pot. Cook the pasta and broccoli together until they are both tender, approximately 3 minutes more. Drain and cool off under running water.

After they have been thoroughly drained, transfer to a large bowl. Set the bowl aside for a moment.

3. To prepare the tofu, heat 1 tablespoon of the canola oil in a wok over medium-high heat. Place the tofu on a kitchen towel. With the heal of your hand, gently press on the tofu to remove the excess moisture. Cube the tofu. Place it on a plate and toss with the sesame seeds.

4. When the oil is hot, carefully place the tofu in the wok. Cook until golden. Pour 4 tablespoons of the sauce onto the tofu and cook for another minute. Transfer the tofu to a plate. Set it aside for a moment.

5. Heat the remaining tablespoon of oil in the wok over medium-high heat. When the oil is hot, add the ginger and garlic. Cook for 15 seconds. Add the red bell pepper and bok choy stems. Cook until they begin to soften, tossing often, approximately 3 minutes. Add the bok choy leaves and cook until they are wilted and tender, tossing often, approximately 3 minutes.

6. Pour the remaining sauce into the wok. Cook the ingredients for another minute.

7. Pour the sauce and vegetables onto the noodles and broccoli. Toss the salad thoroughly. Season with sea salt. Garnish with the tofu and cashews. Serve cold or at room temperature.

❧ Chilled Pasta with Tuna, Tomatoes, Olives, and Capers

Since this classic combination of ingredients makes a wonderful hot pasta dish, we decided to use it in a cold version. It is an ideal dish to prepare earlier in the day and enjoy as a light supper or to carry along on a picnic. Canned tuna is a great and convenient source of omega-3 fatty acids. The cherry tomatoes are rich in Vitamin C.

Tip: During the final seasoning, keep in mind that both capers and olives contain a fair amount of salt.

PREPARATION:
15 MINUTES

COOKING:
10 MINUTES

CHILLING:
2 HOURS

YIELD:
6 MAIN-COURSE
SERVINGS

     Sea salt to taste
 1 pound large elbow macaroni
 2 6.5-ounce cans water-packed tuna, drained and flaked
 4 tablespoons capers, drained and rinsed
24 Kalamata olives, pitted and chopped
 1 pint cherry tomatoes, halved
 ½ cup fresh basil, snipped
 2 teaspoons Dijon mustard
 2 tablespoons red wine vinegar
 4 tablespoons olive oil
     Black pepper to taste

1. Bring a large pot of water to a boil. Add sea salt to the water followed by the pasta. Cook the pasta until tender. Drain and rinse under cold water. Transfer to a large bowl.
2. Add the tuna, capers, olives, tomatoes, and basil. Toss the salad.
3. To prepare the dressing, whisk together the mustard, vinegar, and olive oil.
4. Pour the dressing onto the salad. Toss the salad thoroughly. Season to taste with sea salt and black pepper.
5. Cover the salad and refrigerate for 2 hours or until well chilled.

❧ Chilled Israeli Couscous Salad

PREPARATION:
15 MINUTES

COOKING:
15 MINUTES

CHILLING:
2 HOURS

YIELD:
4 MAIN-COURSE
SERVINGS

A chilled Israeli couscous salad is a creative alternative to a traditional pasta salad. Israeli couscous is quick to prepare and combines well with a variety of vegetables, herbs, and seasonings. When preparing an Israeli couscous salad, the only rule we have is that the vegetables be cut into small enough pieces so that they mesh well with the couscous and not overwhelm it. Here we use great summer vegetables and garnish them with avocado slices and lemon-infused tofu to create a delectable salad that is ideal for a picnic or light lunch. It is rich in phytoestrogens and vitamins C and E.

Tip: *Since we love the starchiness of Israeli couscous, steaming is the way we choose to prepare it. If you want to eliminate the majority of the starch, cook it like traditional pasta and rinse after it has been drained.*

½ pint cherry tomatoes, halved
1 cup fresh basil, snipped
   Sea salt to taste
   Black pepper to taste
2 tablespoons olive oil
4 cloves garlic, peeled and sliced
1 red bell pepper, seeded and diced
1 small zucchini, diced
2 ears fresh corn, kernels removed
2 cups Israeli couscous
2½ cups water
   Juice of 1½ lemons
1 pound extra-firm tofu
1 tablespoon sugar
1 avocado, peeled and sliced

1. Combine the tomatoes and basil in a large bowl. Season with sea salt and black pepper. Set the bowl aside for a moment.
2. Heat 1 tablespoon of the olive oil in a Dutch oven over medium heat. When the oil is hot, add the garlic and cook for 30 seconds.
3. Add the bell pepper. Cook for 2 minutes, stirring often. Add

the zucchini. Sprinkle the vegetables with sea salt. Cook the ingredients until they begin to soften, stirring often, approximately 3 minutes.

4. Add the corn and couscous. Cook for a minute. Raise the heat to high. Add the water and juice of 1 lemon. Bring the water to a boil. Season the liquid with sea salt and black pepper.

5. Cover the pot and turn off the heat. Allow the couscous to steam until all of the liquid has been absorbed, approximately 15 minutes.

6. While the couscous is steaming, prepare the tofu. Heat the remaining tablespoon of olive oil in a wok over medium-high heat. Place the tofu on a kitchen towel. With the heal of your hand, gently press on the tofu to remove the excess moisture. Cube the tofu.

7. When the oil is hot, carefully place the tofu in the wok. Sprinkle with sea salt. Cook until golden, tossing occasionally. Add the sugar and cook for another minute. Add the remaining lemon juice. Remove the pan from the heat.

8. To finish the salad, transfer the couscous to the bowl containing the tomatoes. Combine the ingredients. Garnish the salad with the tofu and avocado.

9. Cover the bowl and chill the salad for 2 hours.

ISRAELI COUSCOUS

Israeli couscous, like Moroccan couscous, is made from semolina. Israeli couscous is larger than the Moroccan variety, about the size of a peppercorn, and unlike the Moroccan type, it is toasted. Its large size and nutty flavor make it a versatile food. It can be cooked and tossed with vegetables and a vinaigrette to make a great chilled salad, or it can be added to soups and stews to absorb their wonderful juices. it can also be lightly seasoned and served as a bed for meat or fish.

Chilled Soba Noodles with Bok Choy and Soy Nuts

PREPARATION:
10 MINUTES

COOKING:
15 MINUTES

CHILLING:
2 HOURS

YIELD:
4 MAIN-COURSE
SERVINGS

When we tire of eating Italian pasta, we pick up a package of Japanese soba noodles. They are made from buckwheat flour and have a pronounced nutty taste and starchy texture. In Japan they are most often served in a soup or chilled and accompanied with a dipping sauce. We have prepared them our favorite way: tossed with greens, plenty of garlic, and soy nuts. This dish is packed with fiber, phytoestrogens, and beta-carotene.

Tip: Dark sesame oil is made from toasted sesame seeds; it has a more intense flavor than traditional sesame oil. If you can't locate it, traditional sesame oil can be substituted.

Sea salt to taste
12 ounces soba noodles
⅔ cup roasted soy nuts
⅓ cup tamari
2 tablespoons rice wine vinegar
2 teaspoons dark sesame oil
2 teaspoons sugar
1 tablespoon canola oil
8 cloves garlic, peeled and thinly sliced
1½ pounds bok choy, trimmed, washed, drained, stems and leaves chopped and separated

1. Bring a large pot of water to a boil. Add sea salt to the water followed by the soba noodles. Cook the noodles until tender, approximately 7 minutes. Drain and rinse under cold running water. Transfer them to a large bowl. Set them aside for a moment.
2. Place the soy nuts in a small skillet over low heat. Sprinkle with sea salt. Toast them until they are golden and fragrant, shaking the pan often, approximately 5 minutes. Set them aside for a moment.
3. Whisk together the tamari, vinegar, sesame oil, and sugar. Set the sauce aside for a moment.

4. Heat the canola oil in a Dutch oven over medium-high heat. Add the garlic and cook for 30 seconds. Add the bok choy stems. Cover the pot and cook the stems for 5 minutes or until they begin to soften. Add the bok choy leaves. Cook them until they are wilted and tender, stirring often, approximately 3 minutes. Transfer them to the bowl containing the noodles.
5. Whisk the sauce one more time and pour onto the noodles and bok choy. Toss the salad. Garnish with the soy nuts.
6. Cover the bowl. Refrigerate the salad for 2 hours.

❧ Tomato and Fresh Onion Salad

Sweet, tender, and not at all sharp tasting, a fresh red onion is a real treat. Unfortunately, they are difficult to find. Most supermarkets do not carry them. A farm stand, farmers' market, or specialty produce store are your best choices. If you can't find one, substitute a Vidalia or traditional red onion.

If you seek out great tomatoes, basil, and olive oil, this simple and Vitamin C–rich salad will not disappoint. Accompany it with plenty of rustic bread to soak up all of the delectable juices.

PREPARATION:
20 MINUTES

RESTING:
1 HOUR

YIELD:
4 SIDE-DISH
SERVINGS

1 large fresh red onion, thinly sliced
  Sea salt to taste
3 large ripe tomatoes
2 tablespoons olive oil
½ cup fresh basil, snipped
  Black pepper to taste

1. Place the onion in a colander. Sprinkle with sea salt. Allow the onion to sweat for 15 minutes.
2. Wrap the onion in a kitchen towel. Squeeze the onion to remove as much excess moisture as possible. Transfer the onion to a serving bowl.
3. Add the tomatoes, olive oil, and basil. Season the salad with sea salt and black pepper. Cover the bowl. Allow the salad to rest for 1 hour so the flavors can develop and intensify.

❧❦ Tomato and Fresh Mozzarella Stacks

PREPARATION:
10 MINUTES

COOKING:
10 MINUTES

YIELD:
6 SIDE-DISH
SERVINGS

During the height of tomato season, we can't get enough of them. Initially, we are satisfied with slicing them, drizzling them with olive oil, a sprinkling of sea salt, and a couple grinds of fresh black pepper. As the season progresses, we enjoy creating different ways to enjoy these wonderful gems of summer. One day it might be a tomato and bread salad, and on another we might prepare a salad of tomatoes, cucumbers, onions, and a bit of feta cheese. Here, we have used the classic combination of tomatoes, basil, and fresh mozzarella and placed it atop garlicky bread to create a unique Vitamin C–rich tomato sandwich. If you are like us, one is never enough.

2 tablespoons olive oil
8 cloves garlic, peeled and thinly sliced
Sea salt to taste
6 slices crusty bread, lightly toasted
4 large ripe tomatoes, cored, each cut into 4 slices
6 large fresh basil leaves
4 ounces fresh mozzarella, cut into 6 slices
Black pepper to taste

1. Heat the olive oil in a small skillet over low heat. Add the garlic. Sprinkle with sea salt. Cook the garlic until golden and slightly crisp, stirring occasionally, approximately 10 minutes. Remove the pan from the heat.
2. Place the bread slices on a large serving platter. Divide the garlic among the slices. Place a slice of tomato on each slice. Top each slice of tomato with a basil leaf and a slice of mozzarella. Place a slice of tomato on each portion to complete the stack. Sprinkle with sea salt and black pepper. If desired, drizzle each stack with olive oil. Serve at once.

✿ Tomato and Cucumber Salad with Olives, Mint, and Feta

Crisp cucumbers, sweet and juicy tomatoes, salty olives, and a hint of mint make this quickly prepared salad a great contrast of flavors and textures. A sprinkling of creamy feta brings all of the elements together. Best of all though, the salad is loaded with breast cancer fighting Vitamin C.

PREPARATION:
10 MINUTES

COOKING:
30 MINUTES

YIELD:
4 SIDE-DISH
SERVINGS

- 4 vine-ripened tomatoes, cored and sliced into wedges
- 1 medium cucumber, peeled, seeded, and sliced
- 12 Kalamata olives, pitted and coarsely chopped
- 2 tablespoons fresh mint, chopped
- 2 tablespoons olive oil
- 1 tablespoon top-quality balsamic vinegar
  Sea salt to taste
  Black pepper to taste
- 3 ounces sheep's milk feta, crumbled

1. Combine the tomatoes, cucumber, olives, and mint in a non-reactive serving bowl.
2. To prepare the dressing, whisk together the olive oil and balsamic vinegar. Pour the dressing into the bowl containing the tomato mixture and toss gently. Season the salad with sea salt and black pepper. Garnish with feta.
3. Allow the salad to marinate at room temperature for 30 minutes.

❧❦ Ellie's Chilled Carrot Salad with Cilantro and Garlic

Our brother-in-law Ellie prepares this carrot salad on Friday and serves it on Saturday while he and Vince's sister Kate and their children observe the Sabbath. Carrots are a great source of beta-carotene.

PREPARATION:
10 MINUTES

COOKING:
10 MINUTES

CHILLING:
2 HOURS

YIELD:
4 SIDE-DISH
SERVINGS

1½ pounds carrots, scraped and sliced at an angle
    Sea salt to taste
1   tablespoon canola oil
3   cloves garlic, finely chopped
1   teaspoon cumin
⅓   cup cilantro, chopped
    Black pepper to taste

1. Place the carrots in a medium saucepan. Cover with water. Sprinkle with sea salt. Bring to a boil. Cook until tender, approximately 10 minutes. Drain. Cool under running water. Transfer to a serving bowl. Set aside for a moment.
2. Heat the canola oil in a skillet over medium-low heat. Add the garlic and cook until soft and fragrant.
3. Add the cumin and cook the mixture for 1 minute.
4. Add the mixture to the carrots. Stir in the cilantro.
5. Season the carrots with sea salt and black pepper. Cover the bowl and chill the carrots for 2 hours.

✿ Roasted Sweet Pepper and Tomato Salad

We like to prepare this slightly sweet and intensely flavored dish in early fall when bell peppers are abundant and sweet and there are still a few good tomatoes lurking about. It is a great accompaniment to any grilled meat, fish, poultry, or tofu dish. It can be prepared several days in advance and served at room temperature. Bell peppers and tomatoes are two of the richest sources of Vitamin C and beta-carotene.

PREPARATION:
30 MINUTES

COOKING:
15 MINUTES

YIELD:
4 SIDE-DISH
SERVINGS

1 tablespoon olive oil
2 cloves garlic, peeled and thinly sliced
1 onion, peeled and thinly sliced
  Sea salt to taste
½ teaspoon sweet paprika
1 teaspoon sugar
1 large roasted yellow bell pepper, skin removed and discarded
1 large roasted green bell pepper, skin removed and discarded
1 large roasted red bell pepper, skin removed and discarded
2 ripe tomatoes, diced
  Black pepper to taste

1. Heat the olive oil in a large skillet over low heat. Add the garlic and cook until soft and fragrant. Add the onion. Sprinkle with sea salt. Cook the onion until soft.
2. Add the paprika and sugar. Cook for another minute.
3. Add all of the roasted peppers. Cook for 2 minutes, stirring occasionally.
4. Raise the heat to medium. Add the tomatoes. Cook the salad for 5 minutes, stirring occasionally.
5. Season the salad with sea salt and black pepper. Transfer it to a serving platter. Serve the salad hot, warm, or at room temperature.

ROASTED BELL PEPPERS

6 bell peppers

1. Heat the broiler.
2. Cut the peppers in half lengthwise and remove the stems, seeds, and ribs.
3. Place the peppers on a rack or broiling pan skin side up, approximately 3 inches from the heat. Broil the peppers until the skin is completely charred, approximately 6 minutes.
4. Remove the peppers from the broiler. Place them in a plastic bag. Seal the bag with a tie or twist it tightly closed. Steam the peppers for approximately 10 minutes.
5. Remove the peppers from the bag. Peel the skin off, making sure that all of the charred skin is removed.
6. Use the peppers as directed in your favorite recipe.

Note: An alternative method of roasting bell peppers is to roast them whole over a gas burner on top of the stove. If you use this method, it is necessary to turn them often.

CHAPTER 12

Pizzas and Calzones

Turning your home kitchen into a pizza shop may seem like a daunting task, but it is easier than you think and a fun and rewarding experience. With a few basic techniques, a bit of imagination and a hot oven, you can produce far superior pizzas and calzones than those from any restaurant. Most important, the creative combination of ingredients you can use for your toppings and fillings will contain many breast cancer preventing nutrients.

A few words about cooking pizzas and calzones at home are necessary. The best restaurant pizzas are baked in wood-fired or coal-fired brick ovens. These ovens supply a very hot and dry heat (700° to 800°F) and impart a distinctive flavor and texture to whatever is baked in them. Although it is difficult to achieve the exact same flavor at home, you can duplicate the superb texture in your oven. All that is needed are two inexpensive pieces of equipment: a pizza stone and pizza peel. If you heat a thick, ceramic pizza stone in your oven at 500°F for one hour, your pizzas and calzones will cook in approximately 8 minutes. This quick-cooking will result in a light and crispy crust that is full of a delectable yeasty flavor. A pizza peel is a long-handled, wooden tool used to move pizzas and calzones in and out of the oven. It takes a bit of practice to be able to efficiently slide a pizza or calzone off a peel and onto a stone, but after two or three attempts your technique will be as good as any *pizzaiolo*. If you don't have a stone and peel, very good pizzas can still be made in a pan or on a heavy baking tray. If you choose this method, sprinkle the pan or tray with cornmeal before rolling out the dough. Cook your pizzas at approximately 400°F.

We like to prepare thin-crusted, Neapolitan-syle pizza at home. Our calzones are simply folded pizzas that contain a tasty tofu "ricotta" as the main ingredient in the filling. When preparing our pizzas and calzones or creating your own, keep in mind that the best results are achieved with just a few top-quality ingredients. Fresh vegetables, fruity olive oil, and a little tangy cheese are the basics for great homemade pizzas and calzones.

The ingredients in our pizza and calzone dough are similar to most recipes with one exception: ground flaxseed. The flaxseed adds a distinctive earthy flavor and is one of the few nonfish sources of omega-3 fatty acids. The recipe yields enough dough for two 16-inch thin-crusted pizzas, each serving 3 or 4 as a main course or eight 8-inch main-course calzones. If you don't use all of the dough at once, it can be wrapped tightly and refrigerated for up to 2 days or it can be shaped and baked as bread. Raw dough can also be frozen for up to 2 months. After the kneading is complete, shape the dough into a flat disc, wrap it tightly in plastic wrap, and place in a freezer bag. The dough can be defrosted in 3 hours by setting it in a warm (80°F) place. Waiting for defrosted dough to double in size is not necessary. It can be used as soon as it can be stretched and shaped.

So next time you are craving a pizza or calzone, delight your taste buds and enhance your health by preparing a delectable Pan-Roasted Butternut Squash and Balsamic-Glazed Tofu Pizza or a Roasted Sweet Bell Pepper and Basil Pizza or a hearty Spinach, Provolone, and Tofu-"Ricotta" Calzone.

🌿 Pizza and Calzone Dough

The key to preparing a good pizza and calzone crust is to prepare a moist and sticky dough. Too much flour will produce a tough and dry crust. For this reason, we like to make our dough in a stand-up mixer. The mixer will knead the dough thoroughly and you won't be tempted to add an excessive amount of flour. If you mix the dough by hand, it should feel sticky when it's ready.

We have added ground flaxseed to our basic dough recipe. Flaxseed adds a wonderful earthy flavor and tenderness to the dough without heaviness. It is a great source of fiber, calcium, protein, and omega-3 fatty acids.

PREPARATION:
1½ HOURS

YIELD:
TWO 16-INCH
THIN-CRUSTED
PIZZAS
(8 MAIN-COURSE
SERVINGS)
OR
EIGHT 8-INCH
CALZONES
(8 MAIN-COURSE
SERVINGS)

- 2½ cups warm water (105° to 115°F)
- 1 teaspoon sugar
- 2½ teaspoons active dry yeast
- 1 tablespoon olive oil
- ½ cup flaxseed
- 6–6½ cups unbleached, all-purpose flour
- 2 teaspoons sea salt

1. Combine the water and sugar in the bowl of a stand-up mixer. Add the yeast and stir until it is dissolved. Allow the yeast to proof for 5 minutes. Stir in the olive oil.
2. Pulverize the flaxseed in a coffee grinder until it resembles flour. Transfer to a large mixing bowl. Add 6 cups of the flour to the mixing bowl. Add the sea salt. Combine the ingredients thoroughly.
3. Attach the paddle to the mixer. Turn the machine on low. Add half of the flour mixture to the bowl. Beat the ingredients for 2 minutes. Add the remaining flour mixture. Beat the mixture for 2 minutes more.
4. Replace the paddle with the dough hook. Turn the machine on medium. Knead the dough for 7 minutes more, adding more flour if necessary to create a moist and slightly sticky dough.

5. Transfer the dough to a clean bowl. Cover it tightly with plastic wrap. Allow the dough to rise until it has doubled in size, approximately 1½ hours.

6. Form the risen dough into a ball. Divide the ball into two pieces. On a lightly floured surface, roll each piece into a ball. Place each ball onto a lightly floured surface. Allow the dough to rest until slightly puffed, approximately 15 minutes.

7. Proceed with one of the topping recipes.

FLAXSEED

As the cooking uses and health benefits of flaxseed have become well known, it is becoming more common in our kitchens. Flaxseed adds great texture and flavor to bread doughs, piecrusts, quick breads, and cookie doughs. When using flaxseed in baking, you will need little or no added fats, since flaxseed adds moisture to your baked goods. In a few instances, you can use whole flaxseed, such as in a bread dough, but most often it is ground to resemble flour. The best tool for processing flaxseed is a coffee bean grinder. You can process one-half cup of flaxseed in seconds to use in your recipes. Since ground flaxseed loses nutrients quickly, we suggest only grinding the amount you are going to use immediately.

Flaxseed is available in natural groceries and health-food stores either in bulk containers or one-pound packages. Like all seeds, flaxseed contains a significant amount of oil, and it can turn rancid quickly. Therefore, purchase flaxseed in small amounts (1–2 pounds) and keep it in your refrigerator or freezer.

❦ Pan-Roasted Butternut Squash and Balsamic-Glazed Tofu Pizza

You will not find this supernutritious and tasty pizza topping at your corner pizza shop. The slightly sweet and vinegary flavor of the squash and tofu contrasts beautifully with the earthy crust. The pizza is rich in beta-carotene, omega-3 fatty acids, and phytoestrogens.

PREPARATION:
15 MINUTES

COOKING:
15 MINUTES

YIELD:
ONE 16-INCH
PIZZA

2 tablespoons olive oil, plus additional for drizzling
1 small butternut squash, peeled and cut into ½-inch pieces
Sea salt to taste
1 onion, peeled and thinly sliced
8 ounces extra-firm tofu
2 tablespoons balsamic vinegar
2 tablespoons flat-leaf (Italian) parsley, chopped
Black pepper to taste
1 portion Pizza and Calzone Dough (page 147)
Cornmeal for sprinkling
2 cloves garlic, peeled and finely chopped
4 ounces part-skim mozzarella cheese, grated or sliced

1. Heat the pizza stone in the oven at 500°F for 1 hour.
2. Heat 1 tablespoon of olive oil in a wok over medium-high heat. When the oil is hot, add the squash. Sprinkle with sea salt. Cook the squash until tender and golden, tossing occasionally, approximately 7 minutes. Add the onion and cook the ingredients until the onion is soft, tossing often, approximately 3 minutes. Transfer the ingredients to a bowl.
3. Heat another tablespoon of the olive oil in the wok over high heat. Place the tofu on a kitchen towel. Press it gently with the heel of your hand to remove any excess moisture. Cut the tofu into ½-inch cubes.
4. When the oil is hot, carefully place the tofu into the wok. Sear it until golden, tossing often, approximately 3 minutes. Add the vinegar and cook for another minute.
5. Return the squash to the pan. Add the parsley. Cook the ingredients for another minute. Season with sea salt and

black pepper. Set the pan aside for a moment.

6. Flatten the dough on a lightly floured work surface into a 16-inch circle. Sprinkle a wooden pizza peel with cornmeal. Transfer the dough to the paddle.

7. Drizzle the dough lightly with olive oil. Sprinkle with the garlic. Scatter the topping and spread the cheese onto the pizza.

8. Transfer the pizza to the oven. Cook the pizza until the cheese bubbles and the crust begins to brown, 5 to 8 minutes.

9. Remove the pizza from the oven.

🌿 Broccoli Rabe and Garlic Pizza

PREPARATION:
5 MINUTES

COOKING:
15 MINUTES

YIELD:
ONE 16-INCH
PIZZA

This is the type of pizza you would find at the great pizza shops in New Haven. In keeping with the great New Haven tradition, this simple pizza relies on a few top-quality ingredients to create a memorable pie.

Broccoli rabe is not a common pizza topping. Blanching it beforehand tames its usual pungency, making it the perfect complement to the salty Romano and mellow mozzarella cheeses. The pizza is an excellent source of beta-carotene, omega-3 fatty acids, calcium, and fiber.

1 cup water
Sea salt to taste
1 large bunch broccoli rabe, trimmed, washed, and drained
1 portion Pizza and Calzone Dough (page 147)
Cornmeal for sprinkling
Olive oil for drizzling
3 cloves garlic, peeled and finely chopped
4 tablespoons Romano cheese, grated
4 ounces part-skim mozzarella cheese, grated or sliced

1. Heat the pizza stone in the oven at 500°F for 1 hour.
2. Bring the water to a boil in a Dutch oven. Add sea salt to the water followed by the broccoli rabe. Cover the pot and

steam the rabe until just tender, approximately 4 minutes, tossing it once.

3. Drain the rabe and shock it under cold running water. Squeeze it to remove any excess moisture. Set it aside for a moment.

4. Flatten the dough on a lightly floured work surface into a 16-inch circle. Sprinkle a wooden pizza peel with the cornmeal. Transfer the dough to the paddle.

5. Drizzle the dough lightly with olive oil. Sprinkle with the garlic. Sprinkle with the Romano cheese and scatter on the rabe. Top the pizza with the mozzarella cheese.

6. Transfer the pizza to the oven. Cook the pizza until the cheese bubbles and the crust begins to brown, 5–8 minutes.

7. Remove the pizza from the oven.

🌿 Roasted Sweet Bell Pepper and Basil Pizza

PREPARATION:
10 MINUTES

COOKING:
15 MINUTES

YIELD:
ONE 16-INCH
PIZZA

This quickly prepared sauce is our answer to the ubiquitous tomato sauce. It has a creamy texture and a pronounced roasted bell pepper flavor. It is a great source of Vitamin C, beta-carotene, omega-3 fatty acids, and phytoestrogens.

Tip: *This recipe yields approximately 2 cups of sauce, which is about twice the amount needed for two medium pizzas. The extra can be used as a pasta sauce or sandwich spread.*

1	tablespoon olive oil, plus additional for drizzling
5	cloves garlic, peeled and finely chopped
1	onion, peeled and diced
	Sea salt to taste
1⅓	cups roasted red bell peppers from a jar, chopped
2	tablespoons flat-leaf (Italian) parsley, chopped
6	ounces soft tofu
	Black pepper to taste
1	portion Pizza and Calzone Dough (page 147)
	Cornmeal for sprinkling
4	ounces part skim mozzarella cheese, sliced or grated
10	basil leaves

1. Heat the pizza stone in the oven at 500°F for 1 hour.
2. Heat the tablespoon of olive oil in a skillet over low heat. Add 2 cloves of the garlic. Cook until soft and fragrant. Add the onion and sprinkle with sea salt. Cook the onion until soft.
3. Add the roasted bell peppers and parsley. Cook the ingredients for another minute.
4. Transfer the mixture to a blender or food processor fitted with a metal blade. Add the tofu and puree the mixture. Season with sea salt and black pepper. Transfer to a bowl. Set aside for a moment.
5. Flatten 1 portion of dough on a lightly floured work surface into a 16-inch circle. Sprinkle a wooden pizza peel with the cornmeal. Transfer the dough to the paddle.

6. Drizzle the dough lightly with olive oil. Sprinkle with the remaining garlic. Spread with approximately 1 cup of the roasted bell pepper sauce. Top the pizza with the mozzarella cheese. Arrange the basil leaves on the pizza.
7. Transfer the pizza to the oven. Cook the pizza until the cheese bubbles and the crust begins to brown, 5–8 minutes.
8. Remove the pizza from the oven.

❧ Spinach, Provolone, and Tofu-"Ricotta" Calzone

Whether we toss it with pasta, enjoy it as a side dish, or simply scoop it up with rustic bread, garlicky spinach is one of our favorite vegetable dishes. When tucked into our flaxseed dough along with tofu-"ricotta" and provolone cheese, it makes a delectable beta-carotene, omega-3 fatty acid, and phytoestrogen-rich calzone.

PREPARATION:
15 MINUTES

COOKING:
15 MINUTES

YIELD:
4 8-INCH
CALZONES

TOFU-"RICOTTA"
1 tablespoon olive oil
3 cloves garlic, peeled and thinly sliced
1 onion, peeled and diced
  Sea salt to taste
½ teaspoon dried basil
½ teaspoon dried oregano
2 tablespoons fresh flat-leaf (Italian) parsley, chopped
1 pound extra-firm tofu, squeezed to remove excess moisture and crumbled
⅓ cup Romano cheese, grated
  Black pepper to taste

SPINACH AND DOUGH
 1   tablespoon olive oil
 4   cloves garlic, peeled and thinly sliced
 1½ pounds fresh spinach, trimmed, washed, and spun dry
     Sea salt to taste
     Black pepper to taste
 1   portion Pizza and Calzone Dough (page 147), divided
     into 4 pieces
 4   ounces provolone cheese, sliced
     Cornmeal for sprinkling

1. Heat the pizza stone in the oven at 500°F for 1 hour.
2. To prepare the tofu-ricotta, heat the olive oil in a Dutch oven over medium heat. When the oil is hot, add the garlic. Cook the garlic for 30 seconds. Add the onion and sprinkle with sea salt. Cook the onion until soft.
3. Add the basil, oregano, and parsley. Cook the ingredients for another minute.
4. Add the tofu. Cook the mixture for another minute, stirring often. Transfer it to a bowl. Add the Romano and season with sea salt and black pepper. Set aside for a moment.
5. To prepare the spinach, heat the olive oil in the Dutch oven over high heat. When the oil is hot, add the garlic and cook for 10 seconds. Add the spinach and sprinkle with sea salt. Cook the spinach only until it wilts, stirring constantly. Season with black pepper.
6. To assemble the calzones, flatten 1 piece of dough on a lightly floured work surface into an 8-inch circle. Place one-quarter of the tofu-ricotta onto 1 side of the dough. Top it with one-quarter of the spinach and one-quarter of the provolone. Fold the top half of the dough over the filling. Crimp the edges with a fork.
7. Repeat the procedure with the remaining dough and fillings. With a spatula, carefully transfer each calzone to a pizza peel liberally sprinkled with cornmeal. Transfer the calzones to the oven. Bake the calzones until golden, approximately 12 minutes.

🎕 Sweet Red Pepper, Shiitake Mushroom, and Tofu-"Ricotta" Calzone

Sweet peppers and shiitake mushrooms are a versatile combination. They are wonderful braised with tomatoes and chicken thighs or used as a topping for seared chicken breasts or pizzas. When folded into a calzone, they provide a pleasantly sweet contrast to the earthy-tasting crust. This calzone provides plenty of Vitamin C, beta-carotene, omega-3 fatty acids, and phytoestrogens.

PREPARATION:
30 MINUTES

COOKING:
15 MINUTES

YIELD:
4 8-INCH
CALZONES

TOFU-"RICOTTA"
1 tablespoon olive oil
3 cloves garlic, peeled and thinly sliced
1 onion, peeled and diced
  Sea salt to taste
½ teaspoon dried basil
½ teaspoon dried oregano
2 tablespoons fresh flat-leaf (Italian) parsley, chopped
1 pound extra-firm tofu, squeezed to remove excess moisture and crumbled
⅓ cup Romano cheese, grated
  Black pepper to taste

VEGETABLES AND DOUGH
1 tablespoon olive oil
3 cloves garlic, peeled and sliced
1 onion, peeled and diced
  Sea salt to taste
1 red bell pepper, cored and thinly sliced
8 ounces shiitake mushrooms, stems removed and discarded, caps sliced
2 tablespoons fresh flat-leaf (Italian) parsley, chopped
  Black pepper to taste
4 ounces provolone cheese, sliced
1 portion Pizza and Calzone Dough (page 147), divided into 4 pieces
  Cornmeal for sprinkling

1. Heat the pizza stone in the oven at 500°F for 1 hour.
2. To prepare the tofu-ricotta, heat the olive oil in a Dutch oven over medium heat. When the oil is hot, add the garlic. Cook the garlic for 30 seconds. Add the onion and sprinkle with sea salt. Cook the onion until soft.
3. Add the basil, oregano, and parsley. Cook the ingredients for another minute.
4. Add the tofu. Cook the mixture for another minute, stirring often. Transfer to a bowl. Add the Romano cheese and season with sea salt and black pepper. Set aside for a moment.
5. To prepare the vegetables, heat the olive oil in a wok over medium heat. When the oil is hot, add the garlic. Cook the garlic for 30 seconds. Add the onion and sprinkle with sea salt. Cook the onion until soft.
6. Add the red bell pepper and shiitake mushrooms. Cook the vegetables until soft, stirring occasionally, approximately 7 minutes.
7. Remove the pan from the heat. Add the parsley. Season the vegetables with sea salt and black pepper.
8. To assemble the calzones, flatten 1 piece of dough on a lightly floured work surface into an 8-inch circle. Place one-quarter of the tofu-ricotta onto 1 side of the dough. Top it with one-quarter of the spinach and one-quarter of the provolone. Fold the top half of the dough over the filling. Crimp the edges with a fork.
9. Repeat the procedure with the remaining dough and fillings. With a spatula, carefully transfer each calzone to a pizza peel liberally sprinkled with cornmeal. Transfer the calzones to the oven. Bake the calzones until golden, approximately 12 minutes.

CHAPTER 13

Pastas

We would have no problem eating pasta night after night. A package of dried pasta is one of the world's most versatile foods. Pasta dishes are a great opportunity for a creative cook to use a variety of ingredients to create wonderful meals that are rich in breast cancer preventing nutrients. There is an endless combination of antioxidant-rich vegetables and nuts and phytoestrogen-rich soy products that can be used in quick preparations, "make ahead" meals, and long-simmering delicacies.

If you are the type of person who likes to cook several meals on the weekend to enjoy during the week, try our Pasta Casserole with Chard, Tomatoes, and Mushrooms. It is a wonderful contrast of flavors and textures and provides plenty of antioxidants and phytoestrogens.

When it is prepared in a restaurant, the ubiquitous combination of pasta, chicken, and broccoli is usually loaded with cream and butter. We have created a delightful beta-carotene and phytoestrogen-rich version starring tofu-pesto. You will not miss the cream.

Lentils and pasta are a unique combination. When they are combined with a "creamy" tofu–butternut squash sauce, they make a hearty, cool weather meal. Like all deep orange–fleshed fruits and vegetables, butternut squash is a great source of beta-carotene.

When you are craving a pasta dish with a heady sauce and plenty of flavor, but do not want to take the time to make a ragu, prepare our Spaghetti with Zucchini, Tomatoes, and Anchovies. Canned anchovies are one of the richest sources of omega-3 fatty acids. When they are slowly cooked with a bit of water, wine, or stock, they create a delicious and deceptively rich sauce.

Whether you are cooking ahead, or are in the mood for a rich-tasting pasta dish without the accompanying fat and calories or just want something quick with seasonal vegetables or a bold sauce, the pasta dishes here will delight your palate.

🦋 Fettuccine with Chickpeas, Arugula, and Fried Garlic

With nutty-tasting chickpeas, earthy arugula, and sweet fried garlic, this dish contains a palate-pleasing spectrum of flavors and textures. Arugula is an excellent source of beta-carotene and calcium. Chickpeas provide plenty of fiber, folic acid, and Vitamin E.

PREPARATION:
10 MINUTES

COOKING:
15 MINUTES

YIELD:
4 MAIN-COURSE
SERVINGS

4	tablespoons pine nuts
	Sea salt to taste
2	tablespoons olive oil
10	cloves garlic, peeled and thinly sliced
1	pound fettuccine
1½	pounds arugula, washed, drained, and chopped
1	15-ounce can chickpeas, drained and rinsed
1	cup pasta cooking water
	Black pepper to taste
4	tablespoons Romano cheese, grated

1. Bring a large pot of water to a boil.
2. Meanwhile, place the pine nuts in a small skillet over low heat. Sprinkle with sea salt. Toast them until they are golden, shaking the pan occasionally. Transfer the nuts to a plate.
3. While the pine nuts are toasting, heat the olive oil in a Dutch oven over medium-low heat. Add the garlic and sprinkle with sea salt. Cook the garlic until it is a deep golden color and crisp, stirring it often. With a slotted spoon, transfer the garlic to a plate leaving the oil in the pot.
4. Add sea salt to the boiling water followed by the pasta.
5. Heat the garlic oil in the Dutch oven over high heat. When the oil is hot, add the arugula. Cook the arugula only until it wilts, stirring constantly. Add the chickpeas to the pot and stir thoroughly.
6. Reduce the heat to low and add the cup of pasta cooking water to the pot. When the pasta is tender, drain and add to the arugula mixture.

7. Heat the pasta and arugula together for 2 minutes, stirring occasionally. Season the pasta with sea salt and black pepper.
8. Divide the pasta among 4 large plates. Garnish with pine nuts, fried garlic, and Romano cheese.

GARLIC

The flavor of garlic is easily manipulated by the type of cooking technique you choose. To make nutty-tasting fried garlic, sprinkle whole cloves of peeled garlic with sea salt. Cook the cloves in olive oil over low heat until crisp and golden. Fried garlic is an ideal garnish for a pasta dish or it can be enjoyed as a snack or appetizer on slices of rustic bread. Roasting whole heads of garlic in a slow oven produces mild-flavored garlic pulp with an incredible sweetness. Roasted garlic is a great addition to mashed potatoes. It can also be whisked into a sauce or soup. Sautéed garlic is often the first step in soups, sauces, stews, vegetable, and pasta dishes. It gives the dish a pronounced garlic flavor. The longer you cook the garlic, the mellower its flavor. Garlic cooked to the browning point will be bitter, ruining the flavor of a meal. Your only choice if you "burn the garlic" is to toss it out and begin over. Raw garlic should be used sparingly. It has a very strong and bitter taste. A finely chopped small clove or two is enough to season a pesto or salsa.

🐾 Penne with a White Bean and Spinach Ragu

It is not necessary to make an Italian ragu with meat and cream. A delicious and more healthful vegetarian version can be prepared with white beans and spinach. Rather than being loaded with fat, our leaner version is rich in beta-carotene, calcium, fiber, Vitamin C, and phytoestrogens.

Tip: *The ragu can be prepared a day in advance. Not only is this convenient but a day in the refrigerator allows the flavors to fully develop and marry.*

BEAN SOAKING:
12 HOURS

PREPARATION:
15 MINUTES

COOKING:
1½ HOURS

YIELD:
4 MAIN-COURSE SERVINGS

1 cup navy beans
4 cups water
1 tablespoon olive oil
4 cloves garlic, peeled and sliced
1 onion, peeled and diced
   Sea salt to taste
1 carrot, scraped and diced
6 ounces tempeh bacon, diced
5 tomatoes from a can, seeded and chopped
½ pound spinach, trimmed, washed, and drained
6 ounces soft tofu, pureed
   Black pepper to taste
1 pound penne
2 ounces Parmesan cheese, shaved

1. The night before preparing the ragu, sort and rinse the beans. Cover with water and soak overnight.
2. The following day, pour off the soaking water and discard. Transfer the beans to a medium saucepan. Add the fresh water. Bring the beans to a boil. Cover the pot and reduce the heat. Simmer the beans until tender, approximately 1¼ hours.
3. While the beans are cooking, heat the olive oil in a Dutch oven over low heat. Add the garlic and cook until soft and fragrant.
4. Add the onion and sprinkle it with sea salt. Cook the onion

until it begins to soften. Add the carrot and tempeh. Cover the pot and cook the ingredients until the carrot begins to soften, stirring occasionally. Add the tomatoes.

5. When the beans are tender, transfer them along with their cooking water to the Dutch oven. Raise the heat to high. Bring the mixture to a boil. Reduce the heat and simmer for 10 minutes.

6. Add the spinach to the pot and cook until it wilts, stirring constantly. Add the tofu to the ragu. Reduce the heat to low. Season with sea salt and black pepper.

7. Cook the pasta in boiling salted water until tender. Drain and divide it among 4 large bowls. Ladle the ragu onto the pasta and garnish with the Parmesan cheese.

❧ Linguine with Broccoli Rabe, Glazed Flank Steak, and Fried Garlic

PREPARATION:
10 MINUTES

COOKING:
20 MINUTES

YIELD:
4 MAIN-COURSE
SERVINGS

Balsamic vinegar can be used in both sweet and savory dishes. We have all prepared salad dressings with it and drizzled a syrupy aged vinegar on fresh fruit. It also makes a wonderful glaze for meat. When flank steak is pan-seared and then splashed with balsamic vinegar, it turns out juicy and slightly sweet-tasting. When it is combined with earthy broccoli rabe and nutty-flavored fried garlic, the finished product is delectable. Broccoli rabe is an excellent source of beta-carotene and calcium.

Tip: *Be certain to only cook the garlic until golden and crisp. If it cooks to a deep brown, the flavor will be bitter and you will have to begin again.*

2 tablespoons olive oil
12 cloves of garlic, peeled and sliced
Sea salt to taste
1 pound flank steak
Black pepper to taste
¼ cup excellent-quality balsamic vinegar
1 pound linguine

  1 pound broccoli rabe, trimmed and rinsed
1½ cups pasta cooking water
  1 tablespoon unsalted butter
  4 tablespoons Romano cheese, grated

1. Bring a large pot of water to a boil.
2. Heat the olive oil in a Dutch oven over low heat. Add the garlic and sprinkle with sea salt. Cook the garlic until golden brown and crisp, approximately 8 minutes, stirring occasionally.
3. Remove the garlic from the pot with a slotted spoon, leaving the oil behind. Raise the heat to high. Sprinkle the meat on both sides with sea salt and black pepper.
4. When the oil is hot, place the meat in the pan. Sear the meat on each side, turning it once. Reduce the heat to medium. Add the vinegar. Cook the meat through for another minute, turning 2 or 3 times. Transfer the meat to a plate.
5. Add sea salt to the boiling water followed by the pasta.
6. Raise the heat to high under the Dutch oven. Add the broccoli rabe and sprinkle with sea salt. Add the pasta cooking water and butter to the pot. Cover the pot. Cook the rabe until tender, approximately 5 minutes.
7. When the pasta is tender, drain. Transfer to the Dutch oven. Reduce the heat to low and cook the pasta and sauce together for 2 minutes, stirring often.
8. Divide the pasta among 4 large plates. Thinly slice the flank steak on the bias. Divide the flank steak and accumulated juices among the 4 plates and garnish with Romano cheese.

🍃 Penne with a Tofu "Meat" Sauce

PREPARATION:
10 MINUTES

COOKING:
45 MINUTES

YIELD:
4 MAIN-COURSE
SERVINGS

We have all had those nights when we have opened a near empty refrigerator and a sparse pantry and asked the question: "What are we going to have for dinner?" One such evening, this recipe was the answer. We were able to take some of our food staples: olive oil, garlic, onions, tofu, canned tomatoes, and several other items on hand and create a delicious vegetarian version of a meat sauce. It is a hearty meal and packed with phytoestrogens and antioxidants.

1 tablespoon olive oil
4 cloves garlic, peeled and sliced
1 onion, peeled and diced
 Sea salt to taste
1 pound firm tofu, crumbled
6 ounces soy bacon, chopped
1 35-ounce can whole tomatoes in juice, chopped
1 pound penne or ziti
⅓ cup flat-leaf (Italian) parsley, chopped
¾ cup pasta cooking water
 Black pepper to taste
4 tablespoons Parmesan cheese, grated

1. Bring a large pot of water to a boil.
2. Heat the olive oil in a Dutch oven over low heat. Add the garlic and cook until soft and fragrant.
3. Add the onion to the pot and sprinkle with sea salt. Cook the onion until it begins to soften, stirring occasionally.
4. Raise the heat to medium and add the tofu and soy bacon. Cook for 5 minutes, stirring often.
5. Raise the heat to high. Add the tomatoes. Bring the sauce to a boil. Reduce the heat and simmer for 30 minutes, stirring occasionally.
6. Ten minutes before the sauce is done, add sea salt to the boiling water followed by the pasta. Cook the pasta until tender. Drain the pasta, reserving ¾ cup cooking water.
7. Add the parsley and pasta cooking water to the sauce.

Simmer for 5 minutes more. Season the sauce with sea salt and black pepper.

8. Divide the pasta among 4 large bowls and ladle the sauce onto each. Garnish with Parmesan.

Rigatoni with Sausage, Tomatoes, Tofu, and Broccoli Rabe

This is our version of a common hearty Italian country-style meal. By adding phytoestrogen-rich firm tofu to the recipe, we were able to decrease the amount of sausage without altering the texture or taste of the meal. Broccoli rabe is a great source of antioxidants and calcium and provides an eye-catching color contrast.

Tip: *The recipe can be prepared a day in advance to the stage where the rabe is steamed. The following day, when heating the sauce over low heat, it may be necessary to add a small amount of water to thin it.*

PREPARATION:
10 MINUTES

COOKING:
1 HOUR

YIELD:
4 MAIN-COURSE
SERVINGS

- 2 tablespoons olive oil
- 6 cloves garlic
- 12 ounces sweet Italian turkey sausage, chopped
- 12 ounces firm tofu, crumbled
- 1 35-ounce can whole tomatoes in juice, chopped
- 1 pound broccoli rabe, trimmed and rinsed
  Sea salt to taste
- 1 pound rigatoni
  Black pepper to taste
- 4 tablespoons Parmesan cheese, grated

1. Heat the olive oil in a large Dutch oven over low heat. Add the garlic and cook until soft and fragrant.
2. Raise the heat to medium. Add the sausage to the pot. To prevent the garlic from burning, immediately stir the ingredients. Cook the sausage until golden, stirring often.

3. Add the tofu. Cook for 5 minutes more, stirring often.
4. Raise the heat to high. Add the tomatoes to the pot. Bring the sauce to a boil. Reduce the heat and simmer for 40 minutes, stirring occasionally.
5. While the sauce is simmering, bring a large pot of water to a boil.
6. Fifteen minutes before the sauce is done, place a steamer or colander into the boiling water. Place the rabe into the steamer and cook until tender, approximately 3 minutes. Transfer to a cutting board and allow to cool.
7. Add sea salt to the boiling water followed by the pasta. Cook the pasta until tender. Drain and divide among 4 large plates.
8. Season the sauce with sea salt and black pepper. Coarsely chop the rabe and add to the sauce. Gently stir the sauce.
9. Spoon the sauce onto the pasta and garnish with Parmesan cheese.

Penne with Chicken and Broccoli in a Pesto "Cream" Sauce

PREPARATION:
10 MINUTES

COOKING:
20 MINUTES

YIELD:
4 MAIN-COURSE
SERVINGS

This type of pasta dish is ubiquitous in American-style Italian restaurants. People have asked us how they can prepare a healthful version of this traditionally cream-laden dish at home. We have substituted pureed silken tofu for the cream and added our oil-free basil pesto. The dish retains its creamy texture, but is now low in fat and much more nutritious. Broccoli is a great source of fiber, beta-carotene, and Vitamin C. Tofu is rich in phytoestrogens.

2 tablespoons olive oil
1 pound boneless and skinless chicken breast, trimmed and sliced
  Sea salt to taste
  Black pepper to taste
1 cup chicken stock
1 pound penne

8 ounces silken tofu

4 tablespoons tofu-basil pesto (see page 178)

4 cloves garlic, peeled and sliced

1½ pounds broccoli, trimmed, stems peeled, and sliced into disks, flowers cut into medium pieces

1 15-ounce can diced tomatoes

4 tablespoons Parmesan cheese, grated

1. Bring a large pot of water to a boil.
2. Meanwhile, heat 1 tablespoon of the olive oil in a Dutch oven over medium-high heat. Sprinkle the chicken with sea salt and black pepper. When the oil is hot, carefully place the chicken into the pot. Sear the chicken until golden, stirring 2 or 3 times. Add ⅓ cup of the stock. Cook the chicken for 1 minute more. Transfer the chicken to a bowl.
3. Add sea salt to the boiling water followed by the pasta.
4. Combine the tofu and pesto in a blender or the work bowl of a food processor fitted with a metal blade and puree. Set the puree aside.
5. Heat the remaining tablespoon of olive oil in the Dutch oven over low heat. Add the garlic and cook until soft and fragrant.
6. Raise the heat to high. Add the broccoli. Add the remaining ⅔ cup of chicken stock. Cover the pot. Cook the broccoli until just tender, approximately 5 minutes. Reduce the heat to low.
7. Return the chicken to the pot. Stir in the tofu-pesto mixture. Gently simmer the sauce for 2 minutes. Season with sea salt and black pepper.
8. Drain the pasta. Add to the sauce. Add the diced tomatoes. Cook the pasta and sauce together for 2 minutes, stirring occasionally.
9. Divide the pasta among 4 shallow bowls and garnish with Parmesan cheese.

🦋 Tofu Mozzarella with a Wine, Tomato, and Mushroom Sauce

PREPARATION:
15 MINUTES

COOKING:
35 MINUTES

YIELD:
4 MAIN-COURSE
SERVINGS

Besides crumbling and cubing, firm and extra-firm tofu work well when sliced into ½-inch-thick rectangles. In this recipe we have breaded and baked it. A full-bodied sauce is the perfect complement to the mild-tasting tofu. The sauce is a great source of antioxidants. Also, with 5 ounces of tofu in each serving, you are getting plenty of breast cancer preventing phytoestrogens.

Tip: *The wine and mushroom sauce is versatile. When accompanied with brown rice, polenta, or pasta, it makes a quick and easy dinner. If desired, you can also add any variety of mushrooms, summer squash, or eggplant to the sauce to alter its texture and flavor. Also, 1 teaspoon of dried basil can be substituted for the fresh; add it after the onion is soft and cook for a minute.*

SAUCE
- 1 tablespoon olive oil
- 4 cloves garlic, peeled and sliced
- 1 onion, peeled and diced
  Sea salt to taste
- 1 pound button mushrooms, wiped and sliced
- 1 cup red wine
- 1 35-ounce can whole tomatoes in juice, chopped
- ⅓ cup fresh basil, snipped
  Black pepper to taste

TOFU AND PASTA
- 1 cup unbleached all-purpose flour
  Sea salt to taste
  Black pepper to taste
- 1 egg
- ½ cup milk
- 1½ cups homemade or store-bought Bread Crumbs (page 263)
- 1½ pounds firm or extra-firm tofu, sliced into ½-inch-thick rectangles and patted dry

4 tablespoons olive oil
4 ounces part-skim Mozzarella cheese, sliced or grated
1 pound spaghetti

1. To prepare the sauce, heat the olive oil in a Dutch oven over low heat. Add the garlic and cook until soft and fragrant. Add the onion and sprinkle with sea salt. Cook the onion until soft, stirring often.

2. Raise the heat to medium. Add the mushrooms. Cook the mushrooms until soft.

3. Raise the heat to high. Add the wine. Bring the wine to a boil and simmer for 1 minute.

4. Add the tomatoes. Bring the sauce to a boil. Reduce the heat and simmer for 30 minutes, stirring often. Add the basil to the sauce. Season the sauce with sea salt and black pepper.

5. While the sauce is simmering, prepare the tofu and cook the pasta. Preheat the oven to 425°F. Bring a large pot of water to a boil.

6. Place the flour on a plate. Season it with sea salt and black pepper. Whisk the egg and milk in a shallow bowl. Place the bread crumbs on a plate.

7. Dredge the tofu in the flour. Dip it into the egg wash. Coat with the bread crumbs. Set the tofu aside for a moment.

8. Place the olive oil on a heavy baking tray. Place the tray in the oven and allow the oil to get hot. Carefully remove the tray from the oven. Place the tofu on the tray. Turn the tofu once. Return the tray to the oven. Bake the tofu until golden and crisp, turning once, approximately 15 minutes.

9. Remove the tofu from the oven. Spoon the sauce to cover each portion and sprinkle with the cheese. Return the tray to the oven. Bake the tofu until the cheese melts and bubbles.

10. While the tofu is baking, add sea salt to the boiling water, followed by the pasta. Cook the pasta until tender.

11. Drain and divide among 4 large plates. Spoon the sauce onto each portion.

12. Place a portion of tofu on each plate and serve at once.

🐦 Pasta Casserole with Chard, Tomatoes, and Mushrooms

PREPARATION:
15 MINUTES

COOKING:
45 MINUTES

YIELD:
6 MAIN-COURSE
SERVINGS

By Sunday evening, our pantry and refrigerator are nearly empty. To make dinner on these nights without going to the market is always a challenge. Our only rule is to avoid creating a meal that has a thrown-together look and taste. Some of our best meals on these evenings are concocted from odds and ends. This casserole is a memorable dish. With tomatoes, carrots, chard, and tofu, it is a breast cancer preventing powerhouse.

Tip: *If desired, ground meat or poultry can be added to the sauce. Cook it in a separate pan and drain off all of the drippings before adding it to the sauce.*

2 tablespoons olive oil
6 cloves garlic, peeled and sliced
1 onion, peeled and diced
  Sea salt to taste
¾ pound button, shiitake, or cremini mushrooms, wiped and sliced
½ pound green, red, or yellow Swiss chard, trimmed, washed, and chopped
1 cup white wine
1 pound firm tofu, crumbled
1 28-ounce can whole tomatoes in juice, chopped
  Black pepper to taste
1 pound penne
8 ounces mozzarella, sliced

1. Bring a large pot of water to a boil. Heat the broiler.
2. Heat the olive oil in a large Dutch oven over low heat. Add the garlic and cook until soft and fragrant. Add the onion and sprinkle with sea salt. Cook the onion until soft, stirring occasionally.
3. Raise the heat to medium and add the mushrooms. Cook the mushrooms until soft, stirring often.
4. Raise the heat to high and add the chard. Cook the chard for 1 minute. Add the wine and simmer for 1 minute.

5. Add the tofu and tomatoes to the pot. Bring the sauce to a boil. Reduce the heat and simmer for 15 minutes, stirring occasionally. Season the sauce with sea salt and black pepper.
6. While the sauce is simmering, add sea salt to the water followed by the pasta. Cook the pasta until tender.
7. Drain the pasta and add to the sauce. Cook the sauce and pasta together for 1 minute.
8. Garnish the pasta with the mozzarella. Place the pot under the broiler. Broil the pasta until the cheese is golden and bubbly.

🌿 Rigatoni with Seasoned Lentils and a "Creamy" Squash Sauce

Earthy tasting and quick-cooking lentils not only make a hearty soup but also a wonderful addition to a pasta dish. When combined with "creamy" butternut squash and garnished with tangy goat cheese, it is a meal full of wonderful flavors and textures. The dish is rich in fiber, phytoestrogens, and beta-carotene.

Tips: *This recipe makes approximately 4 cups of butternut squash sauce. You will need only 2½ cups for this recipe. The remainder can be frozen or used as the base for a quick soup. Also, cooking lentils is similar to toasting pine nuts; they can go from being perfectly cooked to being overdone in a matter of minutes. Begin checking them for tenderness after they have been simmering for 15 minutes.*

PREPARATION: 30 MINUTES

COOKING: 15 MINUTES

YIELD: 4 MAIN-COURSE SERVINGS

LENTILS
6 ounces lentils, sorted and rinsed
4 cups water
3 plum tomatoes, diced
½ cup flat-leaf (Italian) parsley, chopped
1 small clove garlic, peeled and minced
2 tablespoons olive oil
2 tablespoons balsamic vinegar
Sea salt to taste
Black pepper to taste

SQUASH AND PASTA

1 tablespoon canola oil
½-inch gingerroot, peeled and chopped
1 small onion, peeled and diced
Sea salt to taste
1 medium butternut squash, peeled and cubed
3 cups water
8 ounces soft tofu
Black pepper to taste
1 pound rigatoni
4 ounces goat cheese, at room temperature

1. To prepare the lentils, place them in a pot and add the water. Bring to a boil. Reduce the heat and simmer until tender, approximately 20 minutes.
2. Drain the lentils and discard their cooking water. Transfer to a large plate. Spread them out so they cool quickly.
3. Combine the tomatoes, parsley, garlic, olive oil, and vinegar in a large bowl. Add the cooled lentils to the bowl and toss. Season with sea salt and black pepper. Set aside.
4. While the lentils are cooking, prepare the squash and pasta. To cook the pasta bring a large pot of water to a boil.
5. Heat the canola oil in a Dutch oven over low heat. Add the ginger. Cook until soft and fragrant. Add the onion and sprinkle with sea salt. Cook the onion until soft, stirring occasionally.
6. Raise the heat to high and add the squash. Add the water. Bring the water to a boil. Reduce the heat and simmer the squash until tender, approximately 20 minutes.
7. Carefully transfer the squash and its cooking water to a blender. Add the tofu and puree. Season with sea salt and black pepper.
8. Add sea salt to the boiling water followed by the pasta. Cook the pasta until tender. Drain and return to the pot. Add 2 ½ cups of the squash sauce to the pasta and toss well. Divide the pasta among 4 large plates. Garnish with the seasoned lentils and goat cheese.

🌿 Linguine with Tomatoes and Clams

Linguine and clams are a classic combination. With briny clams, a healthy dose of garlic, and plenty of fruity olive oil, how can you not love it? We have updated the recipe and made it more healthful by decreasing the olive oil and adding antioxidant-rich tomatoes to the sauce. For convenience, we have substituted frozen chopped clams for fresh. They are a wonderful product. If you can't find them in your market, an equal amount of canned clams can be substituted.

PREPARATION:
10 MINUTES

COOKING:
20 MINUTES

YIELD:
4 MAIN-COURSE
SERVINGS

- 1 tablespoon olive oil
- 6 cloves garlic, peeled and sliced
- 1 cup white wine
- 1 28-ounce can whole tomatoes in juice, drained, liquid reserved for another use, tomatoes chopped
  Sea salt to taste
- 1 pound linguine
- 1 tablespoon unsalted butter
- 24 ounces frozen chopped clams (including their liquid)
- ½ cup fresh flat-leaf (Italian) parsley, chopped
  Black pepper to taste

1. Bring a large pot of water to a boil.
2. Heat the olive oil in a Dutch oven over low heat. Add the garlic and cook until soft and fragrant.
3. Raise the heat to high. Add the wine. Simmer the wine for 2 minutes. Add the tomatoes to the pot. Bring the sauce to a boil. Reduce the heat and simmer for 10 minutes, stirring often.
4. While the sauce is cooking, add sea salt to the water followed by the pasta. Cook the pasta until tender. Drain and set aside for a moment.
5. Raise the heat to high and add the butter, clams, and parsley to the sauce. Cook the clams for 1 minute. Add the pasta to the sauce and toss thoroughly.
6. Reduce the heat to low. Cook the pasta and sauce together for 1 minute. Season the pasta with sea salt and black pepper.
7. Divide the pasta among 4 plates and serve immediately.

🎋 Penne with Asparagus and Shiitake Mushrooms

PREPARATION:
10 MINUTES

COOKING:
20 MINUTES

YIELD:
4 MAIN-COURSE
SERVINGS

When creating a recipe, we almost always are able to predict the outcome. This one was an exception though. On our first attempt, the asparagus was bland and the pasta dry. The recipe was missing something. On our second attempt, we included shiitake mushrooms, lemon, and fresh basil and the result was wonderful. This meal is rich in folic acid and beta-carotene.

Tip: *To enhance the texture of the sauce, choose medium-sized asparagus spears.*

> 2 tablespoons olive oil
> 2 cloves garlic, peeled and sliced
> 12 ounces shiitake mushrooms, stems removed and discarded, caps sliced
> Sea salt to taste
> 1 pound penne
> 1½ pounds asparagus, trimmed and diagonally sliced
> 1 cup vegetable or chicken broth
> Zest of 1 lemon, grated
> ½ cup fresh basil, snipped
> Black pepper to taste
> 4 tablespoons Parmesan cheese, grated

1. Bring a large pot of water to a boil.
2. Heat the olive oil in a Dutch oven over low heat. Add the garlic and cook until soft and fragrant.
3. Raise the heat to medium. Add the mushrooms. Sprinkle with sea salt. Cook until soft, stirring often.
4. Add sea salt to the boiling water followed by the pasta.
5. Raise the heat to high under the Dutch oven. Add the asparagus. Cook for 2 minutes, stirring often. Add the vegetable or chicken stock. Cover the pot and cook until the asparagus is tender, approximately 5 minutes.
6. Drain the pasta and transfer to the Dutch oven. Reduce the heat to low. Add the lemon and basil. Season the pasta with sea salt and black pepper. Cook the pasta for 2 minutes, stirring occasionally.

7. Divide the pasta among 4 large plates. Garnish with Parmesan cheese and serve at once.

❧ Rigatoni with Herb Crusted Chicken, Olives, and Dried Tomatoes

Like tofu, boneless and skinless chicken breasts have a neutral flavor and adapt well to bold seasonings. In this recipe herb-crusted chicken strips are braised with rich Kalamata olives and fresh and dried tomatoes. The resulting sauce is sweet and earthy and a great source of Vitamin C and beta-carotene.

Tip: *Any leftover sauce and chicken make wonderful hot sandwiches on rustic bread with melted provolone or mozzarella.*

PREPARATION:
15 MINUTES

COOKING:
1 HOUR

YIELD:
4 MAIN-COURSE
SERVINGS

	Sea salt to taste
2	teaspoons dried basil
2	teaspoons dried oregano
1	teaspoon dried thyme
1½	pounds boneless and skinless chicken breast, sliced into strips
1	cup water
1	cup dried tomatoes
3	tablespoons olive oil
6	cloves garlic, peeled and sliced
1	onion, peeled and diced
	Reserved dried tomato soaking water
1	28-ounce can whole tomatoes in juice, drained and chopped
½	cup Kalamata olives, pitted and chopped
	Black pepper to taste
1	pound rigatoni
4	tablespoons Romano cheese, grated

1. Combine the sea salt, basil, oregano, and thyme in a bowl. Sprinkle onto the chicken strips. Toss the chicken thoroughly. Set aside for a moment.

2. Boil 1 cup of water. Place the dried tomatoes in a bowl. Pour the boiling water onto them. Soak until soft, approximately 15 minutes. Drain and reserve their soaking water. Set the tomatoes and their soaking water aside.

3. While the tomatoes are soaking, heat 2 tablespoons of the olive oil in a Dutch oven over medium-high heat. When the oil is hot, carefully place the chicken strips into the pot in a single layer. Sear the strips, turning 2 or 3 times. Remove from the pan and set aside.

4. Reduce the heat to low. Add the remaining tablespoon of oil to the pot. Add the garlic and cook until soft and fragrant. Add the onion and sprinkle with sea salt. Cook the onion until soft.

5. Raise the heat to high and add the tomato soaking water to the pot. Add the chopped tomatoes and olives. Return the chicken to the pot. Bring the sauce to a boil. Reduce the heat and simmer the sauce for 45 minutes, stirring occasionally. Season the sauce with sea salt and black pepper.

6. During the last 15 minutes of simmering, cook the pasta until tender.

7. Divide the pasta among 4 plates and spoon a portion of the sauce onto each. Garnish with the Romano cheese.

TO PEEL, SEED, AND CHOP TOMATOES

Bring a pot of water to a boil. Cut an X on the bottom of each tomato, and carefully place each in boiling water for 30 seconds. Remove from the water and allow to cool. Slip off their skins, remove their cores, cut in half, and gently squeeze them to remove the seeds.

✣ Linguine with a Tomato and Basil Sauce

This tomato sauce recipe is almost as quick and simple as opening and heating a sauce from a jar, and it's much tastier and more nutritious. We make this sauce with top-quality canned Italian plum tomatoes for most of the year. In summer though, we love to use peeled and seeded fresh tomatoes (see box, page 176). Although it adds preparation time, the sauce is full of fresh and clean flavors and well worth the extra time. Either version provides abundant amounts of beta-carotene and Vitamin C.

PREPARATION:
10 MINUTES

COOKING:
20 MINUTES

YIELD:
4 MAIN-COURSE
SERVINGS

1 tablespoon olive oil
4 cloves garlic, peeled
1 28-ounce can whole tomatoes in juice, chopped
1 pound linguine
½ cup fresh basil, snipped
  Sea salt to taste
  Black pepper to taste
4 tablespoons Parmesan cheese, grated

1. Bring a large pot of water to a boil.
2. Heat the olive oil in a Dutch oven over medium-low heat. Add the garlic cloves and cook until soft and fragrant, turning occasionally. Remove and enjoy them as a snack with a slice of bread.
3. Raise the heat to high. Add the tomatoes. Bring the sauce to a boil. Reduce the heat and simmer for 20 minutes, stirring occasionally.
4. After 10 minutes, add the sea salt to the boiling water followed by the pasta. Cook the pasta until tender. Drain and divide the pasta among 4 plates.
5. Add the basil to the sauce. Season with sea salt and black pepper. Ladle the sauce onto the pasta. Garnish with the Parmesan cheese and serve at once.

❧ Orecchiette with Tofu-Basil Pesto

PREPARATION:
10 MINUTES

COOKING:
15 MINUTES

YIELD:
4 MAIN-COURSE
SERVINGS

Pasta tossed with a garden-fresh basil pesto and freshly grated Parmesan cheese is one of the all-time great dishes. A tomato salad and a hunk of rustic bread are all that are needed to complete this simple, yet elegant meal. Unfortunately, traditional pesto is made with too much oil to be considered healthful. To make it more nutritious, we have replaced all of the oil with soft tofu. The intense herb flavor is still pronounced, but the pesto is now rich in breast cancer preventing phytoestrogens.

Tip: The pesto is a great substitute for mayonnaise and makes a delightful Romaine salad dressing.

Sea salt to taste
12 ounces orecchiette
2½ cups fresh basil leaves
1 small clove garlic, crushed
3 tablespoons pine nuts
4 ounces soft tofu
¼ cup water
⅓ cup Romano cheese, grated
Black pepper to taste

1. Bring a large pot of water to a boil. Add sea salt to the water followed by the pasta.
2. Combine the basil, garlic, pine nuts, tofu, and water in the work bowl of a food processor fitted with the metal blade. Process until smooth.
3. Transfer the pesto to a bowl. Stir in the Romano cheese. Season the pesto with sea salt and black pepper.
4. When the pasta is tender, drain. Transfer to a large serving bowl. Add the pesto and toss thoroughly. Serve the pasta at once.

🐝 Orecchiette with Dried Tomatoes and Dandelion Greens

This side-dish is full of wonderful tastes and textures. The flavors of nutty garlic, peppery greens, and sweet, dried tomatoes are evident in every forkful. Tomatoes and dandelion greens are a great source of the antioxidants Vitamin C and beta-carotene.

Tip: *Young dandelion greens are tender and mildly flavored; they are a great addition to a green salad. As they mature, their flavors become peppery, making them ideal for braising. Generally, the larger the greens, the more time they will need in the pot to become tender.*

PREPARATION:
15 MINUTES

COOKING:
10 MINUTES

YIELD:
4 SIDE-DISH
SERVINGS

  1 cup dried tomatoes
  1 cup boiling water
     Sea salt to taste
  8 ounces orecchiette
  1 tablespoon olive oil
  6 cloves garlic, peeled and sliced
 12 ounces dandelion greens, trimmed, washed, and drained
     Tomato soaking water
  ½ cup pasta cooking water
  4 ounces Parmesan cheese, grated
     Black pepper to taste

1. Place the dried tomatoes in a bowl. Pour the boiling water on top. Allow to soak until soft, approximately 10 minutes. Drain and reserve their soaking water. Slice and set aside.
2. While the tomatoes are soaking, bring a large pot of water to a boil. Add sea salt to the water followed by the pasta.
3. While the pasta is cooking, heat the olive oil in a Dutch oven over medium heat. When the oil is hot, add the garlic to the pot. Sprinkle it with sea salt. Cook the garlic for 30 seconds.
4. Raise the heat to high. Add the dried tomatoes and dandelion greens to the pot. Cook for 1 minute, stirring often.
5. Add the tomato soaking water and pasta cooking water to the pot. Cover the pot and cook until the greens are tender, stirring often, approximately 5 minutes.

6. Drain the pasta. Transfer to the Dutch oven. Reduce the heat to low. Cook the pasta and sauce together for 2 minutes, stirring occasionally.

7. Stir the cheese into the pasta. Season the pasta with sea salt and black pepper. Transfer to a shallow bowl and serve at once.

❧ Farfalle with Turnip Greens

PREPARATION:
10 MINUTES

COOKING:
15 MINUTES

YIELD:
4 MAIN-COURSE
SERVINGS

Often the best pasta dishes are those that are quickly prepared and use only a few top-quality ingredients. With fruity olive oil, briny anchovies, peppery turnip greens, and assertive Romano cheese, this recipe fits the bill. Anchovies are an oily fish rich in omega-3 fatty acids. Turnip greens, like many deep green vegetables, are a great source of beta-carotene and calcium.

Tip: *It is important to thoroughly cook the turnip greens. Partially cooked, they will be tough and stringy.*

1	tablespoon olive oil
5	cloves garlic, peeled and sliced
5	anchovy fillets, chopped
	Sea salt to taste
1	pound farfalle
1½	cups chicken stock
1½	pounds turnip greens, trimmed, washed, drained, and chopped
⅓	cup Romano cheese, grated
	Black pepper to taste

1. Bring a large pot of water to a boil.

2. Heat the olive oil in a large Dutch oven over low heat. Add the garlic and cook until soft and fragrant.

3. Raise the heat slightly. Add the anchovies. Cook until they begin to dissolve, stirring often, approximately 5 minutes.

4. Add sea salt to the boiling water followed by the pasta.

5. Add the chicken stock to the Dutch oven. Bring to a boil. Add the turnip greens. Cover the pot. Braise the greens until tender, approximately 10 minutes.

6. Drain the pasta. Transfer to the Dutch oven. Reduce the heat to low. Cook the pasta and greens together for 2 minutes, stirring often. Stir in the Romano cheese. Season the pasta with sea salt and black pepper.

7. Divide the pasta among 4 plates. If desired, grate more cheese on each portion.

ANCHOVIES

Has there ever been a time when you have enjoyed a meal that tasted of the sea and loved its briny flavor but had difficulty identifying all of the ingredients? One of the mysterious flavors may have been anchovies.

Anchovies are not just for pizza and Caesar salad. They are a versatile ingredient that can be used in sauces, pasta dishes, and vinaigrettes. Very good pasta dishes can be prepared with simply olive oil, garlic, anchovies, and one other main ingredient such as broccoli or arugula. For quickly prepared and richly flavored side dishes, anchovies can be cooked with garlic until they dissolve and braised with greens such as broccoli rabe, spinach, turnip greens, or chard. Asians use the fermented juice of anchovies in their ubiquitous condiment *nuoc nam* (fish sauce).

Anchovies are available in cans, salted, and as a paste in a tube. We most often use the canned variety. Purchase canned anchovies that are packed in pure olive oil with only salt added. The olive oil they are packed in can be used sparingly to add extra flavor to a dish. Salted anchovies are usually sold in bulk and need to be rinsed and boned. Anchovy paste is convenient but expensive.

🎝🎝 Linguine with Shrimp, Anchovies, Arugula, and Tomatoes

PREPARATION:
10 MINUTES

COOKING:
20 MINUTES

YIELD:
4 MAIN-COURSE
SERVINGS

The sweetness of the shrimp and tomatoes contrasts with the peppery crunch of the arugula and saltiness of the anchovies, making this dish a wonderful combination of flavors from the land and the sea. Anchovies and shrimp are excellent sources of omega-3 fatty acids. Tomatoes are rich in Vitamin C and arugula is a good source of beta-carotene.

Tip: *Sliced squid can be substituted for the shrimp. Add them to the pot at the same time as you would add the shrimp.*

2 tablespoons olive oil
4 cloves garlic, peeled and sliced
6 anchovy fillets, chopped
Pinch of red chili flakes
1 cup dry white wine
1 28-ounce can whole tomatoes in juice, drained and chopped
Sea salt to taste
1 pound linguine
12 ounces arugula, washed, drained, and chopped
1 pound large shrimp, peeled and deveined
Black pepper to taste

1. Bring a large pot of water to a boil.
2. Heat 1 tablespoon of the olive oil in a Dutch oven over low heat. Add the garlic and cook until soft and fragrant. Add the anchovies and cook until they dissolve, stirring often. Add the red pepper flakes.
3. Raise the heat to high. Add the white wine to the Dutch oven. Simmer the wine for a minute. Add the tomatoes. Bring the sauce to a boil. Reduce the heat and simmer for 10 minutes, stirring occasionally.
4. While the sauce is simmering, add sea salt to the boiling water followed by the pasta.
5. Heat the remaining olive oil in a skillet over high heat. Add the arugula to the pan. Season with sea salt. Cook the arugula until wilted and tender, approximately 4 minutes,

stirring often. If necessary, add water to the pan to prevent it from sticking. Set the arugula aside for a moment.

6. Raise the heat to high under the sauce. Add the shrimp. Cook the shrimp only until they turn pink, approximately 1 minute.

7. Drain the pasta. Transfer to the Dutch oven. Reduce the heat to low. Stir in the arugula. Cook the pasta and sauce together for 1 minute, stirring occasionally.

8. Season the pasta with sea salt and black pepper. Divide the pasta among 4 plates and serve at once.

❧ Spaghetti with Zucchini, Tomatoes, and Anchovies

Canned anchovies are a staple in our kitchen. In a pinch, they can transform an everyday meal into something special. Believing they are full of bones, some people may be squeamish about eating anchovies. After several minutes in a warm pan though, anchovies melt into a delightful sauce. Here we combine them with zucchini, tomatoes, and basil, three of our favorite summertime ingredients, to create a quick and delicious pasta meal. It is rich in omega-3 fatty acids and Vitamin C.

Tips: *When seasoning the dish, keep in mind that canned anchovies contain a fair amount of salt. Also, if top-quality fresh tomatoes are not available, use canned Italian plum tomatoes.*

PREPARATION:
10 MINUTES

COOKING:
20 MINUTES

YIELD:
4 MAIN-COURSE
SERVINGS

1	tablespoon olive oil
6	cloves garlic, peeled and thinly sliced
10	anchovy fillets, chopped
	Sea salt to taste
1	pound linguine
3	medium zucchini, sliced into 1-inch pieces
1½	cups pasta cooking water
4	ripe tomatoes, cored and diced
1	cup fresh basil, snipped
	Black pepper to taste
4	tablespoons Romano cheese, grated

1. Bring a large pot of water to a boil.
2. Heat the olive oil in a Dutch oven over low heat. Add the garlic and cook until soft and fragrant. Add the anchovies. Cook the anchovies until they begin to dissolve, stirring often, approximately 5 minutes.
3. Add sea salt to the boiling water followed by the pasta.
4. While the pasta is cooking, finish the sauce. Raise the heat to high under the Dutch oven. Add the zucchini. Cook the zucchini for 3 minutes, stirring often. Add the pasta cooking water. Cover the pot and cook the zucchini until tender, approximately 5 minutes.
5. Add the tomatoes and basil. Cook the sauce for 2 minutes more. Reduce the heat to low.
6. Drain the pasta. Transfer to the Dutch oven. Cook the pasta and sauce together for 2 minutes. Season the pasta with sea salt and black pepper.
7. Divide the pasta among 4 plates. Garnish with the Romano cheese.

🌿 Penne with Chicken and Spinach in a Sweet Carrot Sauce

PREPARATION:
15 MINUTES

COOKING:
30 MINUTES

YIELD:
4 MAIN-COURSE
SERVINGS

When seasoned with garlic and onion and pureed with silken tofu, carrots make a tasty pasta sauce. We have tossed the sauce with spinach and vinegary chicken to create a memorable and healthful meal. Tofu is rich in phytoestrogens. Spinach and carrots are excellent sources of beta-carotene.

Tip: Choose carrots with their tops intact. They will be fresh and sweet tasting. Carrots sold in plastic tend to be woody-textured and bland.

CARROT SAUCE
   1 tablespoon canola oil
   3 cloves garlic, peeled and sliced
   1 onion, peeled and diced
      Sea salt to taste
  12 ounces carrots, scraped and sliced
   1 cup chicken stock
   6 ounces silken tofu
      Black pepper to taste

CHICKEN AND PASTA
   1 pound penne
      Sea salt to taste
   1 tablespoon canola oil
 1½ pounds boneless and skinless chicken breasts, trimmed and thinly sliced
      Black pepper to taste
   3 cloves garlic, peeled and finely chopped
      1-inch piece gingerroot, peeled and finely chopped
   2 tablespoons rice vinegar
  12 ounces fresh spinach, trimmed, washed, drained, and chopped

1. Bring a large pot of water to a boil.
2. To prepare the sauce, heat the canola oil in a Dutch oven over low heat. Add the garlic and cook until soft and fragrant. Add the onion and sprinkle with sea salt. Cook the onion until soft, stirring often.
3. Add the carrots. Cook for 5 minutes, stirring occasionally. Raise the heat to high. Add the stock. Bring the liquid to a boil. Reduce the heat and simmer the carrots until tender, approximately 5 minutes.
4. Transfer the carrots and their cooking liquid to a blender or the work bowl of a food processor fitted with the metal blade. Add the silken tofu and puree. Season the sauce with sea salt and black pepper. Set aside for a moment.
5. Add sea salt to the boiling water followed by the pasta.

6. To prepare the chicken, heat the canola oil in a wok over medium-high heat. Sprinkle the chicken with sea salt and black pepper. When the oil is hot, carefully place the chicken in the pan. Sear the chicken until golden, tossing 2 or 3 times.

7. Reduce the heat to low. Add the garlic and ginger to the pan. Cook until fragrant, stirring constantly.

8. Raise the heat to high. Add the vinegar to the pan. Cook the ingredients for another minute. Add the spinach. Cook the spinach only until it wilts, stirring constantly. Remove the pan from the heat.

9. Drain the pasta and return it to the pot. Add the carrot sauce to the pot. Toss the pasta and sauce.

10. Divide the pasta among 4 large plates. Garnish with the sliced chicken and spinach and serve at once.

❧ Ziti with White Eggplant, Tofu, Tomatoes, and Ricotta Salata

PREPARATION:
15 MINUTES

COOKING:
40 MINUTES

YIELD:
6 MAIN-COURSE
SERVINGS

Prepare this meal during summer when great tomatoes and egg-plants are abundant. White eggplants are denser and contain fewer seeds than the large purple ones, making them ideal for roasting. If you can't find them, substitute the smaller Italian or Japanese egg-plants. Ricotta salata is nothing like the ricotta to which we are all accustomed. It has a flavor similar to sheep's milk feta, but is denser, creamier, and not as salty; a small amount goes a long way. With plenty of tofu and tomatoes, this hearty pasta dish is rich in phy-toestrogens, beta-carotene, and Vitamin C.

1 pound extra-firm tofu
2 large white eggplants (approximately 2 pounds), sliced into 1-inch cubes
4 tablespoons balsamic vinegar
3 tablespoons olive oil
Sea salt to taste
Black pepper to taste

5 cloves garlic, peeled and thinly sliced
4 ripe tomatoes, cored and diced
½ cup fresh basil, snipped
1 pound penne
4 ounces ricotta salata

1. Preheat the oven to 425°F.
2. Bring a large pot of water to a boil.
3. Place the tofu on a kitchen towel. With the heal of your hand, gently press on the tofu to remove the excess moisture. Cube the tofu. Transfer to a large bowl.
4. Place the eggplant in the bowl. Drizzle with the balsamic vinegar and 2 tablespoons of the olive oil. Season with sea salt and black pepper. Place on 1 large or 2 small heavy baking trays.
5. Place the trays in the oven. Roast the ingredients until golden, approximately 40 minutes. Remove the tray from the oven. With the back of a spatula, loosen the eggplant and tofu.
6. During the last 15 minutes of roasting, heat the remaining olive oil in a skillet over medium heat. Add the garlic and cook for 30 seconds. Add the tomatoes and cook for 5 minutes. Remove the pan from the heat. Add the basil. Season with sea salt and black pepper. Set the sauce aside for a moment.
7. Add sea salt to the boiling water followed by the pasta. Cook the pasta until tender. Drain and return to the pot.
8. Add the sauce to the pasta and toss. Divide the pasta among 6 bowls. Garnish with the eggplant-tofu mixture and ricotta salata.

Rigatoni with Chicken Sausage, Collards, and Edamame

PREPARATION:
10 MINUTES

COOKING:
45 MINUTES

YIELD:
4 MAIN-COURSE
SERVINGS

This pasta dish was an improvised meal one Sunday evening. With chicken sausages and edamame from our freezer and collards from our garden, we came up with this dish. It turned out to be delicious, with plenty of beta-carotene and phytoestrogens, and very nutritious as well.

Tips: *Extra-firm tofu can be substituted for the sausage. To make the tofu version, sear 1 pound of cubed and lightly salted extra-firm tofu in a wok. Just before removing it from the pan, drizzle with 3 tablespoons of rice vinegar or balsamic vinegar. Cook the tofu for another minute. Return the tofu to the pot at the same interval as the edamame. Also, spinach, broccoli rabe, mustard greens, or chard can be substituted for the collards. Since they all become tender more quickly than collards, the cooking time will be shorter.*

1 tablespoon olive oil
4 chicken or turkey sausages
4 cloves garlic, peeled and thinly sliced
1 onion, peeled and thinly sliced
Sea salt to taste
1 pound collard greens, trimmed, washed, and drained
1½ cups frozen, shelled, and blanched edamame
1 pound rigatoni
1½ cups pasta cooking water
Black pepper to taste
4 tablespoons Romano cheese, grated

1. Heat the olive oil in a Dutch oven over medium-high heat. When the oil is hot, carefully place the sausages into the pot. Sear the sausages until golden, turning several times. Remove and set aside.

2. Reduce the heat to low. Add the garlic to the pot. Cook the garlic for 30 seconds. Add the onion and sprinkle with sea salt. Cook the onion until soft, stirring occasionally.

3. Raise the heat to high. Add the collard greens to the pot. Stir until they begin to wilt. Return the sausages to the pot. Cover the pot. Reduce the heat to low. Braise the sausages and collards for 30 minutes, adding water if necessary to prevent the greens from sticking.
4. Add the edamame to the pot. Cook for 10 minutes more.
5. Bring a large pot of water to a boil. Add sea salt to the water followed by the pasta. Cook the pasta until tender. Drain the pasta, reserving 1½ cups of its cooking water. Add the cooking water to the collards. Add the pasta to the collards and toss well. Season the pasta with sea salt and black pepper.
6. Transfer the sausages to a cutting board. Slice into rounds.
7. Divide the pasta among 4 large shallow bowls. Garnish with the sausage rounds. Sprinkle with the Romano cheese and serve at once.

❧ Baked Ziti with Tofu-"Ricotta," Fresh Tomatoes, and Edamame

PREPARATION:
20 MINUTES

COOKING:
20 MINUTES

YIELD:
8 MAIN-COURSE
SERVINGS

Like meat loaf and lasagna, baked ziti is a recipe that needs to be revised. Most often prepared with whole milk ricotta and mozzarella cheeses and canned tomato sauce, it is unnecessarily high in fat, calories, and sugar. Our version contains phytoestrogen-rich tofu-"ricotta" and edamame. A garden fresh tomato sauce adds a burst of flavor and is a great source of Vitamin C. Baked ziti has never been so delectable and nutritious.

Tip: *If ripe tomatoes are not available, substitute one 28-ounce can of whole tomatoes in juice.*

TOMATOES

4–5 medium ripe tomatoes, cored and diced (approximately 5 cups)
   2 tablespoons olive oil
   1 clove garlic, peeled and very finely chopped
   ½ cup fresh basil, snipped
      Sea salt to taste
      Black pepper to taste

TOFU-"RICOTTA"

   1 tablespoon olive oil
   3 cloves garlic, peeled and thinly sliced
   1 onion, peeled and diced
      Sea salt to taste
   ½ teaspoon dried basil
   ½ teaspoon dried oregano
   2 tablespoons fresh flat-leaf (Italian) parsley, chopped
   1 pound extra-firm tofu, squeezed to remove excess moisture and crumbled
   ⅓ cup Romano cheese, grated
      Black pepper to taste

      Sea salt to taste
   1 pound ziti
   2 cups frozen, shelled, and blanched edamame
   6 ounces provolone cheese, grated or sliced

1. To prepare the sauce, place the tomatoes in a nonreactive bowl. Add the olive oil, garlic, and basil. Season with sea salt and black pepper. Set aside for a moment.
2. Bring a large pot of water to a boil. Preheat the oven to 400°F.
3. To prepare the tofu-ricotta, heat the olive oil in a Dutch oven over medium heat. When the oil is hot, add the garlic. Cook the garlic for 30 seconds. Add the onion and sprinkle with sea salt. Cook the onion until soft.
4. Add the basil, oregano, and parsley. Cook for another minute.
5. Add the tofu. Cook for another minute, stirring often. Transfer to a bowl. Add the Romano cheese and season with sea salt and black pepper. Set aside for a moment.
6. Add sea salt to the boiling water followed by the pasta. Cook the pasta for 5 minutes. Add the edamame to the water. Cover the pot. When the water returns to a boil, remove the cover. Cook the pasta and edamame until tender, approximately 6 minutes more. Drain and transfer to a 4-quart oven-proof casserole.
7. Add the tomatoes and tofu-ricotta to the casserole and mix the ingredients. Garnish the casserole with the provolone.
8. Transfer the casserole to the oven. Bake for 15 minutes. Turn on the broiler and broil until the cheese is golden, approximately 5 minutes.

Fettuccine with Spinach, Almonds, and Olives

Richly flavored Kalamata olives and toasted almonds are a versatile combination. It can serve as a garnish for a fish or chicken dish, used to stuff mushrooms, added to a lasagna filling or, as we have done here, combined with garlicky spinach in a pasta dish. Spinach is rich in beta-carotene. Almonds are an excellent source of Vitamin E.

PREPARATION:
10 MINUTES

COOKING:
15 MINUTES

YIELD:
4 MAIN-COURSE
SERVINGS

Sea salt to taste
1 pound fettuccine
½ cup sliced almonds
1 tablespoon olive oil
6 cloves garlic, peeled and thinly sliced
1½ pounds spinach, trimmed, washed, drained, and chopped
1½ cups pasta cooking water
Black pepper to taste
½ cup Romano cheese, grated
12 Kalamata olives, pitted and chopped

1. Bring a large pot of water to a boil. Add sea salt to the water followed by the pasta.
2. While the pasta is cooking, place the almonds in a small skillet over low heat. Sprinkle with sea salt. Toast until golden, approximately 5 minutes, shaking the pan occasionally. Set aside for a moment.
3. Heat the olive oil in a Dutch oven over medium heat. When the oil is hot, add the garlic. Cook the garlic for 30 seconds.
4. Raise the heat to high. Add the spinach. Cook the spinach only until it wilts, stirring constantly. Add the pasta cooking water. Reduce the heat to low. Season the spinach with sea salt and black pepper.
5. When the pasta is tender, drain. Transfer to the Dutch oven. Stir the spinach and pasta together. Cook for 2 minutes. Stir in the cheese. Season with sea salt and black pepper.
6. Divide the pasta among 4 shallow bowls. Garnish with the toasted almonds and olives and serve at once.

CHAPTER 14

Vegetarian Dishes

Y ou don't need to be a vegetarian to prepare and enjoy vegetarian meals. In the past, vegetarian meals were either fat- and calorie-laden affairs or dull and flavorless. With the increasing exposure of the benefits of a well-balanced vegetarian diet, and the availability of excellent-quality soy foods and meat-mimicking products, vegetarian cooking and eating are now much more exciting. Vegetarian meals are also an excellent opportunity to incorporate many breast cancer preventing nutrients into your diet. By cooking with deep orange–fleshed fruits and vegetables, tomatoes, leafy greens, nuts, seeds, dried peas and beans, and soy products, you can prepare creative and lively vegetarian feasts that everyone will love. Most important, these dishes will contain abundant amounts of fiber, calcium, folic acid, phytoestrogens, and antioxidants. Our vegetarian recipes are revised preparations of popular comfort foods, Asian specialties, scrumptious sandwiches, and healthful variations of fast food favorites.

Lasagna is near the top of everyone's favorite comfort food list. When prepared with beef and whole milk cheeses, it is not something you can enjoy on a regular basis. Why not indulge in our wonderful Swiss Chard and Pine Nut Lasagna with a Chickpea and Tomato Sauce? It contains two sources of phytoestrogen-rich tofu, antioxidant-rich chard and tomatoes, and plenty of fiber from the chickpeas. It is a true breast cancer preventing powerhouse meal.

With a laundry list of esoteric ingredients, Asian food can seem intimidating to prepare at home. To create tasty Asian meals at home though, all you have to do is use a recipe as a guideline and make a quick trip to an Asian grocery, or visit the international section of your market to choose a few specialty ingredients. Armed with knowledge and the ingredients, you will be able to prepare authentic tasting Pad Thai and creative delicacies you won't find on many menus, such as Udon Noodles in a Soy Nut Butter Sauce with Tofu and Broccoli. These dishes provide great amounts of breast cancer preventing antioxidants, calcium, folic acid, and phytoestrogens.

With soy foods and antioxidant-rich vegetables, you can create simple or elegant vegetarian sandwiches with an abundance of breast cancer preventing nutrients. Whether you indulge in our phytoestrogen-rich versions of favorites such as Egg Salad Sandwiches or Sloppy Joes or choose a special sandwich, such as Roasted Portobello Mushroom Stacks—a delicious combination of earthy mushrooms and kale, sweet potatoes, and syrupy balsamic vinegar—you will be pleasantly surprised just how tasty, creative, and nutritious meatless sandwiches can be.

Mexican food is rapidly becoming everyone's choice for fast food. As long as you steer away from the sour cream, fatty meats, and fried items and emphasize rice, beans, and vegetables, you can make healthful choices. After a while though, the ubiquitous burritos become predictable. It is time to venture into your kitchen to prepare Roasted Butternut Squash and Tofu Quesadillas. Unlike traditional quesadillas, which are grilled with oil, ours are baked. They are a great source of beta-carotene and phytoestrogens.

We should all strive to view vegetarian food as simply another type of meal. Just as you would have chicken or fish for dinner one evening, why not have a meatless meal based on soy? Vegetarian meals offer interesting contrasts of flavors and textures and provide wonderful breast cancer preventing nutrition.

🌿 Tofu and Squash Quesadillas with a Black Bean and Mango Salsa

PREPARATION:
20 MINUTES

COOKING:
10 MINUTES

YIELD:
8 SIDE-DISH
SERVINGS

Quesadillas are a great snack or light lunch. Since they can be assembled several hours in advance and baked just before serving, they are also an ideal party food. When prepared in a restaurant, they are usually grilled with oil and loaded with cheese. To make them more healthful, we use only a sprinkling of cheese and bake them without oil. Our fillings are unique and tasty and rich in breast cancer preventing phytoestrogens, beta-carotene, Vitamin C, and fiber.

BLACK BEAN AND MANGO SALSA

- 1 15-ounce can black beans, drained and well rinsed
- 1 mango, peeled, pitted, and diced
- 1 tomato, cored and diced
- 1 clove garlic, peeled and finely chopped
- 1 onion, peeled and diced
- 3 scallions, trimmed and thinly sliced
- ⅓ cup cilantro, chopped
- 1 tablespoon olive oil
   Juice of 1½ limes
   Sea salt to taste
   Black pepper to taste

SQUASH AND TOFU

- 1 tablespoon canola oil
- 1 onion, peeled and thinly sliced
- 12 ounces extra-firm tofu, cubed
- 1 small butternut squash, peeled and diced small
   Sea salt to taste
   Black pepper to taste

- 12 medium-sized flour tortillas
- 6 ounces Monterey Jack cheese, grated or sliced

1. To prepare the salsa, in a nonreactive bowl, combine the black beans, mango, tomato, garlic, onion, scallions, cilantro, olive oil, and lime juice. Season with sea salt and black pepper. Set aside for a moment.

2. For the squash and tofu, heat the canola oil in a large skillet over medium heat. Add the onion and sprinkle with sea salt. Cook the onion for 1 minute. Add the tofu and squash. Toss the ingredients thoroughly. Cook until the squash is tender, tossing occasionally, approximately 15 minutes. Remove the pan from the heat.

3. Preheat the oven to 375°F.

4. To assemble the quesadillas, place 6 of the flour tortillas on 1 large or 2 small baking trays. Divide the cheese among the tortillas. Divide the squash mixture among the tortillas. Divide the salsa among the tortillas (there will be a bit leftover). Place one of the remaining tortillas on top of each one on the trays.

5. Place the trays in the oven. Bake the quesadillas until the cheese melts and the tortillas are heated through, approximately 8 minutes.

6. Remove the trays from the oven. Cut each quesadilla into quarters and serve at once.

❧❧ Tofu, Eggplant, Corn, and Spinach Fajitas

PREPARATION:
15 MINUTES

COOKING:
20 MINUTES

YIELD:
4 MAIN-COURSE
SERVINGS

It is not necessary to go out for fajitas. Once you have all of the ingredients prepared, the fajitas can be put together in a snap. We have strayed from the typical meat-based fillings and have prepared a phytoestrogen and antioxidant-rich version, starring tofu, eggplant, and spinach. They are certain to make you pass up fast food versions and entice you to make them again and again in your kitchen.

3 tablespoons canola oil
12 ounces firm tofu, rinsed, dried, and sliced into small cubes
Sea salt to taste
Black pepper to taste
2 tablespoons balsamic vinegar
2 Italian or Japanese eggplants, sliced into small cubes
1 large red bell pepper, cored, seeded, and thinly sliced
4 cloves garlic, peeled and sliced
2 ears fresh corn, kernels removed, or 2 cups frozen corn, thawed
4 plum tomatoes, cored and diced
12 ounces spinach, trimmed, washed, drained, and chopped
½ cup cilantro, chopped
4 ounces goat cheese at room temperature
4 large flour tortillas, warmed

1. Heat 1 tablespoon of the oil in a wok over high heat. Season the tofu with sea salt and black pepper. Carefully place the tofu into the wok. Sear the tofu until golden, stirring 2 or 3 times.
2. Add the vinegar. Cook the tofu for 30 seconds more. Transfer the tofu to a serving platter.
3. Heat another tablespoon of oil in the wok over high heat. When the oil is hot, add the eggplants and bell pepper to the pan. Sprinkle with sea salt. Cook the vegetables until they begin to color and soften, stirring occasionally.

4. Push the vegetables to one side of the wok and add the remaining tablespoon of oil to the pan. Add the garlic. Cook for 10 seconds. Combine the vegetables and garlic.

5. Add the corn, tomatoes, and spinach. Cook the ingredients only until the spinach wilts, stirring constantly. Stir in the cilantro and tofu. Transfer the fajita filling to a serving platter.

6. Spread an equal portion of the goat cheese on each of the tortillas. Place the serving platter and tortillas onto the table and have everyone assemble their own fajitas.

🦋 Roasted Butternut Squash and Tofu Quesadillas

We often roast butternut squash and tofu to use in a pasta dish, but the combination also makes a delicious filling for a quesadilla. With the traditional garnishes of tomatoes and avocado, the meal is rich in beta-carotene, phytoestrogens, and vitamins C and E.

Tips: *Cut the squash and tofu into uniform pieces to assure even cooking. Also, for a smoky flavor, the quesadillas can be grilled or cooked in a skillet on the range.*

PREPARATION:
45 MINUTES

COOKING:
5 MINUTES

YIELD:
4 MAIN-COURSE
SERVINGS

1   medium butternut squash, peeled, seeded, and sliced into ¾-inch pieces
1   pound extra-firm tofu, sliced into ¾-inch cubes
2   tablespoons olive oil
    Sea salt to taste
    Black pepper to taste
3   ounces Monterey Jack cheese, sliced or grated
4   large flour tortillas
4   scallions, trimmed and thinly sliced
4   plum tomatoes, cored and diced
1   avocado, peeled and sliced
⅓   cup cilantro, chopped

1. Preheat the oven to 400°F.
2. Place the squash and tofu on a large baking tray. Drizzle with the olive oil and sprinkle with sea salt and black pepper. Place the tray into the oven. Roast the vegetables until golden and tender, tossing 2 or 3 times, approximately 35 minutes.
3. Remove the tray from the oven. With the back side of a spatula, loosen the squash and tofu. Reduce the oven temperature to 300°F.
4. Divide the cheese among the tortillas. Divide the squash and tofu among the tortillas. Garnish each tortilla with an equal amount of scallions, tomatoes, avocado, and cilantro.
5. Place the quesadillas onto 2 baking trays. Place the trays into the oven. Heat the quesadillas only until the cheese melts, approximately 5 minutes.
6. Divide the quesadillas among 4 plates. Fold in half and serve at once.

❧ Sweet Potato and Tomato Quesadillas

One Sunday in early spring, we were feverishly working to prepare our vegetable garden for the season as it approached noon. We were famished and as on most Sundays, we didn't have much food in the house. Not wanting to take the time to go to the market, we made use of leftover ingredients from the testing of a previous recipe and a few odds and ends. We were able to create a quesadilla that makes a delightful lunch. With sweet potatoes and dried tomatoes as the main ingredients, it is a great source of beta-carotene and Vitamin C.

PREPARATION:
40 MINUTES

COOKING:
5 MINUTES

YIELD:
4 MAIN-COURSE
SERVINGS

- 2 tablespoons olive oil
- 3 cloves garlic, peeled and sliced
- 1 onion, peeled and thinly sliced
- 2 sweet potatoes, peeled and sliced into ½-inch pieces
  Sea salt to taste
  Black pepper to taste
- 3 ounces Monterey Jack cheese, sliced or grated
- 4 large flour tortillas
- 4 scallions, trimmed and thinly sliced
- 4 plum tomatoes, cored and diced
- ⅓ cup cilantro, chopped

1. Heat the olive oil in a large skillet over low heat. Add the garlic. Cook until it is soft and fragrant. Add the onion and cook until soft, stirring occasionally.
2. Raise the heat to high. Add the potatoes. Sprinkle the ingredients with sea salt. Shake the pan several times. Reduce the heat to medium. Cook the potatoes until tender, stirring occasionally, approximately 30 minutes. Season with sea salt and black pepper. Remove the pan from the heat.
3. Preheat the oven to 300°F.
4. Divide the cheese among the tortillas. Divide the potatoes among the tortillas. Garnish each tortilla with an equal amount of scallions, tomatoes, and cilantro.
5. Divide the quesadillas among 2 baking trays. Place the trays

in the oven. Heat the quesadillas only until the cheese melts, approximately 5 minutes.

6. Divide the quesadillas among 4 plates. Fold in half and serve at once.

❧ Spicy Tofu and Black Bean Burritos with a Mango and Tomato Salsa

Mild-tasting tofu is the perfect canvas for a spicy coating. We have combined the tofu with earthy black beans and a mango salsa to make a unique burrito filling. The sweet salsa is the perfect complement to the fiery beans and tofu. The burritos provide a wealth of breast cancer preventing phytoestrogens, fiber, beta-carotene, and Vitamin C.

Tip: *The rice, beans, salsa, and tofu can be prepared a day in advance. With the exception of the salsa, everything can be reheated in the microwave.*

PREPARATION:
15 MINUTES

COOKING:
45 MINUTES

YIELD:
6 MAIN-COURSE
SERVINGS

RICE
5 cups water
2 cups short-grain brown rice

BEANS
1 tablespoon olive oil
4 cloves garlic, peeled and sliced
1 onion, peeled and diced
2 chipotle or jalapeño peppers, finely chopped
   Sea salt to taste
1 teaspoon chile powder
1 teaspoon cumin powder
1 15-ounce can black beans, drained and rinsed
   Black pepper to taste

SALSA
1 medium tomato, cored and diced
1 mango, peeled, pitted, and diced
3 scallions, trimmed and thinly sliced

⅓ cup cilantro, chopped

2 tablespoons balsamic vinegar

   Sea salt to taste

   Black pepper to taste

TOFU AND TORTILLAS

2 tablespoons olive oil

1 tablespoon chile powder

1 tablespoon cumin powder

1 pound extra-firm tofu, cubed

   Sea salt to taste

   Black pepper to taste

3 ounces Monterey Jack cheese, sliced or grated

6 large flour tortillas

1. To prepare the rice, bring the water to a boil in a saucepan. Stir in the rice. Cover the pot. Reduce the heat to low. Simmer the rice until the water is absorbed and the rice is tender, approximately 40 minutes.

2. While the rice is cooking, prepare the beans. Heat the olive oil in a Dutch oven over low heat. Add the garlic. Cook until soft and fragrant. Add the onion and chipotle peppers and sprinkle with sea salt. Cook the ingredients until they are soft, stirring occasionally.

3. Add the chile powder and cumin. Cook the spices for 1 minute. Add the beans. Cook for 5 minutes more, stirring occasionally. Season with sea salt and black pepper.

4. Transfer the mixture to a food processor fitted with a metal blade and puree. Set aside for a moment.

5. To prepare the salsa, combine the tomato, mango, scallions, cilantro, and vinegar in a nonmetal bowl. Season the salsa with sea salt and black pepper. Set aside for a moment.

6. To prepare the tofu, heat the olive oil in a large skillet over medium-high heat. Combine the chile powder and cumin in a small bowl.

7. Place the tofu on a plate and season with sea salt and black pepper. Sprinkle the tofu with the spice mixture and toss thoroughly. When the oil is hot, carefully place the tofu into the pan. Sear it, tossing occasionally. Remove the pan from the heat.

8. To make the burritos, divide the cheese among the tortillas. Microwave the tortillas until the cheese melts, approximately 30 seconds. Place an equal portion of rice, beans, tofu, and salsa in the center of each tortilla and roll them.

🌺 Swiss Chard and Pine Nut Lasagna with a Chickpea and Tomato Sauce

PREPARATION:
30 MINUTES

COOKING:
30 MINUTES

YIELD:
8 MAIN-COURSE
SERVINGS

Whether it is tossed with pasta, served as a side dish, or used as a stuffing for poultry, Swiss chard and toasted pine nuts are a great combination. Here we have pureed the chard and combined it with crumbled tofu, pine nuts, and a bit of Romano cheese to create a unique lasagna filling. A sauce of pureed chickpeas, tomatoes, soft tofu, and fresh basil adds creaminess and a nutty taste. The lasagna is a breast cancer preventing powerhouse. It is rich in beta-carotene, Vitamin C, and fiber and with two sources of tofu, a great source of phytoestrogens as well.

Tips: *This is the ideal dish to serve to a crowd. It can be assembled a day or two in advance and popped into the oven 30 or 40 minutes before serving. The assembled lasagna also freezes well.*

SAUCE
1 tablespoon olive oil
4 cloves garlic, peeled and sliced
2 onions, peeled and diced
  Sea salt to taste
2 28-ounce cans whole tomatoes, chopped
1 16-ounce can chickpeas, drained and rinsed
1 pound soft tofu
1 cup fresh basil, snipped
  Black pepper to taste

FILLING

½ cup pine nuts
 Sea salt to taste
1 tablespoon olive oil
4 cloves garlic, peeled and sliced
1 onion, peeled and diced
1½ pound Swiss chard, trimmed, washed, drained, and chopped
1 pound extra-firm tofu, squeezed to remove excess moisture and crumbled
½ cup Romano cheese, grated
1 cup Homemade Bread Crumbs (page 263)
 Black pepper to taste
1 egg, beaten

1 pound lasagna noodles
1 pound part-skim mozzarella cheese, grated or sliced

1. To prepare the sauce, heat the olive oil in a Dutch oven over medium heat. When the oil is hot, add the garlic. Cook for 30 seconds. Add the onions and sprinkle with sea salt. Cook the onions until soft.
2. Add the tomatoes and chickpeas. Bring the sauce to a boil. Reduce the heat and simmer for 30 minutes, stirring occasionally.
3. Transfer the sauce to the work bowl of a food processor. Add the tofu and basil and puree.
4. Return the sauce to the Dutch oven. Season with sea salt and black pepper.
5. While the sauce is simmering, prepare the filling. Place the pine nuts in a small skillet over low heat. Sprinkle with sea salt. Toast until golden, shaking the pan occasionally, approximately 8 minutes. Remove the pan from the heat and set aside for a moment.
6. To complete the filling, heat the olive oil in another Dutch oven over medium heat. When the oil is hot, add the garlic to the pot. Cook for 30 seconds. Add the onion and sprinkle with sea salt. Cook the onion until soft, stirring occasionally.

7. Bring a large pot of water to a boil.
8. Raise the heat to high under the Dutch oven. Add the chard. Cover the pot and cook the chard until tender, stirring occasionally, approximately 8 minutes.
9. Transfer the chard to the work bowl of a food processor fitted with the metal blade and puree.
10. Transfer the chard to a large mixing bowl. Add the tofu, cheese, bread crumbs, and pine nuts and mix well. Season the filling with sea salt and black pepper. Add the egg.
11. To complete the lasagna, add sea salt to the boiling water followed by the noodles. Cook the noodles until just tender, approximately 6 minutes. Drain. Rinse under cold water.
12. Preheat the oven to 400°F.
13. To assemble the lasagna, cover the bottom of a 4-quart ovenproof casserole with a layer of noodles. Spread one-quarter of the filling onto the noodles. Add one-quarter of the sauce. Sprinkle on one-quarter of the mozzarella cheese. Repeat the pattern 3 more times with the remaining noodles, filling, sauce, and cheese for a total of 4 layers.
14. Transfer the lasagna to the oven. Bake until the edges bubble and the cheese is golden, approximately 30 minutes.
15. Remove the lasagna from the oven. Allow to rest for 5 minutes before slicing.

❧ Eggplant, Chard, and Tofu Lasagna

When we stir-fry eggplant, we choose the smaller and more tender Japanese or Italian variety. When we make an eggplant lasagna, we use the large purple variety. Oven roasting the large ones tames their strong flavor; their large size is ideal for layering. This lasagna, with a wonderful sauce of chard, tofu, and tomatoes, is great to serve to a crowd. It can be assembled a day in advance and popped in the oven 35 minutes before serving time. It is a great source of phyto-estrogens, beta-carotene, and Vitamin C.

PREPARATION:
30 MINUTES

COOKING:
20 MINUTES

YIELD:
8 MAIN-COURSE
SERVINGS

5 tablespoons olive oil
4 large eggplants, sliced into 1-inch rounds
  Sea salt to taste
  Black pepper to taste
4 cloves garlic, peeled and thinly sliced
2 onions, peeled and diced
1 28-ounce can tomatoes in juice, chopped
1 pound chard, trimmed, washed, drained, and chopped
1 pound extra-firm tofu, squeezed to remove moisture and crumbled
1 pound part-skim mozzarella cheese, sliced or grated
2 ounces Romano cheese, grated

1. Preheat the oven to 425°F.
2. Divide 4 tablespoons of the olive oil between 2 large, heavy baking trays. Place the trays into the oven for 5 minutes.
3. Carefully remove the trays from the oven. Divide the eggplant slices between the 2 trays, rubbing each slice in the olive oil. Flip each slice so the side with the olive oil is facing up. Sprinkle the eggplant with sea salt and black pepper. Return the trays to the oven. Roast the eggplant slices until soft and golden, approximately 30 minutes. Remove the trays from the oven. Do not turn off the oven.
4. Meanwhile, heat the remaining tablespoon of olive oil in a large Dutch oven over medium heat. Add the garlic and cook for 30 seconds. Add the onions and sprinkle with sea salt. Cook the onions until soft.

5. Raise the heat to high. Add the tomatoes. Bring the sauce to a boil. Reduce the heat and simmer for 10 minutes.

6. Return the heat to high. Add the chard to the sauce. Cook the chard until it wilts, stirring often, approximately 5 minutes.

7. Add the tofu to the sauce. Cook for 10 minutes more, stirring occasionally. Remove the sauce from the heat. Season with sea salt and black pepper.

8. To assemble the lasagna, place a layer of eggplant on the bottom of a 4-quart casserole. Add a layer of sauce and a layer of mozzarella cheese. Add another layer of eggplant, sauce, and mozzarella cheese. Finish the lasagna with a layer of eggplant. Sprinkle on the Romano cheese.

9. Transfer the lasagna to the oven. Bake until the edges bubble, approximately 20 minutes. Remove the lasagna from the oven. Allow to cool for 5 minutes. Slice into 8 portions and serve at once.

❧ Baked Brown Rice, Tofu, Spinach, and Eggplant

During spring and fall, we like to prepare this casserole with greens from our garden, which are not widely available, such as pak choi, an Asian cooking green, and New Zealand spinach. This recipe is designed to be versatile. Besides spinach, you can use mustard or turnip greens, broccoli rabe, chard, or bok choy. If you choose an Asian green, be creative and vary the seasonings. Cook fresh ginger with the garlic and substitute tamari and a touch of light miso for the vinegar. This meal provides great doses of phytoestrogens and beta-carotene.

 Tip: *To save time, the casserole can be assembled earlier in the day.*

PREPARATION:
45 MINUTES

COOKING:
20 MINUTES

YIELD:
4 MAIN-COURSE
SERVINGS

  5 cups water
    Sea salt to taste
  2 cups short-grain brown rice
  3 tablespoons olive oil
  3 Italian eggplants, cubed
  2 ears fresh corn, kernels removed, or 2 cups frozen corn, thawed
 ⅓ cup cilantro, chopped
  4 cloves garlic, peeled and sliced
 1½ pounds spinach, trimmed, washed, drained, and chopped
  1 pound extra-firm tofu
  1 tablespoon sugar
  2 tablespoons balsamic vinegar
  6 ounces soy Cheddar cheese, sliced

1. Place the water in a saucepan. Bring to a boil. Add sea salt to the water, followed by the rice. Bring the rice to a boil. Cover the pan. Reduce the heat and simmer the rice until tender and all of the water has been absorbed, approximately 45 minutes.

2. Meanwhile, heat 1 tablespoon of the olive oil in a wok over

high heat. Sprinkle the eggplant with sea salt. When the oil is hot, carefully place into the wok. Sear until golden and soft, tossing occasionally, approximately 6 minutes. Add the corn and cilantro and cook for 2 minutes more. Transfer the vegetables to a plate. Set aside for a moment.

3. Heat another tablespoon of the olive oil in the wok over medium-high heat. Add the garlic and cook for 30 seconds. Add the spinach and sprinkle with sea salt. Cook the spinach until it wilts, stirring often. Transfer the spinach to a plate. Set aside for a moment.

4. Preheat the oven to 450°F.

5. To prepare the tofu, heat the remaining tablespoon of olive oil in the wok over medium-high heat. Place the tofu on a kitchen towel. With the heel of your hand, gently press on the tofu to remove the excess moisture. Cube the tofu. Sprinkle it with sea salt.

6. When the oil is hot, carefully place the tofu into the wok. Sear it, tossing occasionally. Sprinkle with sugar and cook for another minute. Drizzle with the vinegar and cook for another minute. Set aside for a moment.

7. To assemble the casserole, place a layer of cooked rice onto the bottom of a 9 by 11-inch ovenproof pan. Add a layer of the eggplant mixture, spinach, and tofu. Add another layer of rice. Then add a final layer of the eggplant mixture, spinach, and tofu. Scatter the cheese onto the last layer of vegetables.

8. Place the casserole into the oven. Bake until the cheese melts and the casserole is heated through, approximately 15 minutes.

9. Divide the casserole among 4 plates and serve at once.

✣ Bread Casserole of Kale, Tomatoes, and Tofu

This casserole is layered like a lasagna, but we have substituted slices of rustic sourdough bread for pasta. It is one of our favorite weekend meals. We can prepare each part earlier in the day and assemble the casserole in the evening. It is a great source of beta-carotene, Vitamin C, and phytoestrogens.

PREPARATION:
40 MINUTES

COOKING:
20 MINUTES

YIELD:
6 MAIN-COURSE
SERVINGS

TOPPING AND BREAD

1 tablespoon olive oil
1 cup Homemade Bread Crumbs (see page 263)
10 4- by 4-inch slices sourdough bread

TOMATO SAUCE

1 tablespoon olive oil
4 cloves garlic, peeled and sliced
1 onion, peeled and diced
   Sea salt to taste
2 teaspoons dried basil
1 teaspoon dried oregano
1 teaspoon dried thyme
1 28-ounce can whole tomatoes in juice, chopped
1 pound extra-firm tofu, squeezed to remove excess moisture and crumbled
   Black pepper to taste

KALE

1 tablespoon olive oil
4 cloves garlic, peeled and sliced
1½ pounds Dinosaur or Red Russian kale, trimmed, washed, drained, and chopped
   Sea salt to taste
   Black pepper to taste

½ cup Kalamata olives, pitted and chopped
3 ounces provolone cheese, sliced or grated

1. Preheat the oven to 400°F.

2. To prepare the topping and bread, heat the olive oil in a skillet over high heat. When it is hot, add the bread crumbs to the pan. Stir and remove the pan from the heat. Set aside. Place the bread slices in the oven. Toast until they are dry, approximately 10 minutes. Remove from the oven and set aside. Do not turn off the oven.

3. While the bread slices are toasting, prepare the sauce. Heat the olive oil in a Dutch oven over low heat. Add the garlic to the pot and cook until soft and fragrant. Add the onion and sprinkle with sea salt. Cook the onion until soft, stirring occasionally.

4. Add the basil, oregano, and thyme. Cook the herbs for 1 minute. Raise the heat to high. Add the tomatoes. Bring the sauce to a boil.

5. Stir in the tofu. Reduce the heat and simmer for 20 minutes, stirring occasionally. Season the sauce with sea salt and black pepper. Set aside.

6. While the sauce is simmering, prepare the kale. Heat the olive oil in a Dutch oven over low heat. Add the garlic. Cook until soft and fragrant.

7. Raise the heat to high. Add the kale to the pot. Stir until it begins to wilt. Reduce the heat to low. Cover the pot. Braise the kale until tender, stirring occasionally, approximately 30 minutes. If necessary, add a bit of water to prevent the kale from sticking. Season with sea salt and black pepper.

8. To assemble the casserole, place 5 slices of bread on the bottom of a rectangular 4-quart casserole. Scatter one-half of the chard on the bread. Spoon one-half of the sauce onto the chard. Sprinkle one-half of the olives onto the sauce. Scatter the cheese on the olives. Create another layer of bread, chard, sauce, and olives. Top the casserole with the bread crumbs. Transfer the casserole to the oven. Bake until heated through, approximately 20 minutes.

✣ Vegetarian Pad Thai

Many of us consider Pad Thai to be too intimidating to prepare at home. It's not. All you need to do is visit an Asian market or the international section of a supermarket and pick up two important ingredients: flat rice noodles and fish sauce. Fish sauce (nuoc nam), a traditional Thai condiment, is strongly flavored and salty—a small amount goes a long way. Rice noodles (sen mee) are made from rice flour and water. They resemble translucent fettuccine. Their neutral flavor makes them an ideal canvas for a tangy sauce. With tofu and edamame, our Pad Thai is a great source of phytoestrogens.

* **Tip:** *To prevent the noodles from clumping, rinse them under cold water after they have been drained.*

PREPARATION:
15 MINUTES

COOKING:
5 MINUTES

YIELD:
4 MAIN-COURSE
SERVINGS

12 ounces flat rice stick noodles
  Sea salt to taste
1½ cups shelled, frozen, and blanched edamame
2 tablespoons canola oil
1 pound extra-firm tofu
2 tablespoons brown sugar
6 tablespoons ketchup
2 tablespoons white vinegar
2 tablespoons sugar
2 teaspoons fish sauce
3 cloves garlic, peeled and finely chopped
2 eggs plus 2 egg whites, whisked
¼ pound bean sprouts, rinsed
4 scallions, thinly sliced
⅓ cup cilantro, chopped
¼ cup unsalted and roasted peanuts, finely chopped
1 lime, quartered

1. Bring a large pot of water to a boil. Remove the pot from the heat. Stir in the noodles. Allow the noodles to soak until tender, approximately 5 minutes. Drain the noodles and rinse under cold water. Set aside.
2. While the noodles are soaking, bring a small pot of water to a boil. Add sea salt to the water, followed by the edamame.

Cook the edamame until tender, approximately 5 minutes. Drain. Set aside.

3. Heat 1 tablespoon of the oil in a wok over medium-high heat. Place the tofu on a kitchen towel. With the heel of your hand, gently press the tofu to remove the excess moisture. Cube the tofu. Sprinkle with sea salt.

4. Carefully place the tofu into the wok. Sear, tossing several times. Sprinkle with the brown sugar. Cook the tofu until the sugar is melted and carmelized, tossing often, approximately 2 minutes. Transfer the tofu to a plate. Set aside.

5. Prepare the sauce by whisking together the ketchup, vinegar, sugar, and fish sauce. Set aside.

6. Heat the remaining tablespoon of oil in the wok over medium heat. When the oil is hot, add the garlic. Cook for 30 seconds. Add the eggs and scramble. Stir in the sauce, edamame, bean sprouts, and scallions. Stir in the noodles. Cook the noodles and sauce together for 1 minute.

7. Transfer the noodles to a large serving platter. Garnish with cilantro, peanuts, and the tofu. Accompany the Pad Thai with the lime wedges. Serve hot or at room temperature.

❧❧ Udon Noodles in a Soy Nut Butter Sauce with Tofu and Broccoli

Soy nut butter is an excellent substitute for peanut butter in a traditional peanut sauce. A soy nut sauce is versatile and quick to prepare. It can be served as a dip for grilled meat and vegetables or used to sauce Asian noodles. Crisp broccoli and sesame-coated tofu add texture and flavor to the noodles. With an abundance of fiber, phytoestrogens, beta-carotene, and vitamins C and E, the meal contains many important breast cancer preventing nutrients.

Tips: *If you can't locate Udon noodles, spaghetti can be substituted. Also, the broccoli, soy nut sauce, and tofu can be prepared several hours in advance.*

PREPARATION:
20 MINUTES

COOKING:
5 MINUTES

YIELD:
4 MAIN-COURSE
SERVINGS

1 cup water
Sea salt to taste
1 large bunch broccoli, trimmed, washed, stems peeled and sliced, florets separated
Reserved broccoli cooking water
⅓ cup soy nut butter
¼ tamari
1 tablespoon sugar
2 tablespoons cider vinegar
2 tablespoons sesame oil
1 pound extra-firm tofu
2 tablespoons unhulled sesame seeds
12 ounces udon noodles
1-inch gingerroot, peeled and finely chopped
2 cloves garlic, peeled and finely chopped
3 scallions, trimmed and thinly sliced
1 cup pasta cooking water
¼ cup roasted and unsalted peanuts, chopped
⅓ cup cilantro, chopped

1. Bring the water to a boil in a Dutch oven. Add sea salt to the water, followed by the broccoli. Cover the pot and steam the broccoli until crisp-tender, approximately 4 minutes. Drain

the broccoli and reserve its cooking water. Cool the broccoli under running water. Set aside for a moment.

2. To prepare the sauce, place the broccoli cooking water in a bowl. Whisk in the soy nut butter, tamari, sugar, and vinegar. Set the sauce aside for a moment.

3. To prepare the tofu, heat 1 tablespoon of the sesame oil in a wok over medium-high heat. Place the tofu on a kitchen towel. With the heel of your hand, gently press on the tofu to remove the excess moisture. Cube the tofu.

4. Sprinkle the tofu with sea salt and sesame seeds and toss well. Carefully place in the wok. Sear the tofu until the seeds are golden, tossing several times. Transfer to a plate and set aside.

5. To cook the noodles, bring a large pot of water to a boil. Add sea salt to the water, followed by the noodles. Cook until tender. Drain. Reserve 1 cup of the cooking water. Set aside for a moment.

6. Heat the remaining oil in the wok over medium-high heat. When the oil is hot, add the ginger and garlic. Cook for 30 seconds.

7. Add the scallions and broccoli. Cook for 1 minute, stirring often. Add the noodles and their cooking water. Cook the ingredients until the noodles are warm.

8. Add the sauce. Combine the noodles and sauce.

9. Transfer the noodles to a large platter. Garnish with the peanuts, cilantro, and tofu. Serve hot or at room temperature.

❧ Rice Noodles with Tofu, Bok Choy, and Edamame

*This quickly prepared dish is equally good hot or at room tempera-
ture. As with Pad Thai, it is critical to prepare the rice noodles correctly. If they are boiled like traditional wheat-based noodles or
soaked too long, they will be too soft to stand up to the sauce and
crisp vegetables. Test the noodles after 5 minutes of soaking. This dish
is an excellent source of breast cancer preventing phytoestrogens,
beta-carotene, and vitamins C and E.*

    Tip: *To prevent the noodles from clumping, rinse under cold
water after they have been drained.*

PREPARATION:
10 MINUTES

COOKING:
10 MINUTES

YIELD:
4 MAIN-COURSE
SERVINGS

12	ounces rice noodles
	Sea salt to taste
1½	cups shelled, frozen, and blanched edamame
2	tablespoons canola oil
1	pound extra-firm tofu
2	tablespoons unhulled sesame seeds
1	teaspoon sesame oil
3	tablespoons white vinegar
3	tablespoons ketchup
3	tablespoons tamari
2	tablespoons sugar
3	cloves garlic, peeled and finely chopped
4	stalks bok choy, trimmed and chopped, stems and leaves separated
1	red bell pepper, cored and diced
4	scallions, thinly sliced
⅓	cup cilantro, chopped

1. Bring a large pot of water to a boil. Remove the pot from the
   heat. Stir in the noodles. Allow the noodles to soak until tender, approximately 5 minutes. Drain the noodles and rinse
   under cold water. Set aside.
2. While the noodles are soaking, bring a small pot of water to
   a boil. Add sea salt to the water, followed by the edamame.

Cook the edamame until tender, approximately 5 minutes. Drain. Set aside.

3. Heat 1 tablespoon of the canola oil in wok over medium-high heat. Place the tofu on a kitchen towel. With the heel of your hand, gently press on the tofu to remove the excess moisture. Cube the tofu.

4. Sprinkle the tofu with sea salt and sesame seeds. Toss well. Carefully place in the wok. Sear the tofu until the seeds are golden, tossing several times. Transfer to a plate. Set aside.

5. To prepare the sauce, whisk together the sesame oil, vinegar, ketchup, tamari, and sugar. Set the sauce aside.

6. Heat the remaining oil in the wok over high heat. When the oil is hot, add the garlic. Cook for 30 seconds. Add the bok choy stems and bell pepper. Cook until they begin to soften, stirring constantly, approximately 2 minutes.

7. Add the bok choy leaves and edamame. Cook for 2 minutes, stirring constantly. Whisk the sauce. Add to the vegetables.

8. Bring the sauce to a boil. Stir in the scallions. Stir in the noodles. Heat the sauce and noodles together for 2 minutes, stirring occasionally.

9. Transfer the noodles to a large platter. Garnish with the cilantro and tofu.

❧❦ Fried Brown Rice with Tofu

When you order fried rice in a restaurant, it is generally made with white rice and contains excessive amounts of oil and salt. In your own kitchen, it is easy to duplicate the restaurant flavors. Most important, you can add your own personal touches and make the meal more healthful. We prepare our fried rice with brown rice. We add tofu, edamame, and a red bell pepper for texture and taste. With plenty of fiber, phytoestrogens, and Vitamin C, it is far more nutritious than a restaurant-made dish.

PREPARATION:
1 HOUR

COOKING:
10 MINUTES

YIELD:
4 MAIN-COURSE
SERVINGS

    5 cups water
      Sea salt to taste
    2 cups short-grain brown rice
  1½ cups shelled, frozen, and blanched edamame
    6 tablespoons tamari
    2 teaspoons sugar
    2 tablespoons canola oil
    1 pound extra-firm tofu
    3 cloves garlic, peeled and finely chopped
      1-inch piece gingerroot, peeled and finely chopped
    1 red bell pepper, cored and diced
    4 scallions, trimmed and thinly sliced
    1 cup frozen peas, thawed
    2 eggs plus 2 egg whites, whisked

1. Bring the water to a boil in a medium saucepan. Add sea salt to the water. Stir in the rice. Bring the rice to a boil. Reduce the heat and cover the pot. Simmer the rice until tender and the water has been absorbed, approximately 1 hour. Transfer the rice to a baking sheet. Spread it so it cools quickly.
2. While the rice is cooking, bring a small pot of water to a boil. Add sea salt to the water, followed by the edamame. Cook the edamame until tender, approximately 5 minutes. Drain. Set aside.
3. While the rice is simmering, whisk together the tamari and sugar. Set aside.
4. Heat 1 tablespoon of the oil in a wok over medium-high

heat. Place the tofu on a kitchen towel. With the heel of your hand, gently press on the tofu to remove the excess moisture. Cube the tofu.

5. Carefully place the tofu into the wok. Sear, tossing several times. Drizzle with 3 tablespoons of the tamari mixture. Transfer to a plate. Set aside while you complete the dish.

6. Heat the remaining oil in the wok over high heat. When the oil is hot, add the garlic and ginger. Cook for 30 seconds. Add the bell pepper. Cook until it begins to soften, approximately 3 minutes, stirring often. Add the scallions, edamame, and peas.

7. Reduce the heat. Whisk the eggs one more time and add them. Scramble the eggs until they are set. Stir in the rice. Stir the ingredients until well combined.

8. Stir in the remaining tamari mixture. Transfer the rice to a large serving platter. Drizzle a bit more tamari onto the rice. Garnish the rice with the tofu and serve at once.

🪲 Curried Tofu, White Beans, and Tomatoes

Dusting tofu with prepared curry powder is a quick way to enhance its flavor and texture. In this recipe the tofu garnishes a vegetarian curry of crisp vegetables and earthy white beans. With plenty of phytoestrogens, beta-carotene, fiber, and Vitamin C, it has the ideal nutritional profile of a breast cancer prevention meal.

*   **Tip:** *Canned white beans tend to be overcooked. In a pinch, they can be substituted for dried. Drain and rinse them thoroughly. To prevent them from becoming mushy, add them at the end of the recipe and stir only until they are incorporated into the sauce.*

PREPARATION:
15 MINUTES

BEAN SOAKING:
12 HOURS

COOKING:
1¼ HOURS

YIELD:
4 MAIN-COURSE
SERVINGS

1   cup dried white beans, sorted, rinsed, and soaked overnight
4   cups water
1   pound extra-firm tofu
2   tablespoons canola oil
    Sea salt to taste
    Black pepper to taste
1   tablespoon plus 2 teaspoons prepared curry powder
4   cloves garlic, peeled and finely chopped
    1-inch piece gingerroot, peeled and finely chopped
1   onion, peeled and thinly sliced
1   red bell pepper, cored and thinly sliced
4   stalks bok choy, trimmed and chopped, leaves and stems separated
1   28-ounce can whole tomatoes in juice, drained and chopped
4   scallions, trimmed and sliced

1. Combine the white beans and water in a medium-sized pot. Bring to a boil. Reduce the heat. Simmer until tender, approximately 1 hour. Drain and set aside.
2. While the beans are cooking, place the tofu on a kitchen towel. With the heel of your hand, gently press on the tofu to remove the excess moisture. Cube the tofu.

3. Heat 1 tablespoon of the oil in a Dutch oven over medium-high heat. Sprinkle the tofu with sea salt and black pepper. Sprinkle with 1 tablespoon of the curry powder and toss to coat well.

4. Carefully place the tofu into the pot. Sear, tossing several times. Remove from the pan and set aside.

5. Reduce the heat to medium. Add the remaining tablespoon of oil to the pot. When the oil is hot, add the garlic and ginger. Cook for 30 seconds.

6. Add the onion and sprinkle with sea salt. Cook the onion until it begins to soften, stirring often. Add the bell pepper and bok choy stems to the pot. Cook until they begin to soften, stirring often, approximately 5 minutes.

7. Add the remaining 2 teaspoons of curry powder. Cook for 2 minutes more.

8. Raise the heat to high. Add the bok choy leaves, tomatoes, and cooked beans to the pot. Bring the sauce to a boil. Reduce the heat. Simmer for 10 minutes, stirring occasionally.

9. Stir in the scallions. Season the curry with sea salt and black pepper. Divide the curry among 4 shallow bowls. Garnish with the tofu. Accompany this dish with brown basmati rice.

🌿 Oven-Roasted Asparagus, Eggplant, and Portobello Sandwiches

Roasting vegetables in the oven with only olive oil, sea salt, and black pepper releases their earthy and naturally sweet flavors. In this recipe the roasted vegetables are layered into sliced baguettes, which have been spread with tangy goat cheese. Sliced tomatoes and a drizzle of top-quality balsamic vinegar add moisture and enhance the wonderful vegetable flavors. Whether you prepare these sandwiches for lunch or a light dinner, their simple preparation will prove that with truly fresh vegetables the less fuss the better. Asparagus and tomatoes are great sources of beta-carotene and Vitamin C.

PREPARATION:
10 MINUTES

COOKING:
30 MINUTES

YIELD:
4 MAIN-COURSE
SERVINGS

1 pound medium-sized asparagus, tough part of the stems snapped off
2 Italian eggplants, sliced lengthwise into 4 pieces each
4 medium-sized portobello mushrooms, stems removed and discarded, caps wiped
Sea salt to taste
Black pepper to taste
Olive oil for drizzling
2 baguettes
4 ounces goat cheese, at room temperature
1 large tomato, cored and sliced
Balsamic vinegar for drizzling

1. Preheat the oven to 425°F.
2. Place the asparagus, eggplants, and mushrooms on 1 large or 2 small heavy baking trays.
3. Sprinkle with sea salt and black pepper. Drizzle with olive oil. Place the tray in the oven.
4. Roast the asparagus until tender, approximately 10 minutes. Remove from the oven. Roast the eggplants until golden, approximately 7 minutes longer. Remove from the oven. Roast the mushrooms until soft, approximately 8 minutes more. Remove from the oven. The total roasting time will be approximately 25 minutes.
5. Slice the baguettes in half lengthwise. Spread with the goat

cheese. Divide the eggplant and asparagus among the baguettes. Slice the mushrooms and divide among the baguettes. Add the sliced tomato. Drizzle the sandwiches with the balsamic vinegar.

6. Slice the baguettes in half. Divide the sandwiches among 4 plates. Serve hot or at room temperature.

❧ Open-Faced Tofu and Pesto Bagel Sandwiches

PREPARATION:
5 MINUTES

COOKING:
10 MINUTES

YIELD:
2 MAIN-COURSE
SERVINGS

With no seasonings, crumbled tofu is bland. When you enhance it with bold flavors, such as basil pesto, it is transformed into something special. Seasoned tofu is a great addition to toasted cheese sandwiches. With two sources of tofu, the sandwiches offer an abundance of breast cancer preventing phytoestrogens.

8	ounces firm tofu, crumbled
3 to 4	tablespoons tofu-basil pesto (see page 178)
	Sea salt to taste
	Black pepper to taste
2	bagels, halved
	Tomato slices
2	ounces Swiss cheese, sliced

1. Preheat the oven to 400° F.
2. Place the tofu into a bowl. Stir in the basil pesto. Season the tofu with sea salt and black pepper.
3. Divide the tofu among the 4 bagel halves. Top each with the tomato slices. Divide the cheese among each bagel half.
4. Transfer the bagels to a tray. Place the tray into the oven. Bake the bagels until the cheese is melted and the bagels are slightly crisp, approximately 12 minutes.

✃ Broiled Soy Cheese Sandwiches with Olives and Dried Tomatoes

We love the combination of salty olives and sweet dried tomatoes. Here we use it to update a child (and adult) favorite: grilled cheese. We substitute soy cheese, crusty bagels, and olive oil for the usual ingredients, and we bake the sandwiches in a pan. They are rich in phytoestrogens and Vitamin C.

Soy cheeses seem to be a food that people either love or loathe. Compared to traditional cheeses, they are significantly lower in fat and calories. We think they work best when they are melted and combined with robustly flavored ingredients.

Tip: *This recipe is meant to be flexible. You can substitute soy Jack or mozzarella cheeses for the Cheddar. The toppings are endless. You can experiment with turnip greens or chard braised with garlic, cooked soy bacon, or sautéed mushrooms. Whichever cheese and topping you choose, you are certain to create a delectable sandwich.*

PREPARATION:
5 MINUTES

COOKING:
10 MINUTES

YIELD:
2 MAIN-COURSE
SERVINGS

2 sesame bagels, halved
  Olive oil for drizzling
4 ounces soy Cheddar, sliced
8 Kalamata olives, pitted and chopped
6 dried tomatoes, softened and sliced
  Sea salt to taste
  Black pepper to taste

1. Preheat the oven to 400°F.
2. Drizzle each bagel half with olive oil. Divide the cheese, olives, and tomatoes among each half. Sprinkle each with sea salt and black pepper.
3. Place the bagels on a baking tray. Bake the sandwiches until the cheese is melted and the bagels are slightly crisp, approximately 10 minutes.
4. Divide the bagels among 2 plates and serve at once.

🐛 Tofu Sloppy Joes

PREPARATION:
15 MINUTES

COOKING:
1 HOUR

YIELD:
4 MAIN-DISH
SERVINGS

When we were kids, the usual Tuesday lunch in our school cafeteria was a Sloppy Joe sandwich. It was made with ground beef, onions, and a too-sweet tomato sauce. Served on a white hamburger bun, it was definitely kid food. Our version is made with crumbled tofu, tomatoes, peppers, onions, and a touch of ketchup to provide a hint of sweetness. This delightful filling is tucked into a crusty baguette. It is certain to please adults and children alike. Tofu Sloppy Joes are a great source of phytoestrogens and Vitamin C.

1	tablespoon olive oil
3	cloves garlic, peeled and sliced
1	onion, peeled and diced
1	green bell pepper, seeded and diced
	Sea salt to taste
1	pound extra-firm tofu, squeezed to remove excess moisture and crumbled
1	28-ounce can whole tomatoes in juice, chopped
⅓	cup ketchup
2	tablespoons brown sugar
1 to 2	tablespoons Worcestershire sauce
1	tablespoon cider vinegar
	Black pepper to taste
4	ounces provolone cheese, grated or sliced
2	medium baguettes

1. Heat the olive oil in an ovenproof Dutch oven over low heat. Add the garlic and cook until soft and fragrant.
2. Raise the heat to medium. Add the onion and bell pepper. Sprinkle with sea salt. Cook until soft, stirring occasionally.
3. Raise the heat to high. Add the tofu and tomatoes. Stir in the ketchup, brown sugar, Worcestershire sauce, and vinegar. Bring the sauce to a boil.
4. Reduce the heat and simmer the sauce for 50 minutes, stirring occasionally. Season with sea salt and black pepper.
5. Heat the broiler. Scatter the cheese onto the sauce. Place the pot under the broiler. Broil the sauce until the cheese is golden and bubbly, approximately 5 minutes.

6. Cut the baguettes in half. Slice open each half lengthwise. Spoon an equal portion of the filling onto each half to make a sandwich.

✣ Seasoned Edamame, Goat Cheese, and Avocado Sandwiches

Whether they are tossed into a pasta dish or a soup or stewed with tomatoes and served as a side dish, we love the earthy flavor and meaty texture of edamame. Here we have mashed them with fruity olive oil, sea salt, and black pepper to create a unique sandwich spread. Tangy goat cheese, creamy avocado, and peppery arugula add great flavor. The sandwiches are an excellent source of phyto-estrogens, beta-carotene, and Vitamin E.

Tip: *The sandwiches can be prepared several hours in advance without the avocado. Just before serving, slice the avocado and tuck it into the baguettes.*

PREPARATION:
5 MINUTES

COOKING:
10 MINUTES

YIELD:
4 MAIN-COURSE
SERVINGS

2   cups water
    Sea salt to taste
2   cups frozen, shelled, and blanched edamame
2   tablespoons olive oil
    Black pepper to taste
2   baguettes
4   ounces goat cheese, at room temperature
1   avocado, peeled, pitted, and sliced
4   cups small arugula, trimmed, washed, and spun dry

1. Bring the water to a boil in a saucepan. Add sea salt to the water, followed by the edamame. Bring the edamame to a boil. Reduce the heat and simmer until tender, approximately 5 minutes. Drain and transfer to a bowl.
2. Drizzle with the olive oil. Mash with a fork until they develop a chunky texture. Season with sea salt and black pepper. Set aside for a moment.
3. Cut the baguettes in half. Slice open each half lengthwise. Spread one side of each baguette with the goat cheese.

Spread an equal amount of the edamame over the goat cheese. Divide the avocado and arugula among the baguettes.

4. Divide the sandwiches among 4 plates and serve at once.

❧ Roasted Portobello Mushroom Stacks

PREPARATION:
15 MINUTES

COOKING:
30 MINUTES

YIELD:
4 MAIN-COURSE
SERVINGS

While shopping for this recipe and walking by the prepared food counter, we noticed they had a similar sandwich in their case. We thought their idea was better than ours. We went back to the produce section and picked up a few more things and modified our recipe to include the best of both. We like to use Red Russian or Dinosaur kale in this recipe. They are more sweet and tender than sharp-tasting Ornamental kale. With sweet potatoes and kale, the stacks contain two of the richest sources of beta-carotene.

Tips: *If you use two smaller trays when roasting the vegetables, it may be necessary to rotate them to ensure even cooking. Also, the recipe can be prepared several hours in advance without the vinegar and served at room temperature. Just before serving, drizzle with the vinegar.*

4 large portobello mushrooms, stems removed and discarded, caps wiped

2 medium sweet potatoes, peeled and sliced into ½-inch discs

1 large red onion, peeled and sliced into 4 ½-inch-thick discs

Sea salt to taste

Black pepper to taste

Olive oil for drizzling, plus 1 tablespoon

4 cloves garlic, peeled and sliced

1 pound Red Russian or Dinosaur kale, trimmed, chopped, washed, and drained

1 cup chicken stock or water

4 ounces goat cheese, at room temperature

Top-quality balsamic vinegar, for drizzling

1. Preheat the oven to 450°F.
2. Place the mushrooms, potatoes, and red onion on a heavy, large baking tray or 2 smaller ones. Sprinkle with sea salt and black pepper. Drizzle with olive oil.
3. Place the tray in the oven. Roast the vegetables until tender, stirring 2 or 3 times, approximately 30 minutes. Remove the tray from the oven. Allow the vegetables to cool for a moment.
4. While the potatoes are cooking, heat the tablespoon of olive oil in a Dutch oven over medium-low heat. Add the garlic and cook until soft and fragrant.
5. Add the kale. Sprinkle with sea salt. Cover the pot and cook the kale for 5 minutes, stirring occasionally.
6. Add the chicken stock or water. Cook the kale until tender, stirring occasionally, approximately 20 minutes more.
7. To prepare the stacks, divide the kale among 4 plates. Place a mushroom on top of each portion of kale. Next, place an equal portion of goat cheese onto each mushroom. Last, place a few potato discs and 1 slice of onion on each. Drizzle with balsamic vinegar. Serve at once.

🌿 Vegetable Burgers

PREPARATION:
45 MINUTES

COOKING:
30 MINUTES

YIELD:
8 MAIN-DISH
SERVINGS

There are many varieties of commercially prepared vegetable burgers available. Some are very good, while others are dry and tasteless; none is inexpensive. Fortunately, they are simple to prepare at home. We base ours on Textured Vegetable Protein (TVP), vegetables, and lentils. They are packed with flavor and with an abundance of beta-carotene, Vitamin C, and fiber, plenty of breast cancer preventing nutrients.

Tip: *The mixture can be prepared a day in advance without the eggs. The following day, before forming the patties, mix the eggs in.*

½ cup brown lentils, sorted and rinsed
4 tablespoons olive oil
3 cloves garlic, peeled and sliced
1 onion, peeled and diced
   Sea salt to taste
1 carrot, scraped and diced
1 red bell pepper, cored and diced
2½ cups water
2 cup TVP
2 cups Homemade Bread Crumbs (page 263)
   Black pepper to taste
2 eggs

1. Place the lentils in a small saucepan. Cover with water. Bring the water to a boil. Cover the pot. Reduce the heat and simmer the lentils until tender, approximately 45 minutes. Drain them of their cooking water. Transfer to a large mixing bowl.
2. While the lentils are cooking, heat 1 tablespoon of the olive oil in a Dutch oven over low heat. Add the garlic and cook until soft and fragrant. Add the onion and sprinkle with sea salt. Cook the onion until it begins to soften.
3. Add the carrot and bell pepper. Cook until very soft, stirring often, approximately 10 minutes. Transfer to the mixing bowl containing the lentils.
4. Bring the water to a boil in the Dutch oven. Add sea salt to

the water. Add the TVP. Cover the pot and remove from the heat. Allow the TVP to rehydrate for 15 minutes. Transfer to the bowl containing the other ingredients.

5. Mix in the bread crumbs. Season the mixture with sea salt and black pepper. Mix in the eggs. Transfer the mixture to a food processor fitted with a metal blade. Pulse the mixture until well combined but still chunky.

6. Form the mixture into 8 tightly packed balls. Flatten the balls to form patties approximately 1 inch thick.

7. Heat the oven to 400°F.

8. Place a heavy baking tray in the oven. After 5 minutes, carefully remove the tray from the oven. Pour the remaining 3 tablespoons of olive oil on the tray. Place the patties on the tray.

9. Place the tray into the oven. Bake the patties for 15 minutes. Flip and bake them for 10 minutes more.

10. Remove the tray from the oven. Transfer the patties to a serving platter. Accompany with crusty rolls and your favorite toppings.

TEXTURED VEGETABLE PROTEIN

Made from defatted soy flakes, textured vegetable protein (TVP) is one of the most versatile soy products. It is a dry and granular product with relatively little taste. It is the primary ingredient in many of the commercially produced soy products that mimic meat products, such as soy hot dogs, soy sausages, and soy bacon.

Before it can be used in a recipe, TVP needs to be rehydrated either in hot water or a flavorful liquid. Its unique ability to absorb flavors makes it ideal for preparing creative meatless dishes and transforming old favorites, such as meat loaf, into vegetarian feasts.

It is generally available in bulk or 1-pound packages in health food stores and supermarkets.

❧ Roasted Red Bell Pepper and Curried Tofu Pitas

PREPARATION:
10 MINUTES

COOKING:
10 MINUTES

YIELD:
4 MAIN-COURSE
SERVINGS

A hummus recipe is versatile. The list of ingredients that can be added to the base of chickpeas and tahini is long. Some great combinations are roasted garlic and balsamic vinegar, Kalamata olive and scallion, and roasted eggplant. This version, made with roasted peppers, canned beans, and seasoned with cumin, not only has great flavor but is convenient as well. When spread into a pita and accompanied with tofu, you have the makings of a tasty and healthful meal. The chickpeas are a great source of fiber, the tofu is loaded with phytoestrogens, and the tomatoes and arugula provide Vitamin C and beta-carotene.

HUMMUS
1 tablespoon canola oil
3 cloves garlic, peeled and sliced
1 onion, peeled and diced
    Sea salt to taste
2 teaspoons cumin
1 15-ounce can chickpeas, drained and rinsed
1 12-ounce jar roasted red bell peppers, drained and chopped
3 tablespoons sesame tahini
2 tablespoons white vinegar
    Black pepper to taste

TOFU
1 tablespoon canola oil
1 pound extra-firm tofu
    Sea salt to taste
    Black pepper to taste
1 tablespoon curry powder
1 tablespoon sugar

4 medium whole-wheat pitas, sliced
1 large bunch arugula, trimmed, washed, and spun dry
1 large tomato, cored and sliced

1. To prepare the hummus, heat the canola oil in a wok over medium heat. Add the garlic and cook for 30 seconds. Add the onion and sprinkle with sea salt. Cook the onion until soft, stirring occasionally.

2. Add the cumin. Cook the ingredients for another minute. Transfer the ingredients to the work bowl of a food processor fitted with a metal blade.

3. Add the chickpeas, roasted peppers, tahini, and vinegar to the bowl and puree. Season the hummus with sea salt and black pepper. Set the hummus aside for a moment.

4. To prepare the tofu, heat the canola in the wok over medium-high heat. Place the tofu on a kitchen towel. With the heel of your hand, gently press on the tofu to remove the excess moisture. Cube the tofu. Sprinkle with sea salt, black pepper, and curry powder.

5. When the oil is hot, carefully place the tofu into the pan. Sear it, tossing occasionally. Add the sugar and cook the tofu for another minute. Remove the pan from the heat.

6. To make the sandwiches, spread an equal amount of the hummus inside the pitas. Divide the tofu, arugula, and tomato among the pitas.

🐾 Egg Salad Sandwiches

PREPARATION:
5 MINUTES

COOKING:
15 MINUTES

YIELD:
2 MAIN-COURSE
SERVINGS

With whole eggs and mayonnaise, a traditional egg salad sandwich is not part of a healthful diet. However, when you reduce the number of eggs, include tofu, and substitute soy mayonnaise for the regular type, you have a phytoestrogen-rich sandwich that you can enjoy often.

4 eggs
6 ounces firm tofu, crumbled
2 tablespoons soy or traditional mayonnaise
1 teaspoon Dijon mustard
  Sea salt to taste
  Black pepper to taste
4 slices whole-wheat bread, toasted
  Lettuce leaves
  Tomato slices

1. Bring a small pot of water to a boil. With a slotted spoon, carefully place the eggs into the water. Reduce the heat to a simmer and cook the eggs for 12 minutes.
2. Plunge the eggs into cold water. Allow them to cool.
3. Peel the eggs. Transfer 2 eggs to a bowl. Remove the yolks from the others and discard. Place the whites into the bowl. Mash the eggs with a fork.
4. Add the tofu to the bowl. Add the mayonnaise and mustard. Season the egg salad with sea salt and black pepper.
5. Divide the egg salad among 2 slices of bread. Garnish with the lettuce leaves and tomato slices. Form sandwiches with the remaining slices of bread.

❧ Zucchini Boats with Sweet Potatoes, Mushrooms, Tofu, and Feta

Throughout the summer we enjoy stuffed zucchini. We always vary the fillings, trying to create something interesting and healthful. This particular version is our favorite. Roasting the zucchini, potatoes, and mushrooms intensifies their flavors. The tofu adds texture and the feta a tangy taste. With plenty of phytoestrogens and beta-carotene, this delightful dish is a great source of breast cancer preventing nutrients.

Tip: *We enjoy the creamy texture of sheep's milk feta. If you can't locate it, cow's milk feta is a fine substitute. It crumbles more easily and is a bit saltier.*

PREPARATION:
45 MINUTES

COOKING:
10 MINUTES

YIELD:
4 MAIN-COURSE
SERVINGS

4 medium zucchini, halved and seeded
  Sea salt to taste
  Black pepper to taste
  Olive oil for drizzling, plus 1 tablespoon
2 sweet potatoes, peeled and cubed
2 medium portobello mushrooms, stems removed and discarded, caps wiped
3 cloves garlic, peeled and sliced
1 onion, peeled and diced
1 pound spinach, trimmed, washed, drained, and chopped
1 pound extra-firm tofu, squeezed to remove excess moisture and crumbled
4 ounces sheep's milk feta, crumbled
½ cup fresh basil, snipped

1. Heat the oven to 400°F.
2. Sprinkle the inside of each zucchini half with sea salt and black pepper. Drizzle each with olive oil. Place cut side down on a heavy baking tray. Transfer the tray to the oven. Roast the zucchini until tender, approximately 15 minutes. Remove the tray from the oven. Do not turn off the oven.
3. While the zucchini are roasting, place the potatoes and mushrooms on another heavy baking tray. Season with sea salt and black pepper. Drizzle with olive oil. Place the tray

into the oven. Roast the vegetables until tender, approximately 20 minutes. Remove the tray from the oven.

4. Transfer the potatoes to a mixing bowl. Slice the mushrooms. Transfer to the bowl.

5. Heat the remaining tablespoon of olive oil in a Dutch oven over medium-low heat. Add the garlic and cook until soft and fragrant. Add the onion and sprinkle it with sea salt. Cook the onion until soft, stirring occasionally.

6. Raise the heat to high. Add the spinach. Cook the spinach only until it wilts, stirring constantly, approximately 2 minutes. Transfer the mixture to the mixing bowl.

7. Add the tofu, feta, and basil to the bowl. Mix the ingredients until they are thoroughly combined. Season with sea salt and black pepper.

8. Divide the filling evenly among the zucchini halves, packing it lightly. Return the tray to the oven. Bake the zucchini boats until heated through, approximately 8 minutes. Serve at once.

🌿 "Meat Loaf"

When we were growing up, meat loaf was not much more than ground beef, ketchup, and a few spices. Now it can be considered a chic meal, one that many cooks like to play with, altering the seasonings and meats to create signature dishes. We have come up with a version that replaces the meat with textured vegetable protein (TVP). A spoonful of miso gives it an earthy and bold flavor. Rather than being laden with fat and calories, our meatless "meat loaf" is rich in phytoestrogens and fiber.

PREPARATION:
20 MINUTES

COOKING:
40 MINUTES

YIELD:
6 MAIN-COURSE
ESERVINGS

1 cup Homemade Bread Crumbs (page 263)
2 eggs
2 cups water
1 tablespoon miso
2 cups textured vegetable protein (TVP)
1 tablespoon olive oil
4 cloves garlic, peeled and finely chopped
1 onion, peeled and diced
 Sea salt to taste
1 stalk celery, finely chopped
1 small green bell pepper, cored and finely chopped
1 red bell pepper, cored and finely chopped
1 small carrot, scraped and finely chopped
½ teaspoon cumin
¼ teaspoon nutmeg
½ cup ketchup
 Black pepper to taste

1. Preheat the oven to 375°F.
2. Combine the bread crumbs and eggs in a large bowl. Set the bowl aside for a moment.
3. Bring the water to a boil in a medium saucepan. Whisk in the miso. Stir in the textured vegetable protein. Cover the pot. Turn off the heat and allow the TVP to steam for 15 minutes.
4. While the TVP is steaming, heat the olive oil in a skillet over medium-low heat. Add the garlic and cook until soft and fra-

grant. Add the onion and sprinkle with sea salt. Cook the onion until it begins to soften.

5. Add the celery, bell pepper, and carrot. Cover the pan and cook the vegetables until soft, stirring occasionally, approximately 10 minutes.

6. Add the cumin and nutmeg. Cook the ingredients for another minute. Transfer to the bowl with the bread crumbs and eggs. Add the ketchup. Add the TVP. Mix the ingredients until well combined.

7. Lightly oil a heavy sheet pan. Transfer the mixture to the pan. With your hands, form the mixture into a tightly packed loaf. Transfer the pan to the oven. Bake the "meat loaf" for 40 minutes.

8. Remove the pan from the oven. Allow the "meat loaf" to cool for 10 minutes. Cut into slices and accompany with Mashed Potatoes with Garlic and Leeks (page 322).

❧ Macaroni and Cheese with Carrots and Edamame

Macaroni and cheese is a true comfort food. With so many high fat dairy products though, a traditional version is not a healthful meal. By substituting soy milk and soft tofu for the usual cream and whole milk, we have created a more nutritious version. A minimal amount of sharp Cheddar cheese provides just the right amount of flavor. Carrots and edamame add texture and a hint of sweetness. Our macaroni and cheese is wonderfully rich tasting and, with plenty of phytoestrogens and beta-carotene, a meal you can enjoy regularly.

PREPARATION:
20 MINUTES

COOKING:
20 MINUTES

YIELD:
8 MAIN-COURSE
SERVINGS

- 2 tablespoons unsalted butter
- 1 onion, peeled and diced
  Sea salt to taste
- 2 tablespoons unbleached, all-purpose flour
- 2 cups soy milk
- 8 ounces soft tofu
- 8 ounces sharp Cheddar cheese, grated or sliced
  Black pepper to taste
- 1 pound carrots
- 2 cups frozen, shelled, and blanched edamame
- 1 pound elbow macaroni
- 2 cups Homemade Bread Crumbs (page 263)

1. Bring a large pot of water to a boil. Preheat the oven to 400°F.
2. Melt the butter in a small Dutch oven over low heat. Add the onion and sprinkle it with sea salt. Cook the onion until soft, stirring often.
3. Whisk in the flour to make a roux. Stir the roux for 2 minutes.
4. Combine the soy milk and tofu in a blender and puree.
5. Raise the heat to medium under the Dutch oven. Gradually whisk the tofu mixture into the roux to create a smooth sauce.
6. Whisk the cheese into the sauce a small amount at a time.

Continue whisking until all of the cheese has melted. Season with sea salt and black pepper. Set the sauce aside for a moment.

7. Add sea salt to the water, followed by the carrots and edamame. Cover the pot. When the water returns to a boil, add the pasta. Cook the pasta and vegetables until tender, approximately 6 minutes.

8. Drain and transfer to a 4-quart ovenproof casserole. Pour the sauce onto the pasta and vegetables. Stir the ingredients thoroughly.

9. Sprinkle the macaroni and cheese with the bread crumbs. Place the casserole in the oven. Bake for 15 minutes. Turn on the broiler and broil until the bread crumbs are crisp.

🦋 "Bacon" and Eggs

PREPARATION:
5 MINUTES

COOKING:
5 MINUTES

YIELD:
2 MAIN-COURSE
SERVINGS

Few people make bacon and eggs a regular part of their diet. Our phytoestrogen-rich version is one you can enjoy more often. We have reduced the number of eggs, substituted tempeh "bacon" for the traditional, and added tofu. "Bacon" and eggs has never tasted better or been more nutritious.

1 tablespoon olive oil
6 ounces tempeh "bacon," diced
1 bunch scallions, trimmed and sliced
2 eggs
4 egg whites
8 ounces tofu, crumbled
  Sea salt to taste
  Black pepper to taste

1. Heat the olive oil in a large nonstick skillet over high heat. When the oil is hot, add the tempeh and scallions. Cook the ingredients until the tempeh begins to brown, stirring often.

2. While the tempeh is cooking, whisk together the eggs, egg whites, and tofu. Season with sea salt and black pepper.

3. Pour the egg mixture into the pan. Stir the ingredients often until set, approximately 2 minutes.
4. Divide the eggs among 2 plates and accompany with toasted whole grain English muffins.

SOY PRODUCTS

It seems that every conventional product now has a soy equivalent. Most markets now carry soy hot dogs and burgers, soy sausage and bacon, and soy-based sour cream, cheese, and yogurt. Many of the products are excellent. We love tempeh "bacon" and the soy yogurts are excellent in smoothies. When cooked in a pan until the exterior is crisp and garnished with all of the usual fixings, soy dogs are great, too. With new soy foods being developed regularly, keep an open mind and try those that seem appealing.

CHAPTER 15

Chicken

The health benefits from eating chicken are well documented. Boneless and skinless chicken breasts are a lean protein source that are rich in niacin, riboflavin, and iron. With their mild taste, chicken breasts go well with a variety of bold flavors and seasonings.

By combining chicken breasts with soy, dried peas, and beans and antioxidant-rich fruits and vegetables, the number of creative and nutritious meals one can make is virtually endless. Searing, stir frying, and grilling are the simplest and best methods of preparing chicken breasts. These quick-cooking techniques seal in the breast's natural juices and prevent them from drying out and becoming tough. A bed of earthy-tasting cooked greens, a savory chutney or salsa, or a velvety tofu sauce are the ideal finishing touches for chicken breasts.

The intense flavor of curry perks up the mild flavor of chicken breasts. Rather than prepare a curry with an abundance of cream or oil, try our Curried Chicken Breasts with a Mango

Chutney, a delicious combination of sweet and savory tastes. Stir frying thinly sliced chicken breasts is a common preparation. Rather than adhere to the common Asian seasonings, prepare our unique Sesame-Crusted Chicken and Tofu with Carrots and Broccoli in a Thai Red Curry Sauce. With plenty of tofu, broccoli, and carrots, this meal is a great source of phytoestrogens and beta-carotene. The next time you grill, pass up the burgers and steaks and opt for our Lime- and Cilantro-Grilled Chicken Breasts with a Mango-Tomato Salsa. The slightly sweet salsa contains plenty of beta-carotene and Vitamin C and contrasts wonderfully with the tangy and smoky chicken.

Although chicken thighs and legs contain slightly more fat than breasts, they are still leaner than every cut of beef except top round. The additional fat naturally makes them flavorful and ideal for braising. Unlike tough cuts of beef and pork that require several hours of slow cooking to become tender, dark meat chicken is fork tender in just an hour. When you next crave a hearty and comforting meal, forget the pot roast and pork roast and prepare our Chicken Thighs Braised with Tomatoes, Kidney Beans, and Pumpkin Seeds. It is a tasty breast cancer preventing meal combining chicken thighs with a smooth-textured sauce of roasted pumpkin seeds and silken tofu.

With a bit of creativity and an emphasis on soy, fruits, vegetables, nuts, seeds, and dried peas and beans, you can transform the humble chicken into great breast cancer preventing feasts.

❧❦ Pan-Seared Chicken Breasts with Peach Chutney, Spinach, and Edamame

PREPARATION:
45 MINUTES

COOKING:
10 MINUTES

YIELD:
4 MAIN-COURSE
SERVINGS

One summer day, faced with a refrigerator full of fresh-picked peaches, the pressure was on to create as many peach-starring recipes as possible. Besides their obvious place in sweet dishes, peaches can also be the main ingredient in savory ones. Here we have used them to prepare a deceptively rich chutney that garnishes quickly cooked chicken breasts. Accompanied with edamame and spinach, this wonderful meal provides plenty of contrasting textures and flavors: sweet and salty, crisp and soft. It is a great source of beta-carotene and phytoestrogens.

Tips: The most sanitary and efficient way to flatten chicken breasts is to place them, one at a time, inside a plastic food storage bag, and pound them with the smooth side of a kitchen mallet. Discard the bag when you are done. Also, if you are grilling outside, it is not necessary to cook the spinach in your kitchen. It can be cooked in a pot on the grill.

3 tablespoons canola oil
   1-inch piece gingerroot, peeled and finely chopped
1 red onion, peeled and diced
   Sea salt to taste
¼ cup balsamic vinegar
2 tablespoons brown sugar
½ cup water
2 teaspoons Worcestershire sauce
4 medium peaches, pitted and sliced
   Black pepper to taste
2 boneless and skinless chicken breasts (1½ pounds),
   trimmed, halved, and pounded to ¼-inch thickness
1 clove garlic, peeled and finely chopped
2 cups shelled, frozen, and blanched edamame
1 cup chicken stock
1 pound fresh spinach, trimmed, washed, and drained

1. To prepare the chutney, heat 1 tablespoon of the oil in a Dutch oven over medium heat. Add the ginger. Cook until soft and fragrant. Add the onion and sprinkle with sea salt. Cook the onion until soft.

2. Add the vinegar, sugar, water, and Worcestershire sauce. Raise the heat to high.

3. Add the peaches. Bring the chutney to a boil. Reduce the heat. Simmer the chutney until thick, stirring occasionally, approximately 35 minutes. Season with sea salt and black pepper.

4. Transfer the chutney to the work bowl of a food processor fitted with a metal blade or a blender and puree. Set aside for a moment.

5. Heat another tablespoon of the oil in a large skillet over medium-high heat. Sprinkle the chicken breasts on each side with sea salt and black pepper. When the oil is hot, carefully place the chicken in the pan. Sear the chicken until golden on each side, turning once, 2 to 3 minutes on each side. Transfer to a plate. Set aside.

6. Heat the remaining tablespoon of oil in the skillet over medium-high heat. Add the garlic. Cook for 30 seconds. Add the edamame. Raise the heat to high. Add the stock. Bring the stock to a boil. Reduce the heat slightly and cook the edamame until tender, approximately 5 minutes.

7. Stir in the spinach. Cook the spinach only until it wilts, stirring often, approximately 3 minutes.

8. Divide the spinach and edamame among 4 plates. Place a portion of chicken onto each bed of the vegetable mixture. Top with the peach chutney and serve at once.

❧ Pan-Seared Chicken Breasts in a Tomato-Basil Sauce

PREPARATION:
10 MINUTES

COOKING:
30 MINUTES

YIELD:
4 MAIN-COURSE
SERVINGS

This velvety-textured sauce will fool you. It is based not on heavy cream but on a phytoestrogen and antioxidant-rich puree of tomatoes and silken tofu. It is a great way to enjoy the texture of a cream sauce without the fat and calories.

Tips: *The sauce can be prepared a day in advance through step 2. Also, the recipe yields 3 cups of sauce. Two cups are needed for this recipe. The remainder makes a tasty pasta sauce.*

SAUCE
- 1 tablespoon olive oil
- 4 cloves garlic, peeled and sliced
- 1 onion, peeled and diced
  Sea salt to taste
- 1 28-ounce can whole tomatoes in juice, drained and chopped
- 1 cup fresh basil
- 12 ounces silken tofu
  Black pepper to taste

CHICKEN
- 1 tablespoon olive oil
- 2 boneless and skinless chicken breasts (1½ pounds), trimmed, halved, and pounded to ¼-inch thickness
  Sea salt to taste
  Black pepper to taste
- 1 cup chicken stock
- 1 cup Kalamata olives, pitted and chopped

1. To prepare the sauce, heat the olive oil in a Dutch oven over low heat. Add the garlic. Cook until soft and fragrant. Add the onion and sprinkle with sea salt. Cook until it begins to soften, stirring occasionally.
2. Raise the heat to high and add the tomatoes to the pot. Bring the sauce to a boil. Reduce the heat and simmer the

sauce until all of the liquid has evaporated, approximately 15 minutes.

3. Transfer the sauce to a blender or the work bowl of a food processor fitted with the metal blade. Add the basil and tofu to the bowl and puree. Set aside for a moment.

4. For the chicken, heat the olive oil in a large skillet over high heat. Sprinkle the chicken breasts on each side with sea salt and black pepper. Sear on each side, turning once, 2–3 minutes on each side. Remove from the pan and keep warm.

5. Add the chicken stock to the pan to deglaze it. Reduce the heat and simmer the stock for 1 minute. Whisk in the tofu sauce. Add the olives. Season with sea salt and black pepper.

6. Divide the chicken among 4 plates and spoon sauce onto each serving.

🍃 Lime- and Cilantro-Grilled Chicken Breasts with a Mango-Tomato Salsa

PREPARATION:
15 MINUTES

MARINATING:
24 HOURS

COOKING:
10 MINUTES

YIELD:
4 MAIN-COURSE
SERVINGS

Whether they are primary seasonings in a pasta sauce or vegetable dish, lime and cilantro are a delightful combination. In this recipe they are the main ingredients in a marinade for chicken. An antioxidant-rich mango and tomato salsa adds a sweet contrast to the slightly tart poultry.

CHICKEN
- 1 clove garlic, peeled and crushed
  Juice and zest of 2 limes
- 1 tablespoon olive oil
- 1½ teaspoons chili powder
- ⅓ cup cilantro, chopped
  Sea salt to taste
  Black pepper to taste
- 2 boneless and skinless chicken breasts (1 ½ pounds), trimmed, halved, and pounded to ¼-inch thickness

SALSA
- 1 ripe mango, peeled and sliced into small cubes
- ⅔ cup cherry tomatoes, halved
- 1 tablespoon balsamic vinegar
- ¼ cup cilantro, chopped
  Sea salt to taste
  Black pepper to taste

SPINACH
- 1 tablespoon olive oil
- 1 clove garlic, peeled and sliced
- 1½ pounds spinach, trimmed, washed, and drained
  Sea salt to taste
  Black pepper to taste

1. The night before serving the chicken, prepare the marinade. Combine the garlic, lime juice and zest, olive oil, chili powder, and cilantro in a large nonreactive bowl. Season the

marinade with sea salt and black pepper. Place the chicken breasts in the bowl and turn to evenly coat with the marinade. Cover the bowl. Refrigerate the chicken for 12 to 24 hours.

2. The following day, prepare the salsa. Combine the mango, tomatoes, vinegar, and cilantro in a nonreactive bowl. Season with sea salt and black pepper. Set aside while you grill the chicken.

3. Heat a grill. When it is hot, remove the chicken from the marinade. Discard the excess marinade. Place the chicken breasts on the hot grill. Grill for approximately 5 minutes on each side. Remove from the grill. Keep warm while you prepare the spinach.

4. Heat the olive oil in a Dutch oven on the grill. When the oil is hot, add the garlic and cook for 30 seconds. Add the spinach and cook until it wilts, stirring constantly. Season the spinach with sea salt and black pepper.

5. To serve, divide the spinach among 4 plates. Place a portion of chicken onto each bed of spinach. Garnish with the salsa and serve at once.

🐦 Curried Chicken Breasts with a Mango Chutney

Chutney, like ketchup, relishes, and mustards, is a condiment that we all seem to prefer to purchase. However, once you prepare one in your own kitchen, you may not buy another from a store. It is simple to make and except for a stir every now and then requires little attention while cooking. We use this antioxidant-rich mango chutney to garnish quickly seared chicken breasts. It also works well with grilled or broiled firm-fleshed whitefish.

Tip: *The chutney can be prepared up to 3 days in advance. Keep it tightly sealed in your refrigerator.*

PREPARATION:
10 MINUTES

COOKING:
30 MINUTES

YIELD:
4 MAIN-COURSE
SERVINGS

CHUTNEY
1 tablespoon canola oil
1 clove garlic, peeled and finely chopped
1 onion, peeled and diced
  Sea salt to taste
1 small green bell pepper, cored and diced
1 small red bell pepper, cored and diced
¼ teaspoon nutmeg
¼ teaspoon cloves
¼ teaspoon cinnamon
2 tablespoons white vinegar
¼ cup sugar
1 large mango, peeled, pitted, and chopped

CHICKEN
1 tablespoon canola oil
2 boneless and skinless chicken breasts (1½ pounds), trimmed, halved, and pounded to ¼-inch thickness
  Sea salt to taste
  Black pepper to taste
1 tablespoon curry powder

1. To prepare the chutney, heat the canola oil in a Dutch oven over low heat. Add the garlic and cook until soft and fra-

grant. Add the onion and sprinkle with sea salt. Cook the
onion until it begins to soften.

2. Add the green and red bell peppers. Cook until they begin
   to soften. Add the nutmeg, cloves, and cinnamon. Cook the
   ingredients for another minute.

3. Raise the heat to high. Add the vinegar, sugar, and mango.
   Bring the chutney to a boil. Reduce the heat and simmer for
   30 minutes, stirring occasionally.

4. During the last 10 minutes of cooking, prepare the chicken.
   Heat the canola oil in a skillet over medium-high heat.
   Sprinkle the chicken breasts on each side with sea salt, black
   pepper, and curry powder.

5. Carefully place the chicken into the pan. Sear on each side,
   turning once. Reduce the heat slightly and cook for another
   2 minutes, or until cooked through.

6. Divide the chicken among 4 plates. Top with the chutney
   and serve at once.

❧❦ Spicy Pan-Fried Chicken Breast Sandwiches with Avocado

PREPARATION:
15 MINUTES

COOKING:
10 MINUTES

YIELD:
4 MAIN-COURSE
SERVINGS

In this recipe a bold blend of spices enhances the mild flavor of boneless chicken breasts. The accompanying avocado sauce adds a velvety texture to the sandwiches and tempers the spiciness of the chicken. These sandwiches are rich in phytoestrogens, Vitamin E, and beta-carotene.

Tips: *The avocado sauce can be prepared a day in advance and refrigerated. Also, like a traditional guacamole, it can be used as a dip and as a garnish for burritos and quesadillas.*

AVOCADO SAUCE
1 avocado, peeled and pitted
4 ounces silken tofu
1 small clove garlic, peeled and minced
  Juice from ½ large lemon
2 scallions, trimmed and thinly sliced
1 large tomato, halved, squeezed to remove seeds and diced
3 tablespoons cilantro, chopped
  Sea salt to taste
  Black pepper to taste

CHICKEN
1 teaspoon chili powder
1 teaspoon cumin
1 teaspoon curry powder
2 small chipotle peppers, finely chopped
2 boneless and skinless chicken breasts (1 ½ pounds), trimmed, halved, and pounded to ¼-inch thickness
  Sea salt to taste
  Black pepper to taste
2 tablespoons olive oil
2 ounces Monterey Jack cheese, sliced
4 Portuguese or hard rolls

1. To prepare the sauce, combine the avocado, tofu, garlic, and lemon in a blender or the work bowl of a food processor fitted with a metal blade and puree.
2. Transfer the puree to a bowl. Add the scallions, tomato, and cilantro. Season with sea salt and black pepper. Set the sauce aside while you prepare the chicken.
3. To prepare the chicken, combine the chili powder, cumin, curry, and chipotle peppers in a small bowl.
4. Sprinkle the chicken breasts on each side with sea salt and black pepper. Sprinkle the spice mixture on one side of each piece of chicken. Press it into the flesh with the heel of your hand.
5. Heat the olive oil over medium-high heat in a large skillet. When the oil is hot, carefully place the chicken breasts, spice side down, in the pan. Sear the breasts until a crust forms, approximately 3 minutes.
6. Turn the breasts. Divide the cheese among the breasts. Cook the breasts for 2–3 minutes more, or until they are cooked through.
7. Slice the rolls in half. Place a portion of chicken on each roll. Garnish with the sauce and serve at once.

🌿 Pan-Seared Chicken Breasts with Fried Leeks and a Tomato Chutney

PREPARATION:
40 MINUTES

COOKING:
10 MINUTES

YIELD:
4 MAIN-COURSE
SERVINGS

We love the sweet and savory flavor of an antioxidant-rich tomato chutney. It is the perfect garnish for chicken breasts. Quickly cooked fried leeks add a great texture and a wonderful sweet onion flavor to this dish.

Tips: As with all chutneys, this one can be prepared up to 3 days in advance and refrigerated. This is not only convenient but it allows the flavors to fully develop and intensify. Also, this recipe makes enough chutney for 2 meals. If you are not going to use the extra within a day or two, freeze it.

3 tablespoons canola oil
   1-inch piece gingerroot, peeled and finely chopped
3 cloves garlic, peeled and sliced
1 onion, peeled and diced
   Sea salt to taste
1 teaspoon dried basil
1 teaspoon cumin
½ teaspoon cinnamon
¼ cup balsamic vinegar
1 tablespoon Worcestershire sauce
2 tablespoons brown sugar
1 28-ounce can whole tomatoes in juice, chopped
   Black pepper to taste
2 boneless and skinless chicken breasts (1 ½ pounds), trimmed, halved, and pounded to ¼-inch thickness
3 medium leeks, trimmed, washed, and thinly sliced

1. To prepare the chutney, heat 1 tablespoon of the oil in a Dutch oven over medium heat. When the oil is hot, add the ginger and garlic. Cook until soft and fragrant. Add the onion and sprinkle with sea salt. Cook the onion until soft.

2. Add the basil, cumin, and cinnamon. Cook the ingredients for another minute. Add the vinegar, Worcestershire sauce, and sugar. Raise the heat to high.

3. Add the tomatoes. Bring the chutney to a boil. Reduce the heat. Simmer the chutney until thick, stirring occasionally, approximately 35 minutes. Season with sea salt and black pepper. Set aside for a moment.

4. Heat another tablespoon of the oil in a large skillet over medium-high heat. Sprinkle the chicken breasts on each side with sea salt and black pepper. When the oil is hot, carefully place the chicken in the pan. Sear on each side, turning once, 2 to 3 minutes on each side. Transfer to a plate. Set aside.

5. Heat the remaining tablespoon of oil in the skillet over medium-high heat. Add the leeks and sprinkle with sea salt. Cook until tender, stirring often, approximately 3 minutes.

6. Divide the leeks among 4 plates. Place a portion of chicken onto each bed of leeks. Top with the tomato chutney and serve at once.

🜲 Sesame-Crusted Chicken and Tofu with Carrots and Broccoli in a Thai Red Curry Sauce

PREPARATION:
25 MINUTES

COOKING:
15 MINUTES

YIELD:
4 MAIN-COURSE
SERVINGS

The neutral flavors of boneless and skinless chicken breasts and tofu make them ideal foods to combine with an assertive sauce. Here they are coated with sesame seeds, quickly stir-fried, and simmered with carrots and broccoli in an authentic-tasting Thai curry sauce.

At first glance, a restaurant-prepared Thai curry containing chicken and fresh vegetables seems like a nutritious meal. However, since it is often based on coconut milk, it is loaded with fat and calories. We make our curry with a combination of light coconut milk and chicken stock. It is just as intensely flavored but much more healthful. This curry is a great source of phytoestrogens, Vitamin C, and beta-carotene.

6	ounces light coconut milk
6	ounces chicken stock
1	teaspoon fish sauce
2	teaspoons Thai red curry paste
1	tablespoon brown sugar
⅓	cup fresh basil, snipped
	Sea salt to taste
2	tablespoons canola oil
1	pound extra-firm tofu
4	tablespoons unhulled sesame seeds
12	ounces boneless and skinless chicken breast, trimmed and sliced
1	cup water
4	carrots, scraped and sliced into ½-inch pieces
1	bunch broccoli, trimmed, stems sliced into discs and florets separated

1. To prepare the sauce, combine the coconut milk, chicken stock, and fish sauce in a bowl. Whisk in the curry paste and sugar. Stir in the basil. Season with sea salt. Set aside for a moment.

2. Heat 1 tablespoon of the oil in a wok over medium-high heat. Place the tofu on a kitchen towel. With the heel of your hand, gently press on the tofu to remove the excess moisture. Cube the tofu. Sprinkle the cubes with sea salt. Toss with 2 tablespoons of the sesame seeds.

3. When the oil is hot, carefully place the tofu into the pan. Sear until golden, tossing occasionally.

4. Drizzle the tofu with 3 tablespoons of the sauce. Cook for another minute. Transfer to a plate and set aside for a moment.

5. Heat the remaining tablespoon of oil in the wok over medium-high heat. Sprinkle the chicken strips with sea salt and the remaining 2 tablespoons of sesame seeds. When the oil is hot, carefully place the chicken strips in the pan. Sear until golden and cooked through, tossing occasionally, approximately 7 minutes. Transfer to a plate and set aside.

6. Bring the water to a boil in the wok. Add sea salt to the water, followed by the carrots. Cover the pot and steam the carrots for 3 minutes. Add the broccoli. Cover the pot and steam the broccoli until tender, approximately 3 minutes more. Drain the vegetables.

7. Pour the sauce into the wok. Bring to a boil. Add the chicken strips and simmer for 2 minutes. Stir in the vegetables. Simmer the curry for 2 minutes more.

8. Transfer the curry to a large platter. Garnish with the tofu and serve at once.

❧ Chicken Thighs Braised with Many Mushrooms

PREPARATION:
15 MINUTES

COOKING:
1 HOUR

YIELD:
4 MAIN-COURSE
SERVINGS

Unlike short ribs of beef, brisket, and veal shanks that require 3 hours of slow cooking to become tender, chicken legs and thighs are meltingly tender after only an hour. In this recipe, whole cloves of garlic, tomatoes, and portobello, shiitake and cremini mushrooms are braised with whole chicken legs to create a wonderfully rich sauce in a short period of time. The dish is a great source of Vitamin C and beta-carotene.

1	tablespoon olive oil
4	whole chicken legs
	Sea salt to taste
	Black pepper to taste
10	cloves garlic, peeled and trimmed
1	onion, peeled and sliced
1	pound portobello mushrooms, stems removed and discarded, caps wiped and thickly sliced
½	pound shiitake mushrooms, stems removed and discarded, caps wiped and halved
½	pound cremini mushrooms, wiped and quartered
1½	cups white wine
1	cup chicken stock
1	35-ounce can whole tomatoes in juice, chopped
1	cup fresh basil, snipped

1. Heat the olive oil in a large Dutch oven over medium-high heat. Sprinkle the chicken with sea salt and black pepper. Carefully place the chicken into the pot and sear on each side turning once. Transfer to a plate and set aside.
2. Reduce the heat to low. Add the garlic cloves to the pot. Cook until golden, turning occasionally. Add the onion and sprinkle with sea salt. Cook the onion until soft, stirring occasionally.
3. Raise the heat to medium. Add the mushrooms to the pot. Sprinkle with sea salt. Cook the mushrooms until soft, stirring occasionally.

4. Raise the heat to high. Add the wine and stock to the pot. Simmer the liquid for 2 minutes.
5. Add the tomatoes to the pot. Return the sauce to a boil. Reduce the heat to low. Simmer the chicken, uncovered, for 1 hour, stirring occasionally.
6. Stir the basil into the sauce. Season with sea salt and black pepper.
7. Divide the chicken among 4 plates and spoon the sauce onto each serving.

🌿 Chicken Thighs Braised with Tomatoes, Kidney Beans, and Pumpkin Seeds

Roasted pumpkin seeds are versatile. When used as a garnish, they add a delightful texture to a dish. In this antioxidant and fiber-rich recipe, we have pureed and combined them with kidney beans and tomatoes to create a flavorful braising liquid for chicken thighs.

Tips: *If all of the chicken thighs do not fit comfortably into your Dutch oven, sear them in two batches. Also, if using a blender to puree the sauce, it may be necessary to do so in two batches.*

PREPARATION:
15 MINUTES

COOKING:
1 HOUR

YIELD:
4 MAIN-COURSE
SERVINGS

1   tablespoon olive oil
8   bone-in chicken thighs, skin removed and discarded
    Sea salt to taste
    Black pepper to taste
4   cloves garlic, peeled and sliced
1   onion, peeled and diced
1   28-ounce can whole tomatoes in juice, chopped
1   cup toasted pumpkin seeds
1   15-ounce can red kidney beans, drained and rinsed

1. Heat the olive oil in a large Dutch oven over medium-high heat. Sprinkle the chicken thighs on each side with sea salt and black pepper.
2. When the oil is hot, carefully place the thighs into the pot.

Sear on each side, turning once. Transfer to a plate. Set aside for a moment.

3. Reduce the heat to low. Add the garlic to the pot. Cook until soft and fragrant. Add the onion and sprinkle with sea salt. Cook until soft, stirring often.

4. Raise the heat to high. Add the tomatoes and pumpkin seeds. Bring the sauce to a boil.

5. Carefully transfer the sauce to a blender or the work bowl of a food processor fitted with a metal blade and puree. Return to the Dutch oven.

6. Bring the sauce to a boil again. Stir in the beans. Return the chicken to the pot along with any accumulated juices from the plate they were resting on.

7. Cover the pot and reduce the heat to very low. Braise the chicken until tender, stirring occasionally, approximately 1 hour. To reduce the sauce, during the final 15 minutes of cooking remove the cover and raise the heat slightly.

8. Transfer the chicken and sauce to a large platter and serve at once.

❧ Chicken and Tofu Meatballs with Lentils, Tomatoes, and Four Spices

The French call a versatile blend of four warm spices quatre epices. *Although the proportion of spices can vary, the four most often included in the mix are cinnamon, nutmeg, cloves, and allspice. In French cooking, they are used to season pâtés and terrines, but they can also add a deep flavor to stews and sauces. In this recipe they season chicken and tofu meatballs. With an abundance of phytoestrogens, Vitamin C, and fiber, the meatballs and sauce provide great breast cancer preventing nutrition.*

Tip: *We love the texture and flavor of tiny French green lentils. If you cannot locate them, the common brown variety is a fine substitute.*

PREPARATION:
30 MINUTES

COOKING:
1 HOUR

YIELD:
8 MAIN-COURSE
SERVINGS

½ cup Homemade Bread Crumbs (page 263)
½ cup milk
3 tablespoons olive oil
6 cloves garlic, peeled and sliced
1 onion, peeled and diced
   Sea salt to taste
1½ teaspoons cinnamon
¼ teaspoon nutmeg
¼ teaspoon ground cloves
¼ teaspoon allspice
1 cup French lentils, sorted and rinsed
3 cups chicken stock
1 28-ounce can whole tomatoes in juice, chopped
1 pound ground chicken (if possible, a mix of white and dark meat)
1 pound extra-firm tofu, squeezed to remove excess moisture and crumbled
2 eggs
1 cup Romano cheese, grated
   Pepper to taste

1. Place the bread crumbs in a large bowl. Add the milk. Set the bowl aside for a moment.
2. Heat 1 tablespoon of olive oil in a large Dutch oven over low heat. Add the garlic and cook until soft and fragrant. Add the onion and sprinkle with sea salt. Cook the onion until soft, stirring occasionally.
3. Add the cinnamon, nutmeg, cloves, and allspice. Cook the spices for 1 minute. Transfer one-half of this mixture to the bowl with the bread crumbs. Set the bowl aside again.
4. Add the lentils to the Dutch oven. Raise the heat to high. Add the chicken stock and tomatoes. Bring the sauce to a boil. Reduce the heat to a simmer.
5. While the sauce is simmering, prepare the meatballs. Add the chicken, tofu, eggs, and cheese to the bowl with the bread crumb mixture. Season the mixture with sea salt and black pepper. With your hands, work the mixture until well combined.
6. Form the mixture into 24 tightly packed balls.
7. Heat another tablespoon of the olive oil in a skillet over medium-high heat. When the oil is hot, add 8 meatballs to the pan. Cook the meatballs until they are deep brown on all sides, turning occasionally, approximately 5 minutes. Add to the sauce. Repeat the procedure with the remaining oil and meatballs.
8. Simmer the meatballs in the sauce for 1 hour, stirring occasionally. Transfer the meatballs and sauce to a serving bowl. A great accompaniment to this meal is Israeli Couscous with Tomatoes and Basil (page 335).

HOMEMADE BREAD CRUMBS

We never toss away stale bread. We cube it and place it in a bowl and allow it to harden. In a day or two, all it takes is a couple of minutes in a food processor to make bread crumbs. We use the bread crumbs as a casserole topping, in meatballs and tofuballs, and to coat chicken breasts and fish fillets.

PREPARATION: 5 MINUTES

YIELD: 3 CUPS

6 cups stale bread cubes (preferably from a rustic loaf)
1 tablespoon dried basil
2 teaspoons dried oregano
Sea salt to taste
Black pepper to taste

1. Place the bread cubes, basil, and oregano in the work bowl of a food processor fitted with the metal blade.
2. Turn on the machine. Process the ingredients until bread crumbs are formed.
3. Transfer the bread crumbs to a plastic container. Season with sea salt and black pepper. Use immediately or cover the container and freeze.

🌿 Chicken Sausages with Shiitake Mushrooms and Onions

PREPARATION:
10 MINUTES

COOKING:
1 HOUR

YIELD:
4 MAIN-COURSE
SERVINGS

Chicken sausages are a healthful alternative to the traditional pork variety. They are leaner and just as flavorful. In this recipe we have braised them in an antioxidant-rich tomato sauce with plenty of sweet onions and earthy shiitake mushrooms. You can accompany them with pasta or, as we prefer, tuck them into a crusty baguette with melted provolone cheese.

1 tablespoon olive oil
1 pound sweet chicken sausages
6 cloves garlic, peeled and thinly sliced
2 large onions, peeled and thinly sliced
 Sea salt to taste
1 teaspoon dried basil
1 teaspoon dried oregano
½ teaspoon dried thyme
1 pound shiitake mushrooms, stems removed and discarded, caps sliced
1 28-ounce can whole tomatoes in juice, chopped
 Black pepper to taste

1. Heat the olive oil in a Dutch oven over medium-high heat. When the oil is hot, carefully place the sausages into the pot. Sear the sausages until golden, turning occasionally, approximately 5 minutes. Transfer to a plate. Set aside.
2. Reduce the heat to low. Add the garlic to the pot. Cook until soft and fragrant. Add the onions. Sprinkle with sea salt. Raise the heat slightly. Cook the onions until they begin to soften, stirring occasionally. Sprinkle with basil, oregano, and thyme.
3. Add the mushrooms to the pot. Cook the mushrooms until soft, stirring occasionally, approximately 5 minutes. Return the sausages to the pot. Cover the pot and cook the sausages for 5 minutes.
4. Raise the heat to high. Add the tomatoes to the pot. Bring the sauce to a boil. Reduce the heat and simmer the sauce for

40 minutes, stirring occasionally. Season with sea salt and black pepper.

5. Divide the sausages and sauce among 4 plates and serve at once.

❧ Quick Cassoulet of Chicken Sausages, Tomatoes, and Lentils

In French cuisine a cassoulet usually contains white beans and a variety of fresh and smoked meats. Our leaner, more healthful, and quick-cooking version contains chicken sausages, turkey bacon, and lentils. The dish is hearty and rich without being heavy and high in fat. It is an excellent source of Vitamin C, folic acid, and fiber.

PREPARATION:
15 MINUTES

COOKING:
1 HOUR

YIELD:
4 MAIN-COURSE
SERVINGS

CASSOULET

1 tablespoon olive oil
3 ounces turkey bacon, chopped
1 pound sweet chicken sausages
4 cloves garlic, peeled and sliced
1 onion, peeled and diced
Sea salt to taste
1½ cups red wine
1 cup chicken stock
⅔ cup lentils, sorted and rinsed
1 28-ounce can whole tomatoes in juice, chopped
Black pepper to taste

GARNISH

1 clove garlic, peeled
¼ cup fresh flat-leaf (Italian) parsley

1. Heat the olive oil in a large Dutch oven over medium heat. When the oil is hot, add the bacon. Render it until crisp, stirring often. With a slotted spoon, transfer the bacon to a plate. Set aside for a moment. Pour off all but 1 tablespoon of the drippings.

2. Raise the heat and add the sausages to the pot. Sear the sausages, turning 3 or 4 times. Transfer to the plate with the bacon.

3. Reduce the heat to low. Add the garlic to the pot. Cook until soft and fragrant. Add the onion and sprinkle with sea salt. Cook the onion until soft, stirring occasionally.

4. Raise the heat to high. Add the wine and stock to the pot. Simmer the liquid for 5 minutes. Add the lentils and tomatoes. Return the bacon and sausages to the pot.

5. Bring the cassoulet to a boil. Reduce the heat and simmer for 45 minutes, stirring occasionally. Season with sea salt and black pepper.

6. To prepare the garnish, mince together the garlic and parsley. Stir into the cassoulet. Divide the cassoulet among 4 large plates. If desired, accompany with rustic bread and egg noodles.

❧ Spicy Chicken and Tofu Quesadillas with Black Bean, Roasted Pepper, and Corn Salsa

PREPARATION:
20 MINUTES

COOKING:
10 MINUTES

YIELD:
6 MAIN-COURSE
SERVINGS

When we prepare quesadillas, we try to be creative and vary the salsas and fillings. One day we may prepare a tomato-based salsa and on another, a bean and fruit one. The fillings can range from butternut squash and tofu to tempeh and beef. In this recipe we have prepared a lively bean and corn salsa and a spicy chicken and tofu filling. Not only are these quesadillas delicious but they are also rich in breast cancer fighting phytoestrogens, Vitamin C, beta-carotene, fiber, and folic acid.

Tip: *The salsa can be prepared a day in advance and refrigerated.*

SALSA
1½ cups frozen corn, defrosted
1 15-ounce can black beans, drained and rinsed
1 12-ounce jar roasted red bell peppers, drained and chopped
1 onion, peeled and finely chopped

1 clove garlic, peeled and finely chopped
3 scallions, trimmed and thinly sliced
½ cup cilantro, chopped
  Juice of 1 lemon
  Sea salt to taste
  Black pepper to taste

CHICKEN AND TOFU FILLING
3 tablespoons canola oil
1 pound boneless and skinless chicken breast, trimmed
  and sliced
1 pound extra-firm tofu, cubed
1 tablespoon cumin
  Sea salt to taste
  Black pepper to taste
4 cloves garlic, peeled and thinly sliced
1 onion, peeled and diced
2 jalapeño peppers, cored, seeded, and finely chopped
4 plum tomatoes, cored and diced
3 scallions, trimmed and thinly sliced
½ cup cilantro, chopped

12 medium flour tortillas
6 ounces Monterey Jack cheese, grated or sliced

1. To prepare the salsa, combine the corn, beans, roasted peppers, onion, garlic, scallions, cilantro, and lemon juice in a large nonreactive bowl. Season the salsa with sea salt and black pepper. Set aside for a moment.
2. Preheat the oven to 375°F.
3. To prepare the chicken and tofu, heat 1 tablespoon of the oil in a wok over high heat. Combine the chicken and tofu in a large bowl. Sprinkle with cumin. Season the mixture with sea salt and black pepper.
4. When the oil is hot, add one-half of the mixture to the pan. Sear the ingredients, tossing them occasionally. Transfer to a bowl. Repeat the procedure with another tablespoon of oil and the remaining chicken and tofu.

5. Reduce the heat to medium. Add the remaining tablespoon of oil to the pan. Add the garlic. Cook for 30 seconds. Add the onion and jalapeños and sprinkle with sea salt. Cook the ingredients until soft.

6. Raise the heat to high. Add the tomatoes. Return the chicken and tofu mixture to the pan. Cook the ingredients for 3 minutes.

7. Stir in the scallions and cilantro. Season with sea salt and black pepper.

8. To assemble the quesadillas, place 6 of the flour tortillas on 1 large or 2 small baking trays. Divide the cheese among the tortillas. Divide the chicken-tofu mixture among the tortillas. Divide the salsa among the tortillas (there will be a bit leftover). Place one of the remaining tortillas on top of each one.

9. Place the trays in the oven. Bake the quesadillas until the cheese melts and the tortillas are heated through, approximately 8 minutes.

10. Remove the trays from the oven. Cut each quesadilla into quarters and serve at once.

🙖 Swiss Chard, Pine Nut, and Dried Tomato-Roasted Chicken

Many stuffed and roasted chicken recipes are based on butter and bread with only a small amount of vegetables. We have taken the opposite approach. Our stuffing is based on vegetables and stock. Homemade croutons are added to enhance its texture. With chard, dried tomatoes, and pine nuts, our roasted chicken is a great source of antioxidants.

Tip: *The recipe yields more than enough stuffing to fill the cavity of a 4-pound chicken. During the final 20 minutes of roasting, place the extra stuffing in an ovenproof casserole and bake it alongside the chicken.*

PREPARATION:
20 MINUTES

COOKING:
1 HOUR

YIELD:
4 MAIN-COURSE
SERVINGS

1	cup dried tomatoes
1⅓	cups boiling water
⅓	cup pine nuts
	Sea salt to taste
2	tablespoons olive oil
6	cloves garlic, peeled and sliced
1½	pounds Swiss chard, washed, trimmed, and chopped
	Tomato soaking water
4	cups Homemade Croutons (see page 271)
	Black pepper to taste
	One 3½- to 4-pound chicken
1	lemon

1. Place the tomatoes in a bowl. Pour the boiling water onto them. Allow them to soak until soft, approximately 10 minutes. Drain and reserve water. Chop and set aside.
2. While the tomatoes are soaking, place the pine nuts in a small skillet over low heat. Sprinkle with sea salt. Toast until golden, tossing often, approximately 5 minutes. Set aside.
3. Preheat the oven to 375°F.

4. Heat the olive oil in a Dutch oven over low heat. Add the garlic and cook until soft and fragrant. Raise the heat to high and add the chard. Sprinkle the chard with sea salt. Cover the pot and cook the chard until tender, approximately 7 minutes, stirring occasionally.

5. Reduce the heat to low. Stir in the dried tomato soaking water, croutons, and pine nuts. Season the mixture with sea salt and black pepper. Set aside for a moment while you refresh the chicken.

6. Rinse and thoroughly dry the chicken. Season with sea salt and black pepper. Squeeze the lemon into the cavity. Discard the lemon.

7. Loosely fill the cavity with the stuffing. Place the remaining stuffing in an ovenproof container to cook alongside the chicken.

8. Place the chicken on the middle rack of the oven, breast side up. Place a roasting pan on the rack below the chicken to catch any drippings. Roast the chicken until the juices run clear when the thigh is pierced or until an internal temperature of 180°F is reached in the thigh, approximately 1 hour.

9. After 30 minutes, place the container with the extra stuffing into the oven.

10. Remove the chicken from the oven, and allow to rest for 10 minutes before carving.

HOMEMADE CROUTONS

These croutons are wonderful in salads, soups, and as an ingredient in a stuffing for poultry or vegetables.

PREPARATION: 5 MINUTES

COOKING: 10 MINUTES

YIELD: 4 CUPS

1   16-inch-long loaf of rustic bread
3   cloves garlic, peeled
2   tablespoons olive oil
    Sea salt to taste
    Black pepper to taste

1. Preheat the oven to 400°F.
2. Cut the bread lengthwise in half. Rub the garlic cloves on the inside of the bread. Drizzle the inside of the bread with the olive oil. Sprinkle the inside of the bread with sea salt and black pepper.
3. Cut the bread into cubes and place on a tray. Transfer the tray to the oven. Bake the cubes until crisp, approximately 10 minutes.
4. Remove the tray from the oven and allow the croutons to cool.

Seafood

Many of us no longer consider seafood something only to be eaten in restaurants. The proliferation of great seafood cookbooks has taken the unknown out of seafood cooking and made it possible to create delectable ocean-fresh dishes in your own kitchen. Because overcooking and too many flavors tend to destroy the texture and distinctive taste of seafood, seafood recipes are naturally quick and simple to prepare. Roasting, pan frying, and grilling are the best techniques for seafood. Fruit and vegetable salsas, light wine–based sauces, seed and herb crusts, or simply a squeeze of lemon are all that are needed to enhance the clean and delicate flavor of seafood.

Seafood is health food. It is a lean protein source and rich in B vitamins, iron, and zinc. Most important, it is one of the richest sources of omega-3 fatty acids. Studies have indicated that omega-3 fatty acids play a critical role in the prevention of heart disease and breast cancer. Oily-fleshed fish, such as salmon, swordfish, tuna, striped bass, anchovies, and bluefish contain the largest quantities of omega-3's. These versatile fish are quick to prepare, are enhanced by a variety of seasonings, and, of course, make wonderful meals. Our Sesame-Crusted Salmon with Seasoned Chard is a great meal of crispy fish and Asian-seasoned Swiss chard. If you prize swordfish, as many of us do, delight in our bold-tasting Mustard-Crusted Swordfish on a Watercress and Tomato Salad. Both of these breast cancer preventing meals combine omega-3 fatty acid–rich fish with antioxidant-rich vegetables. Seafood soups are an ideal way to combine a variety of ocean treasures in one dish. Our Southwestern Swordfish and Clam Soup is a briny corn and tomato broth containing sweet clams and meaty swordfish—a real winner at the table and in the nutrition department.

Even seafood not usually considered rich sources of omega-3 fatty acids, such as scallops, shrimp, mussels, and lean whitefish, contain modest amounts. These types of seafood can be combined with antioxidant-rich ingredients to create delectable breast cancer preventing meals. Chile-Crusted Sea Scallops with Mango and Sweet Peppers is a unique combination of sweet and savory flavors. Haddock Baked with Tomatoes, Zucchini, Basil, and Feta features one of our most popular fish baked in a tomato-basil sauce and garnished with tangy feta cheese.

The next time you are craving seafood, don't make reservations—make one of these delicious recipes. It will be simple, quick, rewarding, and a great breast cancer preventing meal to boot.

❧ Sesame-Crusted Salmon with Seasoned Chard

When pan-fried with a squeeze of lemon, a piece of salmon makes a wonderful and simple meal. Salmon's rich taste is also complemented by earthy and bold flavors. In this recipe we have coated salmon fillets with sesame seeds, quickly pan-fried them, and served them on a bed of Asian-seasoned chard. This dish is a delightful combination of flavors and textures and is a great source of omega-3 fatty acids, Vitamin E, and beta-carotene.

PREPARATION:
10 MINUTES

COOKING:
15 MINUTES

YIELD:
4 MAIN-COURSE
SERVINGS

3	teaspoons canola oil
1½	pounds boneless and skinless salmon fillets, cut from the thick end, sliced into 4 portions
	Sea salt to taste
	Black pepper to taste
¼	cup hulled sesame seeds
2	teaspoons sesame oil
2	teaspoons tamari
1	teaspoon cider vinegar
1	teaspoon sugar
½	cup chicken stock or water
3	cloves garlic, peeled and sliced
1½	pounds Swiss chard, trimmed, washed, drained, leaves and stems separated and chopped

1. Preheat the oven to 400°F.
2. Heat 1 teaspoon of the canola oil in an ovenproof skillet over medium-high heat.
3. Season the salmon fillets on each side with sea salt and black pepper. Coat on each side with the sesame seeds.
4. When the oil is hot, carefully place the fillets into the pan. Sear for 2 minutes on each side or until the sesame seeds are golden, turning once.
5. Transfer the pan to the oven. Roast the fillets until just cooked through, approximately 5 minutes.

6. While the fish is in the oven, prepare the chard. Whisk together the sesame oil, tamari, vinegar, sugar, and stock. Set the sauce aside.

7. Heat the remaining 2 teaspoons of canola oil in a Dutch oven over low heat. Add the garlic and cook until soft and fragrant.

8. Raise the heat to high. Add the chard stems to the pot. Cook for 3 minutes, stirring often. Add the leaves and cover the pot. Cook the chard for 5 minutes or until tender, stirring occasionally.

9. Whisk the sauce. Add to the chard. Divide the chard and sauce among 4 plates. Place a fillet onto each portion of chard and serve at once.

SALMON

With its abundance of omega-3 fatty acids, rich flavor, and firm flesh, salmon makes for great eating. Because of overfishing and pollution, the supply of many species of fish is dwindling. With the explosion of aquaculture, fresh salmon is abundant and widely available. Although the flavor of farm-raised salmon pales in comparison to the wild fish, it is almost always fresh and the price is stable and reasonable. Nutritionally, farm-raised salmon is generally higher in fat than fish found in the wild. Also, since farmed salmon's feed contains omega-3's and beta-carotene, it generally contains a larger amount of these essential nutrients than a wild fish.

When choosing salmon, opt for the fillets. They are more versatile and, because they can be easily boned, make for a better meal. They can be pan-fried, baked, broiled, or steamed. Salsas, citrus sauces, leeks, garlic, seeds, and fresh and dried herbs complement salmon's richly flavored flesh.

The ideal cut of salmon is a 4-inch-wide piece sliced from the thickest part of the fillet. This portion will weigh approximately 6 ounces. The less desirable cuts hail from farther down the fillet. These portions are less uniform in thickness and easy to overcook.

❧ Herb-Crusted Salmon with Balsamic Vinegar and Olive Oil

PREPARATION:
5 MINUTES

COOKING:
15 MINUTES

YIELD:
4 MAIN-COURSE
SERVINGS

Dried herbs are an excellent coating for salmon. When they hit a hot pan, they crisp beautifully, forming a delicious crust. In this recipe we have chosen to leave the skin on the salmon. It will become cracker-crisp, adding great flavor and texture to the fish. A simple vinaigrette provides a burst of flavor. Salmon is one of the richest sources of omega-3 fatty acids.

Tip: *A great accompaniment to the salmon is Brown Rice with Turnip Greens and Fried Garlic (page 325).*

2 tablespoons excellent-quality balsamic vinegar
2 tablespoons plus 1 teaspoon olive oil
1½ pounds skin-on, boneless salmon fillet, cut from the thick end, sliced into 4 portions
Sea salt to taste
Black pepper to taste
1 tablespoon dried basil
1 tablespoon dried oregano
1 teaspoon dried thyme

1. To prepare the vinaigrette, whisk together the vinegar and 2 tablespoons of the olive oil. Set aside.
2. Heat the remaining teaspoon of olive oil in a skillet over medium-high heat. Season the salmon fillets on each side with sea salt and black pepper.
3. Combine the basil, oregano, and thyme on a plate. Place the fillets, skin side up, onto the plate and coat with the herbs. Gently press the herbs into the flesh.
4. When the oil is hot, carefully place the salmon pieces, skin side down, into the pan. Cook three-quarters of the way through, approximately 6 minutes. Turn and continue to cook until the herbs are crisp and the fish is cooked through, approximately 4 minutes.
5. Divide the salmon among 4 plates. Whisk the vinaigrette and spoon onto each portion.

🐟 Oven-Roasted Salmon with a Tomato-Caper Salsa

In this recipe a sweet and slightly salty salsa is the perfect comple-ment to the rich flavor of quickly roasted salmon fillets. The meal is rich in antioxidants and omega-3 fatty acids.

Tip: *The salsa can be prepared several hours in advance. Cover and leave at room temperature. This is not only convenient but the additional time allows the flavors to intensify.*

PREPARATION:
5 MINUTES

COOKING:
10 MINUTES

YIELD:
4 MAIN-COURSE
SERVINGS

4   plum tomatoes, diced
4   teaspoons capers, rinsed
1   tablespoon olive oil
1   tablespoon red wine vinegar
1   small clove garlic, crushed or minced
⅓   cup basil, snipped
    Black pepper to taste
1½ pounds boneless, skin-on salmon fillets, cut from the thick end, sliced into 4 portions
    Sea salt to taste
    Juice of 1 lemon

1. To prepare the salsa, combine the tomatoes, capers, olive oil, vinegar, garlic, and basil in a nonreactive bowl. Season the salsa with black pepper. Set aside for a moment while you prepare the salmon.
2. Preheat the oven to 450°F.
3. Place the salmon fillets on a heavy baking tray. Season with sea salt and black pepper. Drizzle with the lemon juice.
4. Place the tray in the oven. Roast the fillets until just cooked through, approximately 10 minutes.
5. Divide the salmon among 4 plates. Spoon an equal amount of the salsa onto each portion and serve at once.

❧ Salmon with Edamame and Scallions

A combination of finely chopped edamame and scallions is a unique and simple topping for salmon. The soybeans add a crunchy texture and sweet taste; the scallions a mild onion flavor. Salmon is rich in omega-3 fatty acids and edamame is an excellent source of phyto-estrogens.

Tip: *A fiber and beta-carotene-rich accompaniment to the salmon is Brown Rice with Carrots, Scallions, and Cilantro (page 326).*

PREPARATION:
10 MINUTES

COOKING:
15 MINUTES

YIELD:
4 MAIN-COURSE
SERVINGS

Sea salt to taste
2 cups frozen, shelled, and blanched edamame
4 scallions, trimmed and finely chopped
Black pepper to taste
1 tablespoon canola oil
1½ pounds boneless, skin-on salmon fillet, cut from the thick end, sliced into 4 portions

1. Bring a medium saucepan of water to a boil. Add sea salt to the water, followed by the edamame. Cook the edamame until tender, approximately 5 minutes. Drain. Transfer to a cutting board.
2. Finely chop the beans. Transfer to a bowl. Add the scallions. Season with sea salt and black pepper. Set aside for a moment.
3. Heat the canola oil in a large skillet over medium-high heat. Sprinkle the salmon fillets on each side with sea salt and black pepper.
4. When the oil is hot, carefully place the fillets, skin side down, into the pan. Cook three-quarters of the way through, approximately 6 minutes. Turn and continue to cook until cooked through, approximately 4 minutes.
5. Divide the salmon among 4 plates. Pour off all but 1 tablespoon of the accumulated pan drippings.
6. With the pan over high heat, add the edamame mixture. Cook until hot, approximately 1 minute, stirring constantly. Spoon the edamame onto each salmon fillet and serve at once.

🌿 Swordfish au Poivre

Steak au Poivre, the traditional French preparation in which a strip steak is coated with coarsely ground black pepper and pan-fried or grilled, also works well with swordfish. The intense peppery flavor of the crust complements the richness of the fish. Swordfish is an excellent source of breast cancer preventing omega-3 fatty acids.

PREPARATION:
5 MINUTES

COOKING:
10 MINUTES

YIELD:
4 MAIN-COURSE
SERVINGS

   1 tablespoon olive oil
1½ pounds swordfish, sliced into 4 portions
    Sea salt to taste
   4 tablespoons coarsely ground black pepper

1. Heat the olive oil in a skillet over medium-high heat.
2. Sprinkle the swordfish steaks on each side with sea salt. With your fingertips, press the pepper into the flesh of each side of the steaks.
3. When the oil is hot, carefully place the steaks into the pan. Cook for approximately 5 minutes on each side, or until just cooked through, turning once.
4. Divide the steaks among 4 plates and serve at once.

Southwestern Swordfish and Clam Stew

PREPARATION:
10 MINUTES

COOKING:
20 MINUTES

YIELD:
4 MAIN-COURSE
SERVINGS

Fish stews are a delicious way to enjoy a variety of seafood in one meal. This version contains dried chilis, cilantro, and corn, giving it a Southwestern flavor. During the initial testing, we only used swordfish and felt the broth lacked flavor. When we included clams in the recipe, their briny liquid proved to be just what the broth needed. This hearty stew is rich in omega-3 fatty acids, folic acid, and beta-carotene.

*   **Tip:** The sauce can be prepared a day in advance through step 4. The following day, bring the sauce to a boil and proceed with the recipe. This is not only convenient but also improves the flavor of the sauce.*

2 dried ancho chili peppers
1 cup boiling water
2 tablespoons canola oil
4 cloves garlic, peeled and finely chopped
1 onion, peeled and diced
   Sea salt to taste
1 stalk celery, finely chopped
1 carrot, scraped and finely chopped
2 cups dry white wine
1 28-ounce can whole tomatoes in juice, chopped
2 cups fresh or frozen (thawed) corn
½ cup cilantro, chopped
   Black pepper to taste
1¼ pounds swordfish, skin removed and discarded, flesh cut into 2-inch pieces
2 pounds mahogany clams, scrubbed

1. Place the chilis in a bowl. Pour the water over them. Soak until soft, approximately 10 minutes. Drain and discard the soaking water. Cut the peppers in half, remove the seeds, and discard. Finely chop the peppers. Set aside.

2. While the peppers are soaking, heat 1 tablespoon of the oil in a large Dutch oven over medium heat. Add the garlic and

cook for 30 seconds. Add the onion and sprinkle with sea salt. Cook until soft, stirring often.

3. Add the celery and carrot to the pot. Reduce the heat slightly and cook the ingredients until they begin to soften, stirring occasionally, approximately 5 minutes.

4. Raise the heat to high and add the chilis to the pot. Pour in 1 cup of the wine. Simmer the wine for 1 minute. Add the tomatoes. Bring the sauce to a boil. Reduce the heat and simmer for 15 minutes, stirring occasionally.

5. Add the corn and cilantro to the sauce. Season with black pepper.

6. Heat the remaining tablespoon of oil in a skillet over medium-high heat. Sprinkle the swordfish pieces with sea salt and black pepper. When the oil is hot, carefully place into the pan. Sear, turning once. Transfer to the sauce.

7. Raise the heat to high under the skillet. Add the remaining cup of wine to the skillet. When it boils, carefully place the clams into the pan. Cover the pan. Steam the clams until open, approximately 3 minutes.

8. Transfer the clams to the Dutch oven. Stir the soup. Divide the soup among 4 large bowls and serve at once.

MAHOGANY CLAMS

Until two or three years ago, when you wanted clams, your choices were limited. If you wanted to eat raw clams, you chose cherrystones. If you wanted to cook clams, either to serve alone or in stew or pasta sauce, you chose steamers or littlenecks.

There are now more choices. Clams are coming from every coast. Some of the finest are the mahogany clams harvested in the deep and cold waters off the coast of Maine. Named for their striking color, they are the ideal clam to use in a sauce or soup. They are a briny and quick-cooking, hard-shelled clam approximately the size of a littleneck. When purchasing clams, to be certain they are alive, choose those with tightly closed shells that are free of cracks and blemishes.

🐛 Mustard-Crusted Swordfish on a Watercress and Tomato Salad

PREPARATION:
10 MINUTES

COOKING:
10 MINUTES

YIELD:
4 MAIN-COURSE
SERVINGS

Watercress is most often used as a garnish for sandwiches or combined with mild-flavored greens in a salad. On its own, however, its peppery and assertive flavor complements rich foods. In this recipe a lightly seasoned cress and tomato salad serves as a bed for pan-seared swordfish. Cress is a great source of beta-carotene and Vitamin C. Swordfish is rich in omega-3 fatty acids.

Tips: *After you remove the fish from the pan, crisp bits of the coating will remain. This can be spooned onto each portion. Also, for a slightly different flavor and texture, the swordfish can be grilled.*

1	tablespoon Dijon mustard
1	tablespoon whole grain mustard
1	tablespoon lemon juice
1½	pounds swordfish, cut into 4 steaks
	Sea salt to taste
	Black pepper to taste
2	bunches watercress, trimmed, washed, chopped, and spun dry
½	pint red cherry tomatoes, halved
1	tablespoon olive oil
1	tablespoon top-quality balsamic vinegar

1. Heat a skillet over medium-high heat.
2. In a bowl, whisk together the Dijon and whole grain mustards and lemon juice. Set the mixture aside for a moment.
3. Sprinkle the steaks on each side with sea salt and black pepper. Spread the mustard mixture onto each side of the steaks.
4. Place the steaks into the pan. Cook until a crust forms, approximately 5 minutes. Turn and cook until just cooked through, approximately 5 minutes more. Remove the pan from the heat.

5. Place the watercress and tomatoes in a bowl. Sprinkle with sea salt and black pepper. Drizzle with the olive oil and vinegar and toss thoroughly.
6. Divide the salad among 4 plates. Place a swordfish steak onto each portion of salad and serve at once.

✤ Mussels with Tomatoes and Basil

Whether you serve them as a first course or as a main dish, sweet-tasting mussels make for great eating. They require few other ingredients to create a memorable dish. In this quick and easy preparation, their briny liquid flavors an antioxidant-rich tomato and basil sauce. Serve plenty of rustic bread to soak up all of the wonderful juices. Mussels are a good source of omega-3 fatty acids.

PREPARATION:
10 MINUTES

COOKING:
10 MINUTES

YIELD:
4 SIDE-DISH
SERVINGS

1 tablespoon olive oil
4 cloves garlic, peeled and thinly sliced
1 cup dry white wine
1 28-ounce can whole tomatoes in juice, drained and chopped
Sea salt to taste
Black pepper to taste
2 pounds fresh mussels, scrubbed and debearded
⅓ cup fresh basil, snipped

1. Heat the olive oil in a large Dutch oven over high heat. When the oil is hot, add the garlic and cook for 30 seconds.
2. Add the wine. Simmer for 1 minute.
3. Add the tomatoes. Bring the sauce to a boil. Reduce the heat and simmer for 5 minutes. Season with sea salt and black pepper.
4. Raise the heat to high. Add the mussels. Cover the pot. Steam the mussels until open, approximately 6 minutes, shaking the pan occasionally.
5. Stir in the basil. Divide the mussels among 4 large bowls and serve at once.

MUSSELS

In our house, May is mussel month; we eat them as often as possible. Since mussels spawn in June, during May they gorge themselves on algae to build their energy stores. Mussels in May are fat, juicy, and briny.

The majority of mussels in today's markets are farm raised on ropes in the cold waters off the coast of Prince Edward Island. Unlike their counterparts in the wild, they are clean and almost always grit-free. Their one drawback, though, is that they lack the complex flavor and character of wild mussels.

When buying mussels look for shiny black and blue shells that are free of cracks and blemishes. They should smell of the sea and be tightly closed. If they are gaping a bit, tap them with your finger. They should close. If they don't, they are either past their prime or dead.

Steaming mussels is the best method of cooking. Start with a bit of olive oil, and then add an aromatic such as garlic, shallots, scallions, or leeks. Pour in a cup of wine, add the mussels, and cover the pot. Steam the mussels until open. Finish with a fresh herb such as parsley, basil, or cilantro. The wine and the wonderful briny liquid from the open mussels will create a delectable sauce. The mussels can be served with pasta as a main dish or accompanied with bread for a first course.

❧ Chile-Crusted Sea Scallops with Mango and Sweet Peppers

In this recipe we have dusted sea scallops with a heady combination of spices, pan-seared them, and accompanied them with a smooth and sweet-tasting mango sauce. There are plenty of flavors and textures dancing around in your mouth in every forkful. With a velvety sauce containing silken tofu, mango, and red bell peppers, the dish is rich in phytoestrogens, beta-carotene, and Vitamin C.

Tip: *You will only need half the mango puree for this recipe. The extra makes a great romaine lettuce salad dressing.*

PREPARATION:
10 MINUTES

COOKING:
10 MINUTES

YIELD:
4 MAIN-COURSE
SERVINGS

- 1   mango, peeled, pitted, and chopped
- 4   ounces silken tofu
- 1   tablespoon rice wine vinegar
- 2   teaspoons chile powder
- 1   teaspoon cumin
- 1   teaspoon sugar
- ½   teaspoon coriander
- ¼   teaspoon nutmeg
- 1¼ pounds sea scallops, small muscle on side removed and discarded
     Sea salt to taste
     Black pepper to taste
- 2   tablespoons canola oil
- 1   small red bell pepper, cored and diced
- 1½ cups fish or chicken broth
- 2   scallions, trimmed and sliced

1. Combine the mango, tofu, and rice wine vinegar in a blender or the work bowl of a food processor fitted with the metal blade and puree. Set the sauce aside for a moment.
2. Combine the chile powder, cumin, sugar, coriander, and nutmeg in a small bowl. Set the mixture aside for a moment.
3. Thoroughly dry the scallops. Place in a bowl. Sprinkle with sea salt and black pepper. Sprinkle with the spice mixture. Toss thoroughly to coat with the spices.
4. Heat 1 tablespoon of the canola oil in a large skillet over

medium-high heat. When the oil is hot, carefully place the scallops into the pan. Sear on each side until a crust forms, 1–2 minutes, turning once. Transfer to a plate. Set aside while you finish the sauce.

5. Heat the remaining tablespoon of oil in the skillet over medium heat. When the oil is hot, add the bell pepper. Cook until it begins to soften, stirring often. Raise the heat to high. Add the broth. Bring to a boil. Cook the broth for 2 minutes.

6. Reduce the heat to low. Stir in the scallions and approximately one-half of the mango puree. Heat the sauce for 1 minute.

7. Spoon the sauce onto 4 plates. Divide the scallops among the plates and serve at once.

🎋 Haddock Baked with Tomatoes, Zucchini, Basil, and Feta

PREPARATION:
15 MINUTES

COOKING:
30 MINUTES

YIELD:
6 MAIN-COURSE
SERVINGS

Haddock is a versatile fish. It can be baked, broiled, and pan- or deep-fried. Its neutral flavor adapts well to a variety of seasonings. Although haddock is not particularly rich in omega-3 fatty acids, by combining it with beta-carotene–rich zucchini and tomatoes, we have created a delectable breast cancer preventing meal.

Tips: *The zucchini and tomato sauce makes a quick pasta sauce on its own. Also, to be certain that the fish cooks evenly, fold the tail sections under each fillet.*

1½ cups Homemade Bread Crumbs (page 263)
3 tablespoons olive oil
4 cloves garlic, peeled and thinly sliced
1 onion, peeled and sliced
  Sea salt to taste
3 medium zucchini, cut into 1-inch pieces

1 28-ounce can whole tomatoes in juice, drained and
    chopped
2½ pounds haddock fillet, skinned
    Black pepper to taste
1 cup fresh basil, snipped
4 ounces sheep's milk feta, sliced

1. Place the bread crumbs in a bowl. Combine with 2 table-
    spoons of the olive oil. Set aside for a moment.
2. Preheat the oven to 425°F.
3. Heat the remaining tablespoon of olive oil in a Dutch oven
    over medium heat. When the oil is hot, add the garlic. Cook
    for 30 seconds. Add the onion and sprinkle with sea salt.
    Cook the onion until soft.
4. Add the zucchini. Cook the zucchini until it begins to
    soften, stirring often, approximately 5 minutes.
5. Raise the heat to high. Add the tomatoes. Cook the sauce for
    5 minutes, stirring occasionally. Season with sea salt and black
    pepper.
6. Spoon one-half of the sauce onto the bottom of an 8- by 8-
    inch ovenproof casserole dish. Place the fish into the casse-
    role, folding the tail portions under. Scatter the basil and feta
    onto the fish. Add the remaining sauce. Scatter the bread
    crumbs on top.
7. Transfer the casserole to the oven. Bake the fish until the
    sauce bubbles, approximately 25 minutes. Turn on the
    broiler and cook the fish until the topping crisps, approxi-
    mately 5 minutes.
8. Remove the casserole from the oven. Divide the fish among
    6 plates and serve at once.

❧ Ragu of Sea Scallops, Edamame, Tomatoes, and Corn

PREPARATION:
10 MINUTES

COOKING:
20 MINUTES

YIELD:
4 MAIN-COURSE
SERVINGS

In Italian cooking, a classic ragu is a slow-cooked tomato and meat-based dish. We have prepared a quick-cooking version starring sea scallops and edamame. We love to make it during the height of tomato and corn season to take advantage of the sweet flavors of these prized summertime treats. During other times of the year, top-quality canned tomatoes and frozen corn are fine substitutes. The dish is rich in phytoestrogens, folic acid, and Vitamin C.

Tip: Frozen sea scallops are one seafood that we feel retain their just-harvested quality. Be certain the package only contains sea scallops. They should not be processed or injected with any substances to increase their weight or retain their freshness.

2 tablespoons olive oil
1½ pounds fresh or frozen sea scallops, attached muscle removed, rinsed and dried
  Sea salt to taste
  Black pepper to taste
4 cloves garlic, peeled and thinly sliced
1 leek, trimmed, washed, and thinly sliced
1 cup shelled, frozen, and blanched edamame
2 ripe tomatoes, cored and diced
1 cup clam juice or chicken or fish stock
2 ears fresh corn, kernels removed
½ cup cilantro, chopped

1. Heat 1 tablespoon of olive oil in a wok over medium-high heat. Sprinkle the scallops with sea salt and black pepper. When the oil is hot, carefully place into the pan. Sear until golden on each side, 1–2 minutes, turning once. Transfer to a plate. Set aside for a moment.
2. Heat the remaining tablespoon of olive oil in the wok over medium heat. When the oil is hot, add the garlic. Cook for 30 seconds. Add the leek and sprinkle with sea salt. Cook the leek until it begins to soften, stirring occasionally.
3. Add the edamame, tomatoes, and clam juice or stock. Bring

the ragu to a boil. Reduce the heat. Simmer for 10 minutes, stirring occasionally.

4. Add the corn. Return the scallops to the pot along with any accumulated juices. Cook the ragu for another minute. Remove the pan from the heat. Stir in the cilantro. Season the ragu with sea salt and black pepper. Divide among 4 large bowls and serve at once.

❧ Roasted Striped Bass with Tomatoes and Fresh Corn Relish

Until recently, pollution and overfishing had nearly destroyed the wild striped bass population. Fortunately, because of tighter regulations, the species is making a tremendous comeback. With its firm and slightly sweet flesh, we consider wild striped bass to be the best eating fish of all. We have combined this wonderful fish with the tastes of summer to create a simple yet elegant meal. Nutritionally, striped bass is a great source of omega-3 fatty acids. Tomatoes and red bell peppers are rich in Vitamin C and beta-carotene.

PREPARATION:
15 MINUTES

COOKING:
10 MINUTES

YIELD:
4 MAIN-COURSE
SERVINGS

FRESH CORN RELISH
1 tablespoon olive oil
2 cloves garlic, peeled and thinly sliced
1 small red bell pepper, cored and diced
3 ears fresh corn, kernels removed
3 scallions, trimmed and thinly sliced
½ cup cilantro, chopped
  Juice of 2 limes
  Sea salt to taste
  Black pepper to taste

FISH AND TOMATOES
1 tablespoon olive oil
4 6-ounce boneless striped bass fillets with skin intact
  Sea salt to taste
  Black pepper to taste
3 large ripe tomatoes, cored and sliced

1. Preheat the oven to 500°F.
2. To prepare the relish, heat the olive oil in a large and oven-proof skillet over high heat. When the oil is hot, add the garlic. Cook for 30 seconds.
3. Add the red bell pepper. Cook for 1 minute, stirring constantly. Add the corn. Cook the ingredients for 5 minutes, stirring often.
4. Add the scallions, cilantro, and lime juice. Remove the pan from the heat. Season the relish with sea salt and black pepper. Transfer to a bowl. Set aside for a moment while you prepare the fish.
5. To prepare the fish, heat the olive oil in a skillet over high heat. Sprinkle the fillets on each side with sea salt and black pepper. When the oil is hot, carefully place the fillets in the pan, skin side down.
6. Cook the fish until the skin is deep brown, approximately 2 minutes. Transfer the pan to the oven. Roast the fish until just cooked through, approximately 5 minutes.
7. Divide the tomato slices among 4 plates, arranging them like a bed. Place a fillet onto each portion of tomatoes. Spoon the relish onto each piece of fish and serve at once.

❧ Aaron's Spicy Seared Shrimp with Mango, Lime, and Cilantro

Our brother-in-law Aaron Park gave us the idea for this recipe. He served it to Vince's sister Juliet when she was pregnant and craving spicy foods. The versatility of mangoes is evident here. Their sweetness pairs wonderfully with the briny shrimp and spicy jalapeño. Shrimp is a good source of omega-3 fatty acids; the mango provides plenty of beta-carotene.

Tip: *Although not as rich in omega-3 fatty acids, sea scallops can be substituted for the shrimp.*

PREPARATION:
15 MINUTES

COOKING:
5 MINUTES

MARINATING:
2 HOURS

YIELD:
4 MAIN-COURSE
SERVINGS

1   mango, peeled, pitted, and diced small
1   jalapeño pepper, seeded and finely chopped
3   scallions, trimmed and very thinly sliced
1   small clove garlic, peeled and finely chopped
⅓ cup cilantro, chopped
    Juice of 1½ limes
1   tablespoon olive oil
    Sea salt to taste
    Black pepper to taste
1   tablespoon canola oil
1½ pounds large shrimp, peeled and deveined

1. In a nonreactive serving bowl, combine the mango, jalapeño pepper, scallions, garlic, cilantro, lime juice, and olive oil. Toss the ingredients thoroughly. Season with sea salt and black pepper. Set aside for a moment.
2. Heat the canola oil in a large skillet over medium-high heat. Season the shrimp with sea salt and black pepper.
3. When the oil is hot, carefully add the shrimp. Cook the shrimp only until they turn pink, tossing constantly. Transfer to the serving bowl. Toss the ingredients thoroughly.
4. Cover the bowl. Allow the shrimp to marinate for 2 hours. Prior to serving, stir the ingredients.

❧ Shrimp and Israeli Couscous with Spinach and Pine Nuts

Shrimp cook quickly, making them an ideal choice for a weekday dinner. Their mild and slightly sweet flavor combines well with earthy spinach and sweet tomatoes in this recipe. This mixture is spooned onto Israeli couscous to create a memorable meal. Lean shrimp are a surprisingly good source of omega-3s. Spinach and tomatoes are excellent sources of beta-carotene and Vitamin C, and pine nuts are a good source of Vitamin E.

PREPARATION:
15 MINUTES

COOKING:
15 MINUTES

YIELD:
6 MAIN-COURSE
SERVINGS

COUSCOUS
3½ cups chicken stock
    Sea salt to taste
2½ cups Israeli couscous

SHRIMP
⅓ cup pine nuts
    Sea salt to taste
1 tablespoon olive oil
3 cloves garlic, peeled and thinly sliced
2 medium shallots, peeled and chopped
1 cup chicken stock
1 tablespoon unsalted butter
1½ pounds fresh spinach, trimmed, washed, drained, and chopped
1 15-ounce can diced tomatoes, drained
1½ pounds large shrimp, peeled and deveined
    Black pepper to taste

1. To prepare the couscous, bring the chicken stock to a boil in a medium-sized Dutch oven. Add sea salt to the stock. Stir in the couscous. Return the stock to a boil. Boil the couscous for 2 minutes. Turn off the heat. Cover the pot. Steam the couscous until all of the liquid has been absorbed, approximately 10 minutes.

2. While the couscous is steaming, prepare the shrimp. Place the pine nuts in a small skillet over low heat. Sprinkle with

sea salt. Toast until golden, tossing occasionally, approximately 10 minutes.

3. While the pine nuts are toasting, heat the olive oil in a Dutch oven over low heat. When the oil is warm, add the garlic. Cook until soft and fragrant. Raise the heat slightly. Add the shallots. Sprinkle with sea salt. Cook the shallots until soft, stirring occasionally.

4. Raise the heat to high. Add the chicken stock and butter to the pot. Bring the liquid to a boil. Add the spinach. Cook the spinach until wilted, stirring constantly, 2–3 minutes.

5. Stir in the tomatoes and shrimp. Cook the shrimp only until they turn pink, 2–3 minutes, stirring often. Remove the pot from the heat. Season with sea salt and black pepper.

6. To serve, divide the couscous among 6 shallow bowls. Divide the shrimp and spinach among the bowls. Garnish each portion with the pine nuts and serve at once.

🦎 Bluefish with Fried Leeks and Fresh Tomatoes

PREPARATION:

15 MINUTES

COOKING:

10 MINUTES

YIELD:

4 MAIN-COURSE SERVINGS

Bluefish, one of the world's best sport fish, are a great source of omega-3 fatty acids. Once caught, it is critical that bluefish be filleted immediately. Their abundant oil content makes them turn rancid quickly. If cared for properly, bluefish make wonderful eating. They can be baked, grilled, or pan-fried. Acidic sauces complement their distinctive flavor.

Tips: *If fresh tomatoes are not available, substitute an equal amount of top-quality canned plum tomatoes. Also, for the best flavor, prepare the sauce several hours in advance and leave at room temperature. Tuna, swordfish, or salmon can be substituted for the bluefish.*

TOMATO SAUCE

- 4 medium ripe tomatoes, peeled, seeded, and chopped
- 1 tablespoon olive oil
- ½ cup fresh basil, snipped
- 1 small clove garlic, peeled and finely chopped
  Sea salt to taste
  Black pepper to taste

FISH AND LEEKS

- 4 teaspoons canola oil
- 1½ pounds boneless and skinless bluefish fillets, sliced into 4 portions
  Sea salt to taste
  Black pepper to taste
- 4 leeks, trimmed, cleaned, and thinly sliced

1. To prepare the sauce, combine the tomatoes, olive oil, basil, and garlic in a nonreactive bowl. Season with sea salt and black pepper. Set aside while you prepare the fish and leeks.
2. Heat 2 teaspoons of the canola oil in a large skillet over medium-high heat. Sprinkle the fish on each side with sea salt and black pepper.

3. When the oil is hot, carefully place the fish into the pan. Sear the fillets on each side until a crust forms, 3–4 minutes, turning once. Reduce the heat and finish cooking, turning occasionally. Remove the fish from the pan and keep warm.
4. Heat the remaining 2 teaspoons of oil in the skillet over high heat. When the oil is hot, add the leeks. Sprinkle with sea salt. Cook the leeks until wilted, stirring constantly.
5. Divide the leeks among 4 plates. Place a piece of fish onto each portion of leeks. Top each fillet with the tomato sauce and serve at once.

CHAPTER 17

Beef

You may believe that since you have committed to following a breast cancer prevention diet, you will have to eliminate beef from your meals. This is not the case. Although we are proponents of a diet rich in fruits, vegetables, grains, beans, soy, and lean protein sources, there is absolutely nothing wrong with an occasional beef-based meal. It is important though, that when you do indulge, you are conscious of portion size and combine the beef with soy or antioxidant-rich vegetables. We have created quick-cooking steak recipes, braised beef dishes, and even meatballs that contain an abundance of breast cancer preventing nutrients.

Quickly prepared meals such as Pan-Fried Steak with Goat Cheese and Broccoli Rabe and Pan-Fried Steak with Tomatoes, Wilted Greens, and Mozzarella will delight your taste buds and provide your body with healthful doses of antioxidants. For those times you are craving a hearty and comforting beef meal, try our Short Ribs of Beef Braised with White Beans, Shiitake

Mushrooms, and Tomatoes. It combines fork-tender meat with a sauce rich in fiber and antioxidants. Meatballs are one of everyone's favorite meals. When you prepare them next, try Mike's Family Meatballs. The meatballs are a delightful combination of boldly seasoned lean beef and tofu that are simmered in an herbed tomato sauce. Who would have imagined that meatballs could be an estrogenic feast?

With our recipes you will be able to enjoy beef and still reap the benefits of a breast cancer prevention diet.

❧ Pan-Fried Steak with Goat Cheese and Broccoli Rabe

A pan-fried steak is a quick and deceptively rich meal. In this recipe we serve the steak on a bed of antioxidant-rich broccoli rabe. A quick and delicious sauce is made in the pan while the steak rests. A dab of goat cheese is the perfect garnish. Its creamy texture and tangy flavor complement the garlicky rabe and rich meat wonderfully.

Tip: A cast-iron skillet is the best cooking vessel for this recipe. It produces a moist steak with a wonderful crust. Also, this is a messy recipe. Keep the kitchen fans on high and use a splatter screen if you have one.

PREPARATION:
10 MINUTES

COOKING:
20 MINUTES

YIELD:
2 MAIN-COURSE
SERVINGS

STEAK
1 12- to 14-ounce New York strip or Delmonico steak
   Sea salt to taste
   Black pepper to taste
1 tablespoon olive oil
1 ounce goat cheese, at room temperature
1 cup red wine
1 tablespoon unsalted butter

BROCCOLI RABE
1 tablespoon olive oil
2 cloves garlic, peeled and sliced
1 pound broccoli rabe, trimmed and chopped
½ cup water
   Sea salt to taste
   Black pepper to taste

1. Heat a cast-iron skillet over medium-high heat for 5 minutes. Season the steak with sea salt and black pepper.
2. Add the olive oil to the pan. When it is hot, carefully place the steak into the pan. Cook the steak for 5 minutes. Turn and cook for 5 minutes more for a medium steak. If you prefer your steak more well done, reduce the heat and cook several minutes longer.

3. Remove the steak from pan. Top with the goat cheese. Allow to rest while you prepare the sauce and rabe.

4. Add the wine and butter to the pan to deglaze it. With a spoon, scrape the bottom of the pan to dissolve any particles. Simmer the sauce for 2 minutes. Season with sea salt and black pepper. Keep it warm while you prepare the rabe.

5. To cook the rabe, heat the olive oil in a Dutch oven over medium heat. When the oil is hot, add the garlic. Cook for 30 seconds.

6. Raise the heat to high. Add the rabe to the pot, followed by the water. Cook the rabe until tender, approximately 5 minutes, tossing 2 or 3 times. Season the rabe with sea salt and black pepper.

7. To serve, divide the rabe among 2 plates. Cut the steak in half and place a piece onto each portion of rabe. Divide the sauce and any accumulated juices from the plate the steak was resting on among the steaks and serve immediately.

❧ Pan-Fried Steak with Tomatoes, Wilted Greens, and Mozzarella

PREPARATION:
10 MINUTES

COOKING:
15 MINUTES

YIELD:
4 MAIN-COURSE
SERVINGS

Top-quality steaks like New York strip and Delmonico are ideal for a quick dinner. Unlike tougher cuts of beef that require several hours of braising to become edible, these steaks require just several minutes in a pan or on the grill to become juicy and tender. Cooking them in a hot skillet is our favorite technique. A quick sauce of tomatoes and onions and a bed of wilted greens transforms the steaks into a delectable meal rich in antioxidants.

2 tablespoons olive oil
2 1-inch-thick strip steaks (approximately 12 ounces each)
  Sea salt to taste
  Black pepper to taste
1 onion, peeled and thinly sliced
3 ripe tomatoes or 4 tomatoes from a can, diced
⅓ cup fresh flat-leaf (Italian) parsley, chopped
4 ounces fresh mozzarella cheese, sliced
2 cloves garlic, peeled, and thinly sliced
½ pound spinach, trimmed, washed, drained, and chopped
1 large bunch arugula, trimmed, washed, drained, and chopped

1. Heat 1 tablespoon of the olive oil in a large skillet over medium-high heat.
2. Lay the steaks on a cutting board. With a thin and long-bladed knife, slice the steaks in half lengthwise. You now have four ½-inch-thick steaks.
3. Sprinkle the steaks on each side with sea salt and black pepper. When the oil is hot, carefully place them into the pan. Sear on each side for 3 minutes, turning once. Transfer to a plate. Set aside for a moment.
4. Reduce the heat to medium. Add the remaining tablespoon of oil to the pan. When the oil is hot, add the onion to the pan and sprinkle with sea salt. Cook the onion until soft, stir-

ring often. Raise the heat to high. Add the tomatoes. Cook the tomatoes for 5 minutes, stirring occasionally. Season with sea salt and black pepper.

5. Add the parsley. Return the steaks to the pan along with any accumulated juices. Divide the mozzarella among the 4 steaks. Cover the pan and remove from the heat.

6. Heat the remaining olive oil in a wok over high heat. When the oil is hot, add the garlic. Cook the garlic for 10 seconds. Add the spinach and arugula. Cook until wilted, stirring constantly, approximately 2 minutes. Season with sea salt and black pepper.

7. Divide the greens among 4 plates. Place a steak onto each portion of greens. Divide the sauce among the steaks and serve at once.

❧ Short Ribs of Beef Braised with White Beans, Shiitake Mushrooms, and Tomatoes

BEAN SOAKING:
12 HOURS

PREPARATION:
15 MINUTES

COOKING:
4 HOURS

YIELD:
4 MAIN-COURSE
SERVINGS

When we make this meal, Hope says that I'm the only person she knows who prepares dinner before breakfast; there is a reason for such an early start. Short ribs require a long braise to become meltingly tender. Although the dish can be assembled in 15 minutes, it requires 4 hours of slow cooking. Fortunately, you need to pay little attention during braising—just a stir now and then. The delicious sauce is a great source of antioxidants and fiber.

Tips: *During step 6 (stovetop simmering), the fat will float to the surface making it easy to skim. A terrific and phytoestrogen-rich accompaniment to the short ribs is Soy Polenta (page 336).*

SHORT RIBS
  1 cup white beans
  1 tablespoon olive oil
  4 bone-in short ribs of beef, approximately 3 ¼ pounds
     Sea salt to taste
     Black pepper to taste
  5 cloves garlic, peeled and sliced
  1 onion, peeled and diced
 12 ounces shiitake mushrooms, wiped, stems removed and discarded, caps halved
  2 cups red wine
  1 cup chicken stock
  1 35-ounce can whole tomatoes in juice, chopped

GARNISH
  1 clove garlic, peeled
  ⅓ cup flat-leaf (Italian) parsley

1. The evening prior to preparing the ribs, sort and rinse the beans. Cover with cold water and soak for 12 hours.
2. Preheat the oven to 275° F.

3. Heat the olive oil in a large Dutch oven over medium-high heat. Sprinkle the short ribs on all sides with sea salt and black pepper. When the oil is hot, place the meat into the pot. Sear the meat until a deep brown crust forms on all sides, turning 3 or 4 times. Transfer the meat to a plate. Set aside.

4. Reduce the heat to low. Add the garlic to the pot and cook until soft and fragrant. Add the onion and cook until soft.

5. Raise the heat to medium and add the mushrooms to the pot. Cook until soft, stirring occasionally.

6. Raise the heat to high. Add the wine and stock. Simmer the liquid for 5 minutes.

7. Stir in the tomatoes and beans. Return the short ribs to the pot. Bring the sauce to a boil. Reduce the heat and cover the pot. Place the pot in the oven. Braise the ribs for 3 ½ hours, stirring 3 or 4 times.

8. Remove the pot from the oven. Place on the stovetop over medium-low heat. Remove the ribs from the pot and keep warm. Simmer the sauce uncovered for 15 minutes. Skim the surface to remove the fat.

9. Season the sauce with sea salt and black pepper. Prepare the garnish by mincing the garlic and parsley together. Stir the garnish into the sauce.

10. Divide the short ribs among 4 plates. Spoon the sauce onto each portion and serve at once.

❧ Cabbage Rolls with Tofu and Beef

PREPARATION:
30 MINUTES

COOKING:
1 1/2 HOURS

YIELD:
6 MAIN-COURSE
SERVINGS

When developing recipes, it is fun to rework a meal from your child-hood and make it more healthful and creative. Although our mother's meat-filled cabbage rolls were tasty and nutritious, by alter-ing the recipe and adding tofu and carrots to the filling and brais-ing them in a tomato-rich broth, we were able to make them rich in antioxidants and phytoestrogens.

CABBAGE ROLLS
  1 medium green cabbage
     Sea salt to taste
  1 tablespoon olive oil
  3 cloves garlic, peeled and sliced
  1 onion, peeled and diced
  2 carrots, peeled and diced small
 12 ounces lean ground beef
 12 ounces extra-firm tofu, squeezed to remove excess
     moisture and crumbled
 1/3 cup fresh flat-leaf (Italian) parsley, finely chopped
  1 egg
     Black pepper to taste

SAUCE
  1 tablespoon olive oil
  4 cloves garlic, peeled and sliced
  1 onion, peeled and diced
     Sea salt to taste
     Reserved sliced cabbage
  1 35-ounce can whole tomatoes in juice, chopped
     Black pepper to taste

1. Bring a large pot of water to a boil.
2. Remove and discard the outer leaves and core from the cabbage.
3. Add sea salt to the water, followed by the cabbage. Cook the cabbage until the leaves are loose, approximately 5 minutes. Transfer the cabbage to a plate and allow to drain.

4. While the cabbage is draining, prepare the filling. Heat the olive oil in a large Dutch oven over low heat. Add the garlic and cook until soft and fragrant. Add the onion and carrots and sprinkle with sea salt. Cook until soft. Transfer the ingredients to a plate and spread so they cool quickly.

5. In a large bowl combine the beef, tofu, parsley, and egg. Add the cooled vegetable mixture to the bowl. With your hands, thoroughly combine all of the ingredients. Season the filling with sea salt and black pepper.

6. Place the cabbage on a work surface. Carefully separate the large leaves and small leaves. Thinly slice the small leaves and set aside. You will later add them to the sauce. With a paring knife, remove and discard the center rib of each of the large leaves.

7. To make the cabbage rolls, place a large cabbage leaf on a work surface with the core end facing you. Lay another leaf on top to cover the cut area. Place 3 tablespoons of the filling in the center. Fold the sides over the filling. Roll the leaf from the bottom to form a cabbage roll. Secure the roll with toothpicks. Repeat the procedure with the remaining cabbage leaves and filling. Set the rolls aside.

8. To make the sauce, heat the olive oil in a large Dutch oven over low heat. Add the garlic and cook until soft and fragrant. Add the onion to the pot and sprinkle with sea salt. Cook the onion until soft.

9. Add the reserved sliced cabbage to the pot and cook until it begins to soften. Raise the heat to high. Add the tomatoes to the pot. Bring the sauce to a boil.

10. Carefully place the cabbage rolls into the sauce. Return the sauce to a boil. Reduce the heat and braise the cabbage rolls until tender, approximately 1 ½ hours.

11. Transfer the cabbage rolls to a serving platter. Season the sauce with sea salt and black pepper. Ladle the sauce onto the rolls and serve at once.

🐾 Brisket Braised with Tomatoes and Fennel

PREPARATION:
15 MINUTES

COOKING:
3 HOURS

YIELD:
4 MAIN-COURSE
SERVINGS

In the past, when we braised a piece of beef, we chose a rump roast. Now we enjoy a brisket. The cooking techniques are similar, and since they both have large amounts of connective tissue which melts over a long period of cooking, they both become incredibly tender. We prefer the brisket because it tends to be moister and slices more cleanly. The delectable and vegetable-laden braising liquid contains an abundance of antioxidants.

1 tablespoon olive oil
3 pounds of beef brisket
  Sea salt to taste
  Black pepper to taste
5 cloves garlic, peeled and sliced
1 onion, peeled and sliced
1 large or 2 small fennel bulbs, trimmed and sliced
2 carrots, scraped and sliced
2 cups red wine
1 28-ounce can whole tomatoes in juice, chopped

1. Heat the olive oil in a Dutch oven over medium-high heat. Sprinkle the brisket on each side with sea salt and black pepper.
2. When the oil is hot, carefully place the brisket into the pot. Sear the meat on each side until a crust forms, approximately 5 minutes, turning once.
3. Transfer the brisket to a plate. Set aside for a moment. Reduce the heat to low. Add the garlic to the pot. Cook for 30 seconds. Add the onion. Cook until it begins to soften, stirring often. Add the fennel and carrots. Sprinkle with sea salt. Cook until they begin to soften, stirring often.
4. Raise the heat to high. Add the wine. Simmer the wine for 2 minutes. Add the tomatoes. Bring the sauce to a boil. Return the meat to the pot along with any accumulated juices.

5. Bring the sauce to a boil. Reduce the heat to very low. Cover the pot. Braise the meat until very tender, approximately 3 hours, turning 2 or 3 times.

6. Transfer the meat to a cutting board and allow to rest for 10 minutes before slicing. While the meat is resting, simmer the sauce.

7. Slice the meat on the bias. Place on a large platter. Season the sauce with sea salt and black pepper. Spoon the sauce onto the meat and serve at once.

❧ Mike's Family Meatballs

PREPARATION:
30 MINUTES

COOKING:
1 HOUR

YIELD:
8 MAIN-COURSE
SERVINGS

Mike Pfaff, an accomplished runner and cook, passed this recipe to Vince. Since our focus is breast cancer prevention through a diet rich in soy and antioxidants, the tomato-based sauce fit the bill. For the meatballs, we altered the recipe slightly by substituting crumbled tofu for a portion of the meat; we were pleasantly surprised by the results. The meatballs retained their flavor and were tender and moist.

Tip: *Mike suggests removing the meatballs from the sauce after they are cooked and serving the sauce and meatballs separately as in the Italian tradition.*

1 cup Homemade Bread Crumbs (page 263)
1 cup buttermilk
3 tablespoons olive oil
8 cloves garlic, peeled and sliced
2 onions, peeled and diced
  Sea salt to taste
1 teaspoon dried basil
1 teaspoon dried oregano
1 teaspoon dried thyme
2 28-ounce cans whole tomatoes in juice, chopped
1 pound lean ground beef
1 pound extra-firm tofu, squeezed to remove excess
  moisture and crumbled
2 eggs
1 cup Romano cheese
1 cup fresh basil, snipped
  Black pepper to taste

1. Place the bread crumbs in a large mixing bowl. Add the buttermilk. Set the bowl aside for a moment.
2. Heat 1 tablespoon of olive oil in a large Dutch oven over medium-high heat. When the oil is hot, add the garlic. Cook until soft and fragrant. Add the onions and sprinkle with sea salt. Cook the onion until soft, stirring occasionally. Add the

dried basil, oregano, and thyme. Cook the ingredients for another minute.

3. Transfer one-half of this mixture to the bowl with the bread crumbs. Set the bowl aside again.

4. Add the tomatoes to the Dutch oven. Bring the sauce to a boil. Reduce the heat. Simmer the sauce while you prepare the meatballs.

5. To prepare the meatballs, add the beef, tofu, eggs, cheese, and fresh basil to the bread crumb mixture. Season with sea salt and black pepper. With your hands, work the mixture until well combined.

6. Form the mixture into 24 tightly packed balls.

7. Heat another tablespoon of the olive oil in a skillet over medium-high heat. When the oil is hot, add 8 meatballs to the pan. Cook the meatballs until deep brown on all sides, turning occasionally, approximately 5 minutes. Add to the sauce. Repeat the procedure twice more with the remaining oil and meatballs.

8. Simmer the meatballs in the sauce for 1 hour, stirring occasionally. Transfer the meatballs to a platter. Transfer the sauce to a serving bowl. Accompany the meatballs and sauce with pasta or Soy Polenta (page 336).

🌿 Shepherd's Pie

PREPARATION:
40 MINUTES

COOKING:
20 MINUTES

YIELD:
6 MAIN-COURSE
SERVINGS

Shepherd's pie, that comforting mashed potato, beef, and corn casserole, is one of those childhood meals that needs to be updated. To make the filling rich in phytoestrogens, we have substituted extra-firm tofu for a portion of the beef. Our antioxidant-rich sauce contains carrots, tomatoes, and edamame. The potatoes are mashed with olive oil and soy milk. Shepherd's pie has never tasted so good and has never been more nutritious.

POTATOES

- 2 pounds Yellow Finn or Yukon Gold potatoes, scrubbed
  Sea salt to taste
- 1½ cups soy milk
- 2 tablespoons olive oil
  Black pepper to taste

MEAT AND TOFU FILLING

- 1 tablespoon olive oil
- 3 cloves garlic, peeled and thinly sliced
- 1 onion, peeled and diced
  Sea salt to taste
- 12 ounces lean ground beef
- 1 pound extra-firm tofu, squeezed to remove excess moisture and crumbled
  Black pepper to taste

SAUCE

- 1 tablespoon olive oil
- 3 cloves garlic, peeled and thinly sliced
- 1 onion, peeled and diced
  Sea salt to taste
- 2 carrots, scraped and sliced
- 1 cup frozen and blanched edamame
- 1 28-ounce can whole tomatoes in juice, chopped
- 1 cup frozen corn
  Black pepper to taste

1. To prepare the potatoes, place them in a Dutch oven. Cover with water. Season with sea salt. Bring to a boil. Reduce the heat and simmer until tender, approximately 20 minutes.

2. Drain and return to the pot. Add the soy milk and 2 tablespoons of the olive oil. Mash with a hand-held masher. Season with sea salt and black pepper. Set aside for a moment.

3. To prepare the filling, heat the olive oil in a Dutch oven over medium-high heat. When the oil is hot, add the garlic. Cook the garlic for 30 seconds. Add the onion and sprinkle it with sea salt. Cook the onion until soft.

4. Add the beef to the pot. Cook the beef until cooked through. Drain the fat from the pot. Transfer the meat to a bowl. Stir in the tofu. Season with sea salt and black pepper.

5. To prepare the sauce, heat the olive oil in the Dutch oven over medium heat. Add the garlic. Cook for 30 seconds. Add the onion and sprinkle with sea salt. Cook the onion until soft.

6. Preheat the oven to 400°F.

7. Add the carrots and edamame to the pot. Cook for 3 minutes, stirring occasionally. Raise the heat to high. Add the tomatoes. Bring the sauce to a boil. Reduce the heat and simmer for 15 minutes, stirring often.

8. Add the corn. Cook the sauce for 5 minutes more. Season with sea salt and black pepper.

9. To assemble the pie, place one-third of the potatoes on the bottom of a 4-quart casserole. Add half of the meat-tofu mixture. Ladle on half of the sauce. Add another one-third of the potatoes, followed by the remaining meat mixture and sauce. Finish the pie with a layer of the remaining potatoes.

10. Transfer the pie to the oven. Bake for 15 minutes. Turn on the broiler and broil until a crust forms, approximately 5 minutes. Remove the pie from the oven. Allow to rest for 5 minutes before serving.

CHAPTER 18

Side Dishes and Accompaniments

By combining soy foods, nuts, and fresh fruits and vegetables in creative ways, the number of wonderful breast cancer preventing side dishes one can enjoy is virtually endless. Tofu and soy milk can be substituted for high-fat dairy products in your favorite potato and polenta recipes to transform them into phytoestrogen powerhouses. Dark leafy greens and deep orange–fleshed vegetables can be baked, sautéed, or pureed to create simple and delectable antioxidant-rich dishes to accompany your favorite main courses. When preparing the dishes in this chapter, use the recipes as guidelines. Feel free to alter them to your liking. If you are not fond of collards, but enjoy the earthy and sweet flavor of kale, by all means substitute it. If you can't locate Yellow Finn potatoes, Russets are the next best choice. If the peppery taste of broccoli rabe is too powerful for you, try spinach or chard.

The best part of a restaurant meal is often the creatively prepared side dishes. Unfortunately, accompaniments such as mashed potatoes and polenta are delicious and sinfully rich because they are seasoned with an abundance of cream, butter, and cheese. The health of the customer generally takes a backseat to the flavor of the dish. When we prepare mashed potatoes, whether plain or enhanced with garlic or leeks, they are made "creamy" by soft tofu and soy milk. Our Soy Polenta and Sweet Potato and Soy Milk Polenta are prepared with soy milk and are just as creamy and rich-tasting as a traditional version.

Dark leafy greens, such as collards, broccoli rabe, spinach, mustard greens, and Swiss chard, contain great amounts of antioxidants, fiber, calcium, and folic acid. In the kitchen they are simple to prepare and adapt well to many different flavors. Spinach with Fried Garlic and Toasted Almonds is a delightful combination of earthy greens and sweet and crisp garlic and nuts. With a delectable contrast of sweet and savory flavors, Swiss Chard with Chickpeas and Raisins is certain to make your favorites list.

Although beta-carotene is present in many vegetables, those with deep orange flesh contain the greatest amounts. Sweet potatoes, carrots, and butternut squash are important vegetables in a breast cancer preventing diet. With delectable recipes such as Smashed Sweet Potatoes with Broccoli Rabe, Baby Carrots with Cilantro and Pumpkin Seeds, and Carrots and Butternut Squash with Ginger and Orange, including these nutritional powerhouse foods in your diet will be tasty and creative.

One of the best ways to be certain your diet contains a variety of breast cancer preventing nutrients is to combine soy with several vegetables in one preparation. Dishes such as Tofu Ratatouille, Garden Vegetable Bake, and Roasted Summer Vegetables and Tofu not only contain abundant amounts of antioxidants and phytoestrogens but they are hearty enough to serve two or three for a wonderful vegetarian meal.

With creativity, flexibility, and an emphasis on soy foods and antioxidant-rich vegetables, nuts, and seeds, the accompaniments you create may become the stars of your meals.

🌿 Swiss Chard with Chickpeas and Raisins

PREPARATION:
10 MINUTES

COOKING:
10 MINUTES

YIELD:
4 SIDE-DISH
SERVINGS

When we were children, our vegetable garden always had large plots of Swiss chard. Our grandmother would steam and season it with Spanish olive oil. Although we didn't care for it then, we would die for it now.

Chard adapts well to a variety of preparations and seasonings. It can be steamed, pureed, sautéed, or baked. Garlic, onions, olive oil, lemon, tofu, toasted nuts and seeds, tamari, ginger, and raisins all complement chard's earthy flavor. With plenty of calcium, iron, folic acid, and antioxidants, chard is a breast cancer preventing powerhouse.

Tip: *Kale and collard greens can be substituted for the chard. Kale will require 30 minutes to become tender; collards will need approximately 45 minutes. It may be necessary to add a bit of water during the cooking to prevent them from sticking.*

⅔   cup raisins
1   cup water
1   tablespoon olive oil
2   cloves garlic, peeled and thinly sliced
1   onion, peeled and sliced
    Sea salt to taste
1½ pounds Swiss chard, trimmed, leaves chopped and
    stems thinly sliced, washed, and drained
1   15-ounce can chickpeas, drained and rinsed
    Black pepper to taste

1. Combine the raisins and water in a small saucepan. Bring to a boil. Remove the pan from the heat. Set the pan aside while you proceed with the recipe.
2. Heat the olive oil in a large Dutch oven over low heat. Add the garlic and cook until it is soft and fragrant. Add the onion and sprinkle with sea salt. Cook the onion until soft.
3. Raise the heat to high. Add the chard to the pot. Sprinkle with sea salt. Add the raisins and their soaking water to the pot. Cover the pot. Steam the chard until tender, approximately 7 minutes.

4. Add the chickpeas to the pot. Cook the chard for another minute. Season with sea salt and black pepper. Serve hot or at room temperature.

Spinach with Fried Garlic and Toasted Almonds

Whether it is used as a filling for lasagna, a stuffing for mushrooms, or the main ingredients in a pasta dish, spinach, garlic, and almonds are a delectable combination. Spinach is an excellent source of beta-carotene and almonds are rich in Vitamin E.

PREPARATION:
10 MINUTES

COOKING:
20 MINUTES

YIELD:
4 SIDE-DISH
SERVINGS

⅓ cup sliced almonds
Sea salt to taste
1 tablespoon olive oil
6 cloves garlic, thinly sliced
1½ pounds fresh spinach, trimmed, washed, drained, and chopped
Black pepper to taste

1. Place the almonds in a small skillet. Sprinkle with sea salt. Toast over low heat until golden and fragrant, shaking the pan occasionally, approximately 7 minutes. Remove the pan from the heat.
2. Heat the olive oil in a Dutch oven over medium-low heat. Add the garlic. Sprinkle with sea salt. Cook the garlic until golden and crisp, stirring often, approximately 7 minutes. With a small slotted spoon, transfer the garlic to a plate. Set aside for a moment.
3. Raise the heat to high under the Dutch oven. When the oil remaining in the pot is hot, add the spinach. Cook the spinach only until it wilts, stirring constantly, approximately 3 minutes. Season with sea salt and black pepper.
4. Transfer the spinach to a large serving platter. Garnish with the garlic and almonds. If desired, drizzle a bit of olive oil onto the spinach. Serve hot or at room temperature.

🎭 Carrots and Butternut Squash with Ginger and Orange

PREPARATION:
10 MINUTES

COOKING:
30 MINUTES

YIELD:
8 SIDE-DISH
SERVINGS

A hint of ginger and orange are all that are needed to enhance the natural sweetness of carrots and butternut squash. Their deep orange color make these vegetables two of the richest sources of beta-carotene.

Tip: *This recipe yields 8 generous servings. The leftovers can be thinned with water, vegetable, or chicken stock to create a delicious soup. Garnish the soup with fried leeks or pan-fried tofu.*

2 tablespoons canola oil
1-inch piece gingerroot, peeled and sliced
1 medium butternut squash, peeled, seeded, and cubed
6 medium carrots, scraped and sliced into 1-inch pieces
Sea salt to taste
6 cups water
1 cup orange juice
1½ cups vegetable cooking water
⅓ cup cilantro, chopped
Black pepper to taste

1. Heat the canola oil in a large Dutch oven over low heat. Add the ginger and cook until soft and fragrant.
2. Raise the heat to medium. Add the squash and carrots to the pot. Sprinkle the vegetables with sea salt. Cover the pot and steam the vegetables for 10 minutes, stirring occasionally.
3. Raise the heat to high. Add the water to the pot and bring to a boil. Reduce the heat and simmer the vegetables until tender, approximately 20 minutes.
4. Drain the vegetables, reserving their cooking water. Set the cooking water aside. Transfer the vegetables to a blender.
5. Add 1½ cups of the reserved vegetable cooking water and the orange juice to the blender.
6. Puree the ingredients. Transfer to a serving bowl. Stir in the cilantro. Season with sea salt and black pepper and serve at once.

🐦 Kale and Carrots with Toasted Almonds

After braising, kale is sweeter and less earthy tasting. Carrots add a lovely color contrast and the almonds a delectable crunch. Kale and carrots are excellent sources of beta-carotene; the almonds are rich in Vitamin E.

PREPARATION:
10 MINUTES

COOKING:
30 MINUTES

YIELD:
4 SIDE-DISH
SERVINGS

⅓ cup whole almonds, coarsely chopped
Sea salt to taste
1 tablespoon olive oil
1 onion, peeled and thinly sliced
¼ teaspoon nutmeg
1 pound Red Russian or Dinosaur kale, trimmed, washed, drained, and chopped
1 cup water
1 pound carrots, scraped and sliced into rounds
Black pepper to taste

1. Place the almonds in a small skillet over low heat. Sprinkle with sea salt. Toast until golden and no longer raw tasting, shaking the pan occasionally, approximately 7 minutes.
2. While the almonds are toasting, heat the olive oil in a large Dutch oven over medium heat. Add the onion. Sprinkle with sea salt. Cook the onion until soft. Add the nutmeg.
3. Raise the heat to high. Add the kale and water. Stir the kale until it begins to wilt. Cover the pot. Reduce the heat to low. Braise the kale for 15 minutes, stirring occasionally.
4. Add the carrots. Cook the carrots and kale until they are both tender, adding more water if necessary, approximately 15 minutes more.
5. Season the vegetables with sea salt and black pepper. Transfer to a serving bowl. Garnish with the toasted almonds. Serve the dish hot or at room temperature.

🙐 Smashed Sweet Potatoes and Broccoli Rabe

PREPARATION:
10 MINUTES

COOKING:
40 MINUTES

YIELD:
6 SIDE-DISH
SERVINGS

Smashed potatoes are potatoes that have been coarsely mashed and then baked until crusty. In this recipe maple syrup enhances the sweetness of the potatoes and provides just the right amount of contrasting flavor to the peppery rabe. The dish is rich in antioxidants and fiber.

Tip: *The recipe can be prepared a day in advance up to the baking stage. Just prior to baking, drizzle the top of the potatoes with olive oil.*

4   medium sweet potatoes, peeled and cubed
    Sea salt to taste
1   pound broccoli rabe, trimmed
½   cup soy milk
6   tablespoons maple syrup
    Olive oil for drizzling

1. Preheat the oven to 400°F. Place the potatoes in a Dutch oven. Cover with cold water and season with sea salt. Bring to a boil. Reduce the heat and simmer until tender, approximately 20 minutes.
2. While the potatoes are simmering, place an inch of water in a large skillet or Dutch oven. Bring the water to a boil. Add the broccoli rabe. Cover the pan and steam the rabe until tender, approximately 3 minutes. Drain the rabe and cool under running water. Coarsely chop and set aside.
3. When the potatoes are tender, drain and return them to the pot. Place the pot over low heat. Allow the remaining moisture to evaporate.
4. Add the soy milk and syrup to the potatoes. Coarsely mash with a fork or hand-held masher. Mix the rabe into the potatoes. Season with sea salt.
5. Lightly coat a baking dish with olive oil. Transfer the potatoes to the dish. Drizzle the potatoes with olive oil. Bake until a crust forms, approximately 20 minutes.

❧ Pan-Fried Sweet Potatoes with Red Bell Peppers and Scallions

Sweet potatoes are most often baked or mashed; they are also delicious pan-fried. When cooked with sweet bell peppers and scallions, they make a wonderful alternative to traditional homefries. This dish is a great source of beta-carotene and Vitamin C.

Tip: *While cooking the potatoes, monitor the heat closely. High heat will cause the sugars in the potatoes to carmelize too quickly. The potatoes will burn before they are thoroughly cooked.*

PREPARATION:
10 MINUTES

COOKING:
30 MINUTES

YIELD:
4 SIDE-DISH
SERVINGS

2 tablespoons olive oil
2 medium sweet potatoes, peeled and sliced into ½-inch cubes
1 red bell pepper, cored and thinly sliced
Sea salt to taste
4 scallions, trimmed and thinly sliced
⅓ cup cilantro, chopped
Black pepper to taste

1. Heat the olive oil in a large skillet over high heat. Add the potatoes and bell pepper. Sprinkle with sea salt. Toss the ingredients.
2. Reduce the heat to medium. Cook the potatoes until golden and tender, approximately 25 minutes, tossing occasionally.
3. Add the scallions and cilantro to the pan. Cook the potatoes for 2 minutes more.
4. Season the potatoes with sea salt and black pepper and serve at once.

❧ Spiced Sweet Potato "Fries"

Our oven "fries," sliced Russet potatoes that are tossed with olive oil and baked until golden brown, are a healthful alternative to French fries. For a more boldly flavored and antioxidant-rich accompaniment, we enjoy Spiced Sweet Potato "Fries." Although sweet potatoes don't crisp as well as Russet potatoes, they are more tender.

PREPARATION:
10 MINUTES

COOKING:
30 MINUTES

YIELD:
4 SIDE-DISH
SERVINGS

¾ teaspoon cumin
¾ teaspoon curry powder
¾ teaspoon chili powder
4 medium sweet potatoes, scrubbed, dried, each cut lengthwise into 8 wedges
2 tablespoons olive oil
Sea salt to taste
Black pepper to taste

1. Preheat the oven to 400°F.
2. In a small bowl, combine the cumin and curry and chili powders.
3. Place the potatoes in a large mixing bowl. Drizzle with the olive oil. Season with sea salt and black pepper. Toss the ingredients thoroughly.
4. Transfer the potatoes to 1 large baking tray or 2 smaller ones, spreading them in a single layer.
5. Bake until tender, approximately 30 minutes.
6. With the back of a spatula, loosen the potatoes. Transfer to a platter and serve at once.

❧ Oven-Roasted Asparagus with Olive Oil

The initial steps in many asparagus recipes call for either steaming or boiling and then shocking them in an ice bath. This technique produces soggy asparagus. Two of the best and simplest methods, which produce asparagus with a wonderfully smoky and pure flavor, are grilling and oven roasting. A drizzle of fruity olive oil, a sprinkling of sea salt, and a few grinds of black pepper are all that are needed to create savory asparagus to enjoy on their own or to use in your favorite recipes. Asparagus are rich in folic acid and beta-carotene.

PREPARATION:
5 MINUTES

COOKING:
10 MINUTES

YIELD:
4 SIDE-DISH
SERVINGS

1½ pounds asparagus, tough stems snapped off and discarded
1–2 tablespoons olive oil
     Sea salt to taste
     Black pepper to taste
     Juice of 1 lemon, optional

1. Preheat the oven to 400°F.
2. Place the asparagus on a baking tray. Drizzle with the olive oil. Sprinkle with sea salt and black pepper.
3. Transfer the tray to the oven. Roast the asparagus until tender, approximately 10 minutes.
4. Transfer to a serving platter. If desired, drizzle with lemon juice and serve at once.

❧❧ Mashed Potatoes with Garlic and Leeks

PREPARATION:
15 MINUTES

COOKING:
35 MINUTES

YIELD:
6 SIDE-DISH
SERVINGS

Whether plain or seasoned with garlic and leeks, mashed potatoes are one of everyone's favorite comfort foods. When prepared with the usual cream and butter, they cannot be considered part of a healthful diet. When made with soy milk and tofu, they are transformed into a breast cancer preventing delicacy that can be enjoyed regularly.

Tips: *We always mash potatoes with a handheld masher. If you mash the potatoes with an electric mixer, don't overmix them or they will be gooey. A few lumps are fine. Also, the potatoes can be made ahead of time and kept warm in a double boiler.*

1½ cups plain soy milk
6 ounces silken tofu
2½ pounds Yellow Finn potatoes
    Sea salt to taste
1 tablespoon olive oil
4 cloves of garlic, peeled and thinly sliced
2 leeks, trimmed, washed, and thinly sliced
    Black pepper to taste

1. Combine the soy milk and tofu in a blender and puree. Set the puree aside for a moment.
2. Place the potatoes in a Dutch oven. Cover with water. Season with sea salt. Bring the water to a boil. Reduce the heat and simmer the potatoes until tender, approximately 25 minutes.
3. While the potatoes are simmering, heat the olive oil in a skillet over medium heat. When the oil is hot, add the garlic. Cook the garlic for 30 seconds. Add the leeks and sprinkle with sea salt. Cook the leeks until tender, stirring often. Remove the pan from the heat.
4. Drain the potatoes and return to the pot. Reduce the heat to low. Shake the potatoes over low heat to remove any excess moisture. Add the soy milk–tofu mixture and the garlic-leek combination to the pot.

5. Mash the potatoes with a masher until smooth. Season with sea salt and black pepper. Transfer to a serving bowl and serve at once.

❧ Asparagus with Shallots, Pine Nuts, and Lemon

Some recipes are created by chance. One morning while food shopping, we had a list of recipes we were planning to test. None of them contained asparagus. While walking down the produce section, we could not pass up the beautiful and deep green asparagus. We brought them home and paired them with ingredients we already had on hand. The dish turned out to be a winner.

Asparagus are a great source of beta-carotene and folic acid. Pine nuts are rich in Vitamin E.

Tip: *Since pine nuts tend to burn easily, monitor them closely and toss often.*

PREPARATION:
10 MINUTES

COOKING:
10 MINUTES

YIELD:
4 SIDE-DISH
SERVINGS

⅓ cup pine nuts
Sea salt to taste
1 tablespoon olive oil
2 medium shallots, peeled and chopped
1½ pounds asparagus, tough stems snapped off and discarded
⅔ cup water
1 tablespoon butter
Juice from 1 lemon
Black pepper to taste

1. Place the pine nuts in a small skillet over low heat. Sprinkle with sea salt. Toast until golden, tossing often, approximately 6 minutes. Set aside.
2. Heat the olive oil in a large Dutch oven over medium heat. Add the shallots. Cook until soft, stirring often.

3. Raise the heat to high. Add the asparagus to the pot. Add the water and butter. Cover the pot. Cook the asparagus until tender, turning occasionally, approximately 5 minutes.
4. Transfer to a large platter. Squeeze the lemon onto them. Season with sea salt and black pepper. Garnish with the pine nuts and serve immediately.

❧ Baby Carrots with Cilantro and Pumpkin Seeds

PREPARATION:
5 MINUTES

COOKING:
10 MINUTES

YIELD:
4 SIDE-DISH
SERVINGS

Besides being a perfect snack, baby carrots are ideal to use in a quickly prepared side dish. To retain their nutrients, we have steamed them in a minimal amount of water and used the water as the base of the sauce. Carrots are one of the richest sources of beta-carotene. Pumpkin seeds are an excellent source of Vitamin E.

½ cup water
    Sea salt to taste
1 pound baby carrots
1 tablespoon unsalted butter
2 scallions, trimmed and thinly sliced
¼ cup cilantro, chopped
4 tablespoons roasted pumpkin seeds
    Black pepper to taste

1. Bring the water to a boil in a medium saucepan. Add sea salt to the water, followed by the carrots.
2. Add the butter. Cover the pot and steam the carrots until tender, stirring occasionally, approximately 5 minutes.
3. Remove the pan from the heat. Stir in the scallions, cilantro, and pumpkin seeds. Season the carrots with sea salt and black pepper. Transfer to a bowl and serve at once.

❧ Brown Rice with Turnip Greens and Fried Garlic

Although not used as often as other cooking greens, peppery-tasting turnip greens are great on their own and can be added to soups, stews, and pasta dishes. Here we have tossed them with brown rice to create a unique accompaniment. Fried garlic adds texture and a burst of flavor. Turnip greens are one of the most nutritious greens. They are a very rich source of calcium, beta-carotene, and Vitamin C.

Tips: *As with many greens, turnip greens tend to be sandy. Wash them in two or three changes of water. Also, the older the turnip greens, the longer they will need to cook to become tender. Plan on approximately 5 minutes for young greens and 10 for older ones.*

PREPARATION:
10 MINUTES

COOKING:
45 MINUTES

YIELD:
4 SIDE-DISH
SERVINGS

5 cups water
Sea salt to taste
2 cups short-grain brown rice
2 tablespoons olive oil
8 large cloves garlic, peeled and halved
1 pound turnip greens, trimmed, washed, drained, and well chopped
Black pepper to taste

1. Bring the water to a boil in a small Dutch oven. Add sea salt to the water. Stir in the rice. Cover the pot and bring the rice to a boil. Reduce the heat and simmer the rice until the water is absorbed and the rice is tender, approximately 45 minutes.
2. While the rice is cooking, heat the olive oil in a Dutch oven over medium-low heat. Add the garlic and sprinkle with sea salt. Cook the garlic until golden and slightly crisp, turning occasionally, approximately 10 minutes. Remove the garlic from the pot. Set aside.
3. Raise the heat to high under the garlic-flavored oil remaining in the Dutch oven. Add the turnip greens to the pot. Stir thoroughly. Cover the pot. Reduce the heat to low. Braise the greens until tender, stirring occasionally, approximately 15

minutes. If necessary, add a small amount of water to the greens to prevent them from sticking.

4. Fluff the rice with a fork. Stir the rice into the turnip greens. Season the rice with sea salt and black pepper.

5. Divide the rice among 4 plates. Garnish each portion with the fried garlic and serve at once.

🐾 Brown Rice with Carrots, Scallions, and Cilantro

PREPARATION:
10 MINUTES

COOKING:
45 MINUTES

YIELD:
4 SIDE-DISH
SERVINGS

In this Asian-influenced recipe, we simmer the rice in the same water in which the carrots are boiled. This technique not only retains the nutrients from the carrots but also flavors the rice. Carrots are one of the richest sources of beta-carotene. Tamari and miso contain modest amounts of phytoestrogens.

2 tablespoons tamari
2 teaspoons dark miso
1 teaspoon sugar
3 tablespoons hot water
5 cups water
  Sea salt to taste
1 pound carrots, peeled and sliced at a diagonal into 1-inch pieces
1½ cups short-grain brown rice
1 tablespoon canola oil
  ½-inch piece gingerroot, peeled and finely chopped
2 cloves garlic, peeled and finely chopped
4 scallions, trimmed and thinly sliced
⅓ cup cilantro, chopped

1. In a small bowl, whisk together the tamari, miso, sugar, and hot water. Set the bowl aside.

2. Prepare an ice bath.

3. Bring the 5 cups of water to a boil in a medium-sized Dutch oven. Add sea salt to the water, followed by the carrots.

Cover the pot. Reduce the heat and simmer the carrots until tender, approximately 5 minutes. With a slotted spoon, transfer the carrots to the ice bath.

4. Return the water to a boil. Add the rice to the pot. Cover the pot and bring the rice to a boil. Reduce the heat. Simmer the rice until the water is absorbed and the rice is tender, approximately 45 minutes.

5. While the rice is simmering, heat the oil in a skillet over low heat. Add the ginger and garlic to the skillet. Cook until soft and fragrant. Raise the heat to medium. Add the carrots to the skillet. Cook the carrots for 3 minutes, tossing occasionally.

6. Whisk the sauce and add it to the carrots. Cook the ingredients for 2 minutes. Remove the pan from the heat. Stir in the scallions and cilantro.

7. When the rice is tender, stir in the carrot mixture. Transfer the rice to a bowl and serve hot or at room temperature. It is a great accompaniment to Salmon with Edamame and Scallions (page 278).

✃ Colorful Rice

PREPARATION:
5 MINUTES

COOKING:
45 MINUTES

YIELD:
4 SIDE-DISH
SERVINGS

With brown rice, red and yellow bell peppers, and bright green scallions and parsley this tasty dish is also eye-catching. It contains a great amount of fiber and antioxidants.

Tip: *Double the recipe and use the extra rice to prepare Fried Brown Rice with Tofu (page 219).*

5 cups water
  Sea salt to taste
2 cups short-grain brown rice
1 tablespoon olive oil
2 cloves garlic, peeled and sliced
1 red bell pepper, cored and diced
1 yellow bell pepper, cored and diced
⅓ cup flat-leaf (Italian) parsley, chopped
4 scallions, trimmed and thinly sliced

1. Bring the water to a boil in a medium-sized Dutch oven. Add sea salt to the water, followed by the rice. Bring the rice to a boil. Cover the pot. Reduce the heat and simmer the rice until tender and all of the water has been absorbed, approximately 45 minutes.
2. While the rice is cooking, heat the olive oil in a skillet over medium heat. When the oil is hot, add the garlic and cook for 30 seconds. Add the bell peppers. Sprinkle with sea salt. Cook the peppers until they begin to soften, approximately 6 minutes, tossing often.
3. Remove the pan from the heat. Stir in the parsley and scallions.
4. Spoon the vegetable mixture onto the cooked rice. Cover the pot. Allow the rice and vegetables to rest for 5 minutes. With a fork, stir the rice and vegetables together. Serve at once or at room temperature.

✌ Tofu Ratatouille

In the past, we prepared our ratatouille as we would a stew. We cooked the vegetables in one pot, adding them in intervals according to their cooking time. The ratatouille was good but not great. When the vegetables are simmered together, they lose their identities. By cooking each separately, as we now do, and combining them in the last step, they maintain their distinct flavors and textures.

Tofu is not a typical ingredient in a classic Provençal ratatouille. Besides its unique texture and ability to absorb flavors, it adds an abundance of phytoestrogens. Tomatoes and bell peppers are great sources of antioxidants.

Tip: *Eggplant tends to absorb a large amount of oil when cooked in a pan. To reduce the amount of oil needed, start with a well-seasoned wok over high heat. Add oil to the pan and allow it to get hot. Carefully place the eggplant into the pan in a single layer. Cook over high heat, tossing occasionally until golden and soft.*

PREPARATION:
15 MINUTES

COOKING:
20 MINUTES

YIELD:
6 SIDE-DISH
SERVINGS

4 tablespoons olive oil
1 pound extra-firm tofu
  Sea salt to taste
1 tablespoon sugar
3 cloves garlic, peeled and sliced
1 onion, peeled and thinly sliced
1 red bell pepper, cored and thinly sliced
1 green bell pepper, cored and thinly sliced
6 plum tomatoes, diced
2 Italian eggplants, cubed
2 zucchini, cubed
½ cup fresh basil, snipped
  Black pepper to taste

1. Heat 1 tablespoon of the olive oil in a wok over medium-high heat. Place the tofu on a kitchen towel. With the heel of your hand, gently press on the tofu to remove the excess moisture. Cube the tofu. Sprinkle the cubes with sea salt.
2. When the oil is hot, carefully place the tofu into the wok. Sear until golden, tossing occasionally. Sprinkle with sugar.

Cook for another minute. Transfer to a plate. Set aside for a moment.

3. Heat another tablespoon of olive oil in the wok over medium heat. When the oil is hot, add the garlic. Cook for 30 seconds. Add the onion and bell peppers. Sprinkle with sea salt. Cook until soft, stirring often, approximately 6 minutes.

4. Add the tomatoes. Raise the heat to high. Cook the ingredients for 5 minutes, stirring occasionally. Transfer the ingredients to a bowl. Set the bowl aside for a moment.

5. Heat another tablespoon of olive oil in the wok over high heat. When the oil is hot, add the eggplant. Sprinkle with sea salt. Cook the eggplant until golden and soft, tossing occasionally, approximately 5 minutes. Transfer to a plate. Set aside for a moment.

6. Heat the remaining tablespoon of olive oil in the wok over medium-high heat. Add the zucchini. Sprinkle with sea salt. Cook the zucchini until golden and tender, tossing occasionally, approximately 5 minutes. Transfer to a plate. Set aside for a moment.

7. Reduce the heat to medium. Return the bell pepper–tomato mixture to the wok. Return the tofu, eggplant, and zucchini to the wok. Cook the ratatouille until hot, stirring occasionally. Add the basil. Season with sea salt and black pepper.

8. Transfer the ratatouille to a serving platter. Serve hot or at room temperature.

❧ Barbecued Chickpeas

Whether you serve these beans as a side dish or as a main course accompanied with brown rice, they are sure to be a hit at your next cookout. The sauce, when prepared without the beans, can be used as a traditional barbecue or grill sauce. It pairs especially well with grilled tofu and chicken and barbecued pork, beef, and turkey. The chickpeas are a great source of fiber, folic acid, and beta-carotene.

PREPARATION:
15 MINUTES

COOKING:
1 HOUR

YIELD:
4 SIDE-DISH
SERVINGS

1 tablespoon canola oil
4 cloves garlic, peeled and finely chopped
1 large onion, peeled and diced
Sea salt to taste
2 fresh jalapeño peppers, seeded and finely chopped
2 teaspoons chili powder
1 teaspoon cumin
½ teaspoon cinnamon
¼ teaspoon nutmeg
¼ teaspoon cloves
¼ cup white vinegar
¼ cup cider vinegar
¼ cup ketchup
2 tablespoons brown sugar
2 tablespoons Dijon mustard
2 tablespoons orange juice concentrate
2 tablespoons Worcestershire sauce
1 28-ounce can whole tomatoes in juice, chopped
2 15-ounce cans chickpeas, drained and rinsed
Black pepper to taste

1. Heat the canola oil in a large Dutch oven over medium heat. When the oil is hot, add the garlic. Cook for 30 seconds.
2. Add the onion and sprinkle with sea salt. Cook the onion until it begins to soften, stirring often.
3. Reduce the heat to low. Add the jalapeños, chili powder, cumin, cinnamon, nutmeg, and cloves. Cook the ingredients for 2 minutes, stirring often.
4. Raise the heat to high. Add the vinegars, ketchup, brown

sugar, mustard, orange juice concentrate, and Worcestershire sauce. Cook the ingredients for 2 minutes.

5. Add the tomatoes and beans. Bring the sauce to a boil. Reduce the heat. Simmer the sauce for 1 hour, stirring occasionally.

6. Transfer the beans to a large serving bowl. Serve hot or at room temperature.

🌿 Braised Bok Choy with Red Bell Peppers and Ginger

PREPARATION:
10 MINUTES

COOKING:
10 MINUTES

YIELD:
4 SIDE-DISH
SERVINGS

We love the versatility of bok choy. It is a wonderful addition to soups, pastas, cold dishes, and, of course, stir fries. With its sweet and crisp stems and earthy-tasting leaves, its flavor is similar to chard. It can be the supporting ingredient in a recipe or as seen here, the star. This quickly prepared accompaniment is full of breast cancer preventing beta-carotene, Vitamin C, calcium, and phytoestrogens.

3 tablespoons tamari
2 tablespoons rice wine vinegar
1 tablespoon sugar
1 tablespoon canola oil
2 cloves garlic, peeled and finely chopped
   1-inch piece gingerroot, peeled and finely chopped
1 large red bell pepper, seeded and diced
1½ pounds bok choy, trimmed, stems and leaves separated, chopped, washed, and drained
⅓ cup roasted soy nuts, chopped

1. To prepare the sauce, whisk together the tamari, rice wine vinegar, and sugar. Set the sauce aside.

2. Heat the canola oil in a wok over medium-high heat. When the oil is hot, add the garlic and ginger. Cook for 15 seconds.

3. Add the bell pepper and bok choy stems. Cook the ingredients until they begin to soften, tossing often, approximately 4 minutes.

4. Add the bok choy leaves. Cook until tender, tossing often, approximately 3 minutes.

5. Add the sauce to the pan. Cook the vegetables for another minute. Transfer to a serving platter. Garnish with the soy nuts. Serve hot or at room temperature.

❧ Spinach and Edamame with Olive Oil and Garlic

One of the quickest, tastiest, and most healthful methods in which to cook spinach is in a pan with olive oil and garlic. In this recipe the salty and sweet flavor of edamame contrasts beautifully with the robust flavors of the spinach and garlic. This dish is rich in phyto-estrogens, beta-carotene, and calcium.

Tip: *To prepare a quick pasta dish from this recipe, double the proportion of ingredients and toss with 1 pound of cooked penne. It may be necessary to add 1 cup of pasta cooking water to the vegetables to create a bit more sauce.*

PREPARATION:
10 MINUTES

COOKING:
10 MINUTES

YIELD:
4 SIDE-DISH
SERVINGS

    2 cups water
      Sea salt to taste
    2 cups frozen, shelled, and blanched edamame
    1 tablespoon olive oil
    4 cloves garlic, peeled and thinly sliced
    1 pound spinach, trimmed, washed, drained, and chopped
      Black pepper to taste

1. Bring the water to a boil in a small saucepan. Add sea salt to the water, followed by the edamame. Cook the edamame until tender, approximately 5 minutes. Drain. Set aside for a moment.

2. Heat the olive oil in a Dutch oven over medium heat. When the oil is hot, add the garlic and cook for 30 seconds.

3. Raise the heat to high. Add the spinach. Cook the spinach until it wilts, stirring constantly, approximately 2 minutes.

4. Add the edamame to the pan. Season the vegetables with sea salt and black pepper.
5. Transfer to a platter and serve at once.

❧ Asian Kale

PREPARATION:
10 MINUTES

COOKING:
30 MINUTES

YIELD:
4 SIDE-DISH
SERVINGS

Although you do not often find kale cooked with Asian seasonings, its earthy flavor is enhanced by the sweet and salty flavors of rice vinegar and tamari. Kale is one of the richest sources of beta-carotene; sesame seeds are an excellent source of Vitamin E.

4 tablespoons unhulled sesame seeds
1 tablespoon canola oil
3 cloves garlic, peeled and minced
    1-inch piece gingerroot, peeled and minced
1½ pounds Red Russian or Dinosaur kale, trimmed, washed, drained, and chopped
2 tablespoons tamari
1 tablespoon rice vinegar
1 tablespoon sugar
1 teaspoon sesame oil

1. Place the sesame seeds in a small skillet over low heat. Toast until golden, shaking the pan occasionally, approximately 5 minutes.
2. Heat the oil in a large Dutch oven over high heat. When the oil is hot, add the garlic and ginger. Cook for 15 seconds.
3. Add the kale to the pot. Stir the kale until it begins to wilt. Reduce the heat to low. Cover the pan. Cook the kale until tender, stirring occasionally, approximately 30 minutes. If necessary add water to prevent it from sticking.
4. In a small bowl whisk the tamari, rice vinegar, sugar, and sesame oil. Add to the kale. Cook the kale for another minute.
5. Transfer to a platter. Garnish with the sesame seeds and serve hot or at room temperature.

✿ Israeli Couscous with Tomatoes and Basil

Israeli couscous, like Moroccan couscous, is made from semolina. Israeli couscous is larger than the Moroccan variety, about the size of a peppercorn, and unlike the Moroccan variety, it is toasted. It is quick to prepare and versatile. It can be added to soups and stews and makes a wonderful chilled salad. In this recipe we have combined it with basil and antioxidant-rich tomatoes to create a delightful accompaniment to a braised meal or quickly cooked fish dish.

PREPARATION:
5 MINUTES

COOKING:
10 MINUTES

YIELD:
4 SIDE-DISH
SERVINGS

    1   tablespoon olive oil
    3   cloves garlic, peeled and sliced
    1   onion, peeled and diced
        Sea salt to taste
    2   cups Israeli couscous
    3   cups chicken stock or water
    3   plum tomatoes, diced
    ½   cup fresh basil, snipped
        Black pepper to taste

1. Heat the olive oil in a medium saucepan over low heat. Add the garlic. Cook until soft and fragrant. Add the onion and sprinkle with sea salt. Cook the onion until soft, stirring occasionally.
2. Stir in the couscous. Cook the couscous for 1 minute, stirring often. Raise the heat to high.
3. Add the stock or water. Bring the liquid to a boil. Turn off the heat and cover the pot.
4. Steam the couscous until all of the liquid has been absorbed, approximately 10 minutes.
5. Stir in the tomatoes and basil. Season the couscous with sea salt and black pepper.

❧ Soy Polenta

PREPARATION:
10 MINUTES

COOKING:
45 MINUTES

YIELD:
4 SIDE-DISH
SERVINGS

Polenta is the Italian answer to mashed potatoes. It is a true comfort food and one of our favorite side dishes. This version is made creamy by the addition of soy milk and soft tofu.

Tip: *No shortcuts or quick methods are available for making polenta. It needs to be cooked for 45 minutes over low heat and stirred often. Shorter cooking time and less attention produces raw-tasting polenta.*

1 cup soy milk
6 ounces soft tofu
4 cups water
   Sea salt to taste
1 cup stone-ground yellow cornmeal
   Black pepper to taste

1. Combine the soy milk and tofu in a blender and puree. Set the mixture aside.
2. Bring the water to a boil in a heavy-bottomed pan. Add sea salt. Slowly whisk in the cornmeal. When all of the cornmeal has been added, stir the polenta with a wooden spoon for 2 minutes more.
3. Reduce the heat to low. Cook the polenta until creamy and no longer raw tasting, stirring every 5 minutes. The process will take approximately 45 minutes.
4. Stir in the soy milk and tofu mixture. Season with sea salt and black pepper.
5. Transfer the polenta to a serving bowl and serve at once.

🌺 Sweet Potato and Soy Milk Polenta

One evening on a whim, we altered our basic polenta recipe. We added a leftover sweet potato puree and cooked the cornmeal in soy milk. We loved the flavor contrast between the potatoes and cornmeal. Cooking the polenta in soy milk rather than plain water made it richer tasting and more nutritious. This version is a great source of folic acid, phytoestrogens, and beta-carotene.

Tips: *The potatoes can be prepared up to 2 days in advance and refrigerated. Also, spread any leftover polenta onto a sheet pan and refrigerate it overnight. The following day, for a great snack, slice the polenta into squares, rub with olive oil, and bake until golden. Or try substituting the squares for bread in your favorite sandwich or spread them with jam for a creative breakfast treat.*

PREPARATION:
15 MINUTES

COOKING:
45 MINUTES

YIELD:
6 SIDE-DISH
SERVINGS

2 medium sweet potatoes, peeled and diced
4 cups soy milk
   Sea salt to taste
1 cup stone-ground yellow cornmeal
3 tablespoons honey
   Black pepper to taste

1. Place the potatoes in a pot. Cover with water. Bring the water to a boil. Reduce the heat. Simmer the potatoes until tender, approximately 15 minutes. Drain the potatoes, reserving 1 cup of their cooking water.
2. Transfer the potatoes to the work bowl of a food processor fitted with a metal blade. Add the reserved water. Puree the potatoes. Transfer to a bowl and set aside.
3. Bring the soy milk to a gentle boil in a heavy-bottomed pan. Add sea salt. Slowly whisk in the cornmeal. When all of the cornmeal has been added, stir the polenta with a wooden spoon for 2 minutes more.
4. Reduce the heat to low. Cook the polenta until creamy and no longer raw tasting, stirring every 5 minutes. This process will take approximately 45 minutes.

5. Stir in the sweet potatoes. Cook the polenta for 2 minutes more. Add the honey. Season the polenta with sea salt and black pepper.
6. Divide the polenta among 4 plates and serve at once.

🐾 Garden Vegetable Bake

PREPARATION:
20 MINUTES

COOKING:
15 MINUTES

YIELD:
6 SIDE-DISH
SERVINGS

Often the best and most creative dishes are the result of combining odds and ends from the refrigerator. One summer in Maine, on our last evening of vacation, we had a mélange of fresh vegetables that we did not want to see wasted. This antioxidant-rich side dish is what we created. It is so hearty and tasty, you may even want to serve it as a main course.

1½ cups water
    Sea salt to taste
8 ounces green beans, trimmed
1 cup frozen, shelled, and blanched edamame
1 large bunch broccoli, trimmed, florets and stems separated, stems peeled and sliced
1 tablespoon olive oil
6 cloves garlic, peeled and thinly sliced
2 onions, peeled and thinly sliced
3 medium zucchini, cut into 1-inch pieces
1 28-ounce can whole tomatoes in juice, chopped
1 cup fresh basil, snipped
    Black pepper to taste
4 ounces mild Cheddar cheese, grated or sliced

1. Preheat the oven to 400°F.
2. Bring the water to a boil in a large saucepan. Add sea salt to the water, followed by the green beans and edamame. Cover the pan and steam the vegetables for 2 minutes. Add the broccoli and steam the vegetables for 3 minutes more. Drain. Cool under cold running water. Set aside for a moment.

3. Heat the olive oil in a large Dutch oven over medium heat. When the oil is hot, add the garlic. Cook until soft and fragrant. Add the onions and sprinkle with sea salt. Cook the onions until they begin to soften. Add the zucchini. Cook for 5 minutes, stirring occasionally.

4. Raise the heat to high. Add the tomatoes to the pot. Bring the sauce to a boil. Reduce the heat. Simmer the sauce for 15 minutes, stirring often.

5. Season the sauce with sea salt and black pepper. Stir in the basil. Stir in the steamed beans, edamame, and broccoli.

6. Transfer the vegetables to an 8- by 8-inch ovenproof casserole. Scatter the cheese onto the vegetables. Place the casserole into the oven. Bake until the cheese melts and bubbles, approximately 15 minutes.

7. Remove the casserole from the oven. Serve the vegetables hot or at room temperature.

❧ Roasted Summer Vegetables and Tofu

PREPARATION:
10 MINUTES

COOKING:
45 MINUTES

YIELD:
4 SIDE-DISH
SERVINGS

Strolling through a farmer's market and choosing the freshest vegetables for dinner is something we look forward to doing every summer. For all of the wonderful vegetable flavors to have an opportunity to shine, we prepare the vegetables with little fuss or additional ingredients. Oven roasting them with olive oil, sea salt, and black pepper is a great technique. The high heat draws out their natural sugars and allows them to carmelize.

In this recipe we have combined oven-roasted tofu with eggplant, zucchini, and tomatoes. A garnish of pan-seared fresh corn and cilantro adds just the right texture and fresh herb flavor. It is an excellent dish to serve with grilled chicken or fish. Also, when accompanied with bread or tortillas, it can be a meal in itself. It is a great source of antioxidants, phytoestrogens, and folic acid.

3 Japanese or Italian eggplants, cubed
3 medium zucchini, cubed
  Sea salt to taste
  Black pepper to taste
4 tablespoons olive oil
3 medium tomatoes, cored and quartered
1 pound extra-firm tofu, cubed and dried in a towel
3 ears fresh corn, kernels removed
½ cup cilantro, chopped
3 ounces sheep's milk feta

1. Preheat the oven to 425°F.
2. Place the eggplants on one-half of a heavy baking tray. Place the zucchini on the other half. Sprinkle with sea salt and black pepper. Drizzle with 2 tablespoons of the olive oil. Toss thoroughly. Set the tray aside for a moment.
3. Place the tomatoes on one-half of another heavy baking tray. Place the tofu on the other half. Sprinkle with sea salt and black pepper. Drizzle with the remaining 2 tablespoons of olive oil. Toss thoroughly.
4. Place both trays in the oven. Roast both trays of ingredients

until the vegetables are tender and golden, tossing occasionally, approximately 45 minutes.

5. Remove the trays from the oven. With the back of a spatula,
loosen the vegetables and tofu. Transfer to a large serving
bowl. Set the bowl aside for a moment while you prepare the
corn.

6. Heat a well-seasoned wok over medium-high heat. When
the pan is hot, add the corn. Cook the corn until slightly
charred, tossing often, approximately 5 minutes. Add the
cilantro. Transfer the corn to the serving bowl and toss.

7. Garnish the vegetables and tofu with the feta. Serve hot or
at room temperature.

🌣 Braised Collard Greens with Garlic and Rice Vinegar

*In the South, collards are a prized green. They are often braised and
served as an accompaniment to barbecue. We prize them for their
unique flavor and first-class nutrition. Like most cooking greens, collards adapt well to a variety of seasonings. In this recipe the sweet
and slightly tart flavor of rice vinegar enhances the earthy taste of the
greens. Collards are an excellent source of antioxidants and calcium.*

PREPARATION:
5 MINUTES

COOKING:
30 MINUTES

YIELD:
4 SIDE-DISH
SERVINGS

1   tablespoon canola oil
6   cloves garlic, peeled and thinly sliced
1½   pounds collard greens, trimmed, washed, and drained
     Sea salt to taste
3   tablespoons rice vinegar
1   cup water
     Black pepper to taste
⅓   cup roasted and salted soy nuts

1. Heat the canola oil in a Dutch oven over medium heat. Add
the garlic. Cook for 30 seconds.

2. Raise the heat to high. Add the collards to the pot. Sprinkle with sea salt. Stir until they begin to wilt.

3. Add the vinegar. Cover the pot. Reduce the heat. Braise the collards until tender, adding water as necessary to prevent them from sticking, approximately 30 minutes. Season with sea salt and black pepper.

4. Transfer the collards to a serving bowl. Garnish with the soy nuts and serve at once.

❧ Stewed Edamame with Tomatoes and Parsley

PREPARATION:
10 MINUTES

COOKING:
20 MINUTES

YIELD:
4 SIDE-DISH
SERVINGS

The versatility of edamame is amazing. They are a wonderful addition to soups, stews, and pasta dishes. Also, they can be boiled, drizzled with sesame or olive oil, and served as a snack or appetizer. In this recipe we have stewed them with tomatoes to create a phytoestrogen and antioxidant-rich side dish.

1 tablespoon olive oil
4 cloves garlic, peeled and sliced
1 onion, peeled and sliced
  Sea salt to taste
3 cups frozen, shelled, and blanched edamame
1 28-ounce can whole tomatoes in juice, drained and chopped
⅓ cup flat-leaf (Italian) parsley, chopped
  Black pepper to taste

1. Heat the olive oil in a Dutch oven over medium heat. When the oil is hot, add the garlic. Cook for 30 seconds. Add the onion and sprinkle with sea salt. Cook the onion until soft.
2. Add the edamame. Cook the ingredients for 2 minutes.
3. Raise the heat to high. Add the tomatoes. Bring the mixture to a boil. Reduce the heat. Simmer the edamame until tender, stirring occasionally, approximately 15 minutes.
4. Add the parsley. Season the edamame with sea salt and black pepper. Transfer the edamame to a serving bowl. Serve hot or at room temperature.

Sweets and Goodies

You may believe that since you are adhering to a breast cancer preventing diet, that you will have to forgo sweets and
goodies. Well, thanks to phytoestrogen-rich soy and flaxseed and
antioxidant-rich fruits, delicious treats can very much be part of
your day.

When we began developing recipes for this chapter, we had
several goals in mind. First, we wanted to substitute ground
flaxseed and soy products for the butter and oil in quick breads
and muffins. Flaxseed-laced bake goods are incredibly moist and
tender. We also wanted to create fresh and dried fruit-based
recipes using silken or soft tofu. Last, we wanted to include several frozen treats with soy milk as the base. In the past, we have
steered away from frozen concoctions since they required an ice-
cream maker. However, very good ice-cream machines can now
be purchased for about the same price as an average-quality drip
coffee maker.

Traditional chocolate chip and oatmeal cookies contain large amounts of butter. Our Chocolate Chip Cookies and Oatmeal Raisin Cookies are made with soybean butter and ground flaxseed. They are delectably moist and rich and you will never miss the fat.

One of our favorite activities is to go to a farm to pick seasonal fruits. It is great to see the trees bursting with perfectly ripe apples, pears, and peaches and the branches of the fruit bushes bent over with deep red strawberries and raspberries. And if you are lucky enough to be in Maine during August, you know what truly fresh and sweet blueberries taste like. With this bounty of fresh fruit, creating treats is a joy. Raspberries are the star in our tofu-laced Raspberry "Cream." Apples and beta-carotene-rich peaches are combined in our delectable Peach-Apple Sauce. Our Fresh Fruit Parfait with Tofu Yogurt and Blueberry Sauce will trick you into believing you are overdosing on sugar and cream.

We love ice cream but try to avoid the full fat varieties. The problem, though, is that light ice cream is light in texture and flavor. Soy ice "creams" are a great alternative. With an inexpensive ice-cream maker, soy-based frozen desserts are simple to prepare at home. Our Rocky Road Ice "Cream" and Orange-Mango Ice "Cream" are based on soy milk and tofu. They are decadently rich and, because they are low in fat and rich in phytoestrogens, can be enjoyed all the time.

With our healthful and delectable goodies, your sweet tooth and nutritional requirements will always be satisfied when you are following a breast cancer preventing diet.

⸞ Peach-Apple Sauce

PREPARATION:
10 MINUTES

COOKING:
40 MINUTES

YIELD:
3 CUPS

Once you have prepared homemade applesauce, you won't purchase a mass-produced variety again. It is simple to make and there is much room to improvise. You can vary the type of apple, seasonings, and texture to create several different recipes. One of our favorite and most nutritious versions contains peaches. Not too sweet and with a pronounced peach flavor, it is sure to please you. Try spreading it on toast, pancakes, or French toast or serve it as an accompaniment to your favorite pork or chicken dish. Peaches, like all orange-fleshed fruits and vegetables, are a great source of beta-carotene. Apples are high in fiber.

Tip: *If you prefer your applesauce smooth, puree it in a food processor or blender. If you like it a bit chunky, mash it with a potato masher.*

⅔ cup water
¼ cup white sugar
¼ cup brown sugar
1 teaspoon cinnamon
½ teaspoon nutmeg
   Juice of ½ lemon
3 peaches, pitted and sliced
3 sweet-tart apples, such as Rhode Island Greening, Jonathan, or Macoun, cored and sliced

1. Place the water in a small Dutch oven. Bring to a boil. Whisk in the white and brown sugars. Add the cinnamon, nutmeg, and lemon juice.
2. Add the peaches and apples. Bring the sauce to a boil. Reduce the heat. Simmer the sauce until thick and all of the liquid has evaporated, stirring occasionally, 30 to 40 minutes.
3. Transfer the sauce to a bowl. Allow to cool at room temperature. Cover the sauce and refrigerate.

❧ Fresh Fruit Parfait with Tofu Yogurt and Blueberry Sauce

Desserts don't have to be heavy, rich, and calorie-laden to be satisfying. During any season, fresh fruit is an ideal way to end a meal. When fruit is perfectly ripe and presented in a creative manner, the results are memorable. Sweet and juicy cantaloupe and mango combine with tart raspberries in this delectable dessert. A blend of vanilla yogurt and soft tofu adds a velvety texture. A delectable blueberry sauce adds just the right amount of sweetness. This treat is rich in antioxidants and phytoestrogens.

PREPARATION:
15 MINUTES

COOKING:
20 MINUTES

CHILLING:
30 MINUTES

YIELD:
6 SERVINGS

  3 cups fresh or frozen (thawed) blueberries
½ cup sugar
  3 tablespoons water
16 ounces nonfat vanilla yogurt
  6 ounces soft tofu
  4 cups cantaloupe chunks
  3 cups fresh or frozen (thawed) raspberries
  2 cups mango chunks

1. To prepare the blueberry sauce, combine the blueberries, sugar, and water in a saucepan over medium heat. Bring the mixture to a boil. Reduce the heat and simmer the mixture until a thick sauce forms, stirring occasionally, approximately 20 minutes. Allow the sauce to cool.
2. While the sauce is cooling, combine the yogurt and tofu in a blender or the work bowl of a food processor fitted with the metal blade and puree. Transfer the mixture to a bowl and set aside for a moment.
3. To assemble the parfaits, place a layer of cantaloupe chunks on the bottom of a large wineglass or similar shaped glass. Spoon a portion of the yogurt-tofu mixture onto the cantaloupe. Add a layer of raspberries and another layer of yogurt-tofu. Add a final layer of mango. Spoon a portion of the blueberry sauce onto the top. Repeat the assembling 5 times for the remaining parfaits. Serve the parfaits at once.

🍃 Raspberries with Tofu Yogurt and Toasted Pecans

PREPARATION:
10 MINUTES

YIELD:
4 SERVINGS

We are fortunate to have a small plot of raspberry plants in our yard. Through the years, the plants have become extremely productive. When we are faced with an abundance of berries, we try to create simple ways to prepare them that allow their freshness to shine. A slightly sweet blueberry tofu–yogurt sauce and a sprinkling of toasted pecans enhance the natural sweet-tart flavor of the berries. It makes a guilt-free dessert or quick and nutritious snack. The tofu-yogurt sauce is rich in phytoestrogens. The berries provide Vitamin C and the pecans are an excellent source of Vitamin E.

½ cup pecans, coarsely chopped
16 ounces nonfat blueberry yogurt
6 ounces soft tofu
2 tablespoons honey
4 cups fresh or frozen (thawed) raspberries

1. Place the pecans in a small skillet over low heat. Toast until fragrant and no longer raw tasting, shaking the pan occasionally, approximately 10 minutes. Remove the pan from the heat.
2. Combine the yogurt, tofu, and honey in a blender or the work bowl of a food processor fitted with the metal blade and puree. Set the mixture aside for a moment.
3. Divide the raspberries among 4 dessert cups or glasses. Divide the tofu-yogurt sauce among the glasses. Sprinkle each portion with the pecans. Serve at once.

🌿 Apple and Maple Tofu Spoonbread

A spoonbread can either be a healthful dessert or a fat and calorie nightmare. Many recipes call for buttery and eggy bread, a heavy cream-based custard, and far too many egg yolks. Our version uses whole-wheat bread and soy milk; it is enhanced by a filling of sweetened apples and cinnamon-flavored tofu. This delectable and healthful dessert is rich in fiber and phytoestrogens.

PREPARATION:
15 MINUTES

COOKING:
45 MINUTES

YIELD:
8 SERVINGS

TOFU

1 tablespoon canola oil
1 pound extra-firm tofu
3 tablespoons white sugar
2 tablespoons maple syrup
½ teaspoon cinnamon

SPOONBREAD

3 cups vanilla soy milk
½ cup sugar
1 tablespoon vanilla extract
4 eggs
2 teaspoons cinnamon
¼ teaspoon nutmeg
2 teaspoons canola oil
12 ounces country-style whole-wheat bread, cut into
½-inch slices (approximately 6 slices)
2 Granny Smith apples, cored and diced

1. Preheat the oven to 350°F.
2. To prepare the tofu, heat the canola oil in a wok over medium-high heat. Place the tofu on a kitchen towel. With the heel of your hand, gently press on the tofu to remove the excess moisture. Cube the tofu. Toss with 2 tablespoons of the sugar.
3. Carefully place the tofu into the wok. Cook the tofu until the sugar carmelizes, tossing occasionally, approximately 10 minutes.
4. Drizzle the tofu with the maple syrup and cook for another minute. Transfer to a bowl.

5. Combine the remaining tablespoon of sugar and the cin-namon. Sprinkle onto the tofu and toss thoroughly. Mash the tofu with a fork. Set aside for a moment.

6. For the spoonbread, whisk together the soy milk, sugar, vanilla extract, eggs, cinnamon, and nutmeg.

7. Oil a 2-quart loaf pan with the canola oil. Place a layer of bread onto the bottom of the pan. Add half of the apples and half of the tofu. Add another layer of bread and the remaining apples and tofu. Add a final layer of bread.

8. Slowly pour the soy milk mixture into the loaf pan. Set the pan aside for 5 minutes to allow the bread to soak up all of the liquid.

9. Place the pan in the oven. Bake the spoonbread only until it is set, approximately 40 minutes.

10. Remove the pan from the oven. Allow to cool on a wire rack. When cool, slice into 8 portions. If desired, drizzle maple syrup or your favorite fruit sauce onto each portion.

❧❦ Raspberry "Cream"

PREPARATION:
5 MINUTES

CHILLING:
2 HOURS

YIELD:
4 SERVINGS

The most difficult part of this recipe is waiting the 2 hours for the dessert to chill. With a dessert containing so few ingredients, the main ingredient has to be of the highest quality. Frequent a farmers' market for the freshest and sweetest raspberries. This quick and easy dessert is extremely healthful. It contains abundant amounts of Vitamin C and phytoestrogens.

  2 cups fresh raspberries
10 ounces silken tofu
⅓ cup sugar
½ teaspoon vanilla extract

1. Place all of the ingredients into a blender. Process until smooth.

2. Divide the raspberry "cream" among 4 dessert glasses. Cover the glasses with plastic wrap. Refrigerate the dessert for 2 hours.

❧ Raspberry-Poppy Muffins

The majority of store-bought muffins are more like cake than muffins; they are loaded with fat, sugar, and preservatives. Our muffins are far less sweet and more healthful. Their tender crumb and moistness results not from butter but ground flaxseed. They are easy to prepare and freeze well so you can always have one for a quick breakfast or snack. With fresh and dried raspberries and poppy seeds these muffins offer great taste and texture. They are rich in phytoestrogens, folic acid, and Vitamin C.

Tip: *When you combine the wet and dry ingredients in muffins and quick breads, stir the ingredients only enough to moisten them. Overmixing the batter will toughen the final product.*

PREPARATION:
10 MINUTES

COOKING:
25 MINUTES

YIELD:
9 MUFFINS

⅓   cup flaxseed
1¾ cup unbleached all-purpose flour
½   cup sugar
1½ teaspoons baking powder
¼   teaspoon salt
2   eggs
1   teaspoon vanilla extract
1   cup soy milk
1   cup dried raspberries
1   cup fresh raspberries
¼   cup poppy seeds
    Canola oil for greasing muffins tins

1. Preheat the oven to 350°F.
2. Place the flaxseed in a coffee grinder. Pulverize until it resembles flour. Transfer to a large mixing bowl.
3. Add the flour, sugar, baking powder, and salt to the large bowl. Mix the ingredients thoroughly.
4. In another bowl, beat the eggs. Whisk in the vanilla and soy milk.
5. Make a well in the center of the dry ingredients. Pour the wet ingredients into the well. Gently mix the ingredients. Fold in the dried and fresh raspberries and the poppy seeds.
6. Lightly oil a muffin tin. Divide the muffin batter among 9

of the muffin cups. Place the trays into the oven. Bake the muffins until they are cooked through, approximately 25 minutes.

7. Remove from the oven. Allow to cool. With a knife, cut around the perimeter of each muffin and remove from the trays. Serve warm or serve later sliced in half and lightly toasted.

🐦 Lemon-Blueberry Muffins

Everyone loves blueberry muffins. We have added a hint of lemon and cinnamon and a healthy dose of ground flaxseed to a basic muffin recipe and created wonderfully earthy and unique-tasting muffins that will top your favorites list. They are rich in antioxidants and phytoestrogens.

PREPARATION:
10 MINUTES

COOKING:
25 MINUTES

YIELD:
9 MUFFINS

⅓ cup flaxseed
2 cups flour
½ cup sugar
1½ teaspoons baking powder
1 teaspoon cinnamon
¼ teaspoon salt
2 eggs
1 cup soy milk
1 teaspoon vanilla extract
1 tablespoon grated lemon zest
1½ cups fresh or frozen (defrosted) blueberries
Canola oil for greasing muffin tins

1. Preheat the oven to 350°F.
2. Place the flaxseed in a coffee grinder. Pulverize until it resembles flour. Transfer to a large mixing bowl.
3. Add the flour, sugar, baking powder, cinnamon, and salt to the bowl. Mix the ingredients thoroughly.
4. In another bowl, beat the eggs. Whisk in the soy milk, vanilla, and lemon zest.

5. Make a well in the center of the dry ingredients. Pour the wet ingredients into the well. Gently mix the ingredients. Fold in the blueberries.

6. Lightly oil a muffin tin. Divide the muffin batter among 9 of the muffin cups. Place the muffins into the oven. Bake the muffins until cooked through, approximately 25 minutes.

7. Remove from the oven. Allow to cool. With a knife, cut around the perimeter of each muffin and remove from the cups. Serve warm or serve later sliced in half and lightly toasted.

&ℰℓ Linda's Pumpkin Bread

PREPARATION:
10 MINUTES

COOKING:
1 HOUR

YIELD:
2 LOAVES

Our first experiment with pumpkin bread was a disaster. It was undercooked and contained far too much pumpkin. We were not going to make another attempt until our good friend Linda DelVecchio offered us her recipe. For it to be part of a breast cancer preventing diet, we needed to slightly alter the ingredients. We omitted the canola oil and reduced the amount of sugar. We added ground flaxseed and soy milk. This wonderfully moist and healthful treat is rich in phytoestrogens and Vitamin E.

Tip: *After the loaves have cooled, they can be sliced into individual portions. Each piece can then be individually wrapped and frozen.*

> Canola oil for greasing loaf pans
> ½ cup flaxseed
> 3 cups unbleached all-purpose flour
> 1½ cups sugar
> 1 teaspoon cinnamon
> ½ teaspoon nutmeg
> ½ teaspoon allspice
> 2 teaspoons baking soda
> 1 teaspoon baking powder
> 1½ teaspoons salt
> 3 eggs
> 1⅔ cups soy milk
> 1 15-ounce can pumpkin
> 1½ cups raisins
> 1 cup walnuts, coarsely chopped

1. Preheat the oven to 350°F.
2. Lightly oil two 2-quart loaf pans. Set aside for a moment.
3. Place the flaxseed in a coffee grinder. Pulverize until it resembles flour. Transfer to a large mixing bowl.
4. Add the flour, sugar, cinnamon, nutmeg, allspice, baking soda, baking powder, and salt to the bowl. Whisk the ingredients thoroughly.
5. In another bowl, whisk the eggs and soy milk. Whisk in the pumpkin.

6. Make a well in the center of the dry ingredients. Pour the wet ingredients into the well. Gently mix the ingredients. Fold in the raisins and walnuts.

7. Divide the batter among the 2 prepared loaf pans.

8. Transfer the pans to the oven. Bake the breads until a toothpick inserted in the middle comes out clean, approximately 1 hour.

9. Remove from the oven. Allow to cool. Remove the breads from the pans. Slice and serve warm spread with soy cream cheese.

🐝 Banana Bread

When those bananas sitting on your counter are past their prime for peeling and eating, they can either be frozen and used in smoothies or mashed and used in quick breads. Linda DelVecchio passed this old family recipe on to us. By eliminating the oil and adding ground flaxseed and soy milk, we turned it into a delightful breast cancer preventing treat.

PREPARATION:
10 MINUTES

COOKING:
1 HOUR

YIELD:
1 LOAF

Canola oil for greasing a loaf pan
½   cup flaxseed
2   cups unbleached all-purpose flour
1   cup sugar
1   teaspoon baking soda
1   teaspoon baking powder
1   teaspoon salt
3   eggs
1½ cups soy milk
5   very ripe bananas, peeled and mashed
1   cup walnuts, coarsely chopped

1. Preheat the oven to 350°F.

2. Lightly oil a 2-quart loaf pan. Set aside for a moment.

3. Place the flaxseed in a coffee grinder. Pulverize until it resembles flour. Transfer to a large mixing bowl.

4. Add the flour, sugar, baking soda, baking powder, and salt to

the bowl. Whisk the ingredients thoroughly.

5. In another bowl, whisk the eggs and soy milk. Whisk in the bananas.

6. Make a well in the center of the dry ingredients. Pour the wet ingredients into the well. Gently mix the ingredients. Fold in the walnuts.

7. Transfer the batter to the prepared loaf pan.

8. Transfer the pan to the oven. Bake the bread until a toothpick inserted in the middle comes out clean, approximately 1 hour.

9. Remove the bread from the oven. Allow to cool. Remove the bread from the pan. Slice and serve warm spread with soy cream cheese.

❧ Chocolate Chip Cookies

PREPARATION:
10 MINUTES

COOKING:
8 MINUTES

YIELD:
2 DOZEN
COOKIES

It is a challenge to make great cookies without using an abundance of butter and sugar. We tried to make cookies that people will eat without realizing they are eating something that is healthful. We think we may have succeeded. By using ground flaxseed, soybean butter, and roasted soy nuts, we have created cookies that are moist, tasty, and incredibly healthful. They are full of fiber and phytoestrogens and will certainly win over even those with the sweetest of sweet tooths.

6	tablespoons soybean butter
½	cup sugar
½	cup brown sugar
2	eggs
1	teaspoon vanilla extract
⅓	cup flaxseed
1½	cups unbleached, all-purpose flour
2	teaspoons baking soda
¼	teaspoon salt
1	cup chocolate chips
⅓	cup roasted soy nuts

1. Preheat the oven to 350°F.
2. In a large mixing bowl, cream together the soybean butter, sugar, and brown sugar. Beat in the eggs and vanilla. Set the bowl aside for a moment.
3. Place the flaxseed in a coffee grinder. Pulverize until it resembles flour. Transfer to a large bowl.
4. Add the flour, baking soda, and salt to the large bowl. Whisk the ingredients thoroughly. Add to the mixing bowl containing the soybean butter mixture. Combine the ingredients thoroughly.
5. Fold in the chocolate chips and soy nuts. Shape the dough into 1-inch balls. Place the balls onto a cookie sheet 2 inches apart. If necessary, use 2 cookie sheets.
6. Transfer the cookies to the oven. Bake for 7 to 9 minutes. Remove the tray from the oven. Allow the cookies to cool for a minute. With a spatula loosen the cookies from the tray. When completely cool, transfer to a cookie jar.

❧ Oatmeal Raisin Cookies

PREPARATION:
10 MINUTES

COOKING:
10 MINUTES

YIELD:
20 COOKIES

We love oatmeal cookies. Unfortunately, commercially produced ones contain too much butter to be considered a healthful snack. In our recipe we substitute soybean butter for the butter. Although this is not a low fat substitution, the nutritional difference is significant. Butter contains no nutritional value, while soybean butter is an excellent source of phytoestrogens. Once you make these cookies, you will always want to keep a few in your cookie jar.

6 tablespoons soybean butter
⅔ cup sugar
⅓ cup brown sugar
2 eggs
¼ cup soy milk
1 teaspoon vanilla extract
½ cup flaxseed
1¼ cups unbleached, all-purpose flour
1 cup old-fashioned oats
1 teaspoon baking powder
¼ teaspoon salt
1 teaspoon cinnamon
½ teaspoon nutmeg
1½ cups raisins

1. Preheat the oven to 350°F.
2. In a large mixing bowl, cream together the soybean butter, sugar, and brown sugar. Beat in the eggs, soy milk, and vanilla. Set the bowl aside for a moment.
3. Place the flaxseed in a coffee grinder. Pulverize until it resembles flour. Transfer to a large bowl.
4. Add the flour, oats, baking powder, salt, cinnamon, and nutmeg to the bowl of flaxseed. Whisk the ingredients thoroughly. Add to the mixing bowl containing the soybean butter mixture. Combine the ingredients thoroughly.
5. Fold in the raisins. Shape the dough into 1-inch balls. Place them on a cookie sheet 2 inches apart. If necessary, use 2 cookie sheets.

6. Transfer the cookies to the oven. Bake for 7 to 9 minutes. Remove the tray from the oven. Allow the cookies to cool for a minute. With a spatula loosen the cookies from the tray. When they are completely cool, transfer to a cookie jar.

❧ Dried Cranberry, Orange, and Almond Biscotti

Biscotti are low in fat and calories. When prepared with phytoestrogen-rich tofu and flaxseed and Vitamin E-rich almonds, they are a wonderful breast cancer preventing goodie. Since they are baked twice, much of their moisture is removed, so they never go stale and will keep for weeks in an airtight container.

PREPARATION:
15 MINUTES

BAKING AND
COOLING:
1 HOUR,
45 MINUTES

YIELD:
24 BISCOTTI

2 eggs
8 ounces soft tofu
¾ cup sugar
2 teaspoons vanilla extract
2 tablespoons orange zest, finely chopped
½ cup flaxseed
2¾ cup unbleached, all-purpose flour
2 teaspoons baking powder
¼ teaspoon salt
1½ cups dried cranberries
1 cup whole almonds, coarsely chopped
Egg wash made by beating 1 egg with 2 teaspoons water

1. Preheat the oven to 300°F.
2. Lightly grease a large baking sheet.
3. Combine the eggs, tofu, sugar, vanilla, and orange zest in a blender and puree. Set the mixture aside for a moment.
4. Grind the flaxseed in a coffee mill until it resembles flour. Transfer to the bowl of a standup mixer fitted with the paddle attachment.
5. Add the flour, baking powder, and salt to the bowl. Turn the machine on low and mix the ingredients for 30 seconds.

6. With the machine running, gradually add the tofu mixture to the bowl. Add the dried cranberries and almonds. Mix the ingredients only until a dough forms, approximately 45 seconds.

7. Turn the dough out onto a lightly floured surface and knead for 1 minute. Divide the dough in half. Form each half into a log 10 inches long and 3 inches wide, approximately the size of a baguette. Transfer the loaves to the prepared baking sheet, separating them by 3 inches. Brush the loaves with the egg wash.

8. Bake the loaves in the center of the oven for 50 minutes. Remove the tray and place it on a rack for 15 minutes to cool.

9. Transfer the logs to a cutting board. Cut the logs on the diagonal into ¾-inch slices. Place the biscotti back on the tray with the cut side down.

10. Bake the biscotti for 15 minutes. Turn the biscotti over and bake 15 minutes longer. Transfer the biscotti to a rack to cool. Store the cookies in airtight containers.

❧ Raisin and Pecan Rolls

In the past, we prepared our raisin-pecan rolls with a sourdough starter. The process was time consuming, but it was well worth it. The rolls had great flavor and wonderful texture. We wanted to include the recipe here, but we realized not everyone has a sourdough starter in their refrigerator. So we revised the recipe and decreased the production time to 2 hours. Although these rolls don't have the same character as the slow-rising ones, they are still delectable. With plenty of flaxseed and pecans, they are rich in phytoestrogens and Vitamin E.

PREPARATION:
2 HOURS

COOKING:
15 MINUTES

YIELD:
12 ROLLS

   Tip: *This recipe yields 12 rolls but it can easily be doubled. After the rolls have cooled, they can be individually wrapped and frozen.*

1½	cups warm water (105–115°F)
⅓	cup raw sugar
2¼	teaspoons active dry yeast
½	cup flaxseed
3¼	cups unbleached, all-purpose flour, plus additional for dusting
2	teaspoons salt
1	cup raisins
1	cup pecans, coarsely chopped

1. Combine the water and sugar in the bowl of a standup mixer. Add the yeast and stir until dissolved. Allow the yeast to proof for 5 minutes.
2. Pulverize the flaxseed in a coffee grinder until it resembles flour. Transfer to a large mixing bowl. Add the flour and salt. Combine the ingredients thoroughly.
3. Attach the paddle to the mixer. Turn the machine on low. Add half of the flour mixture to the bowl. Beat the ingredients for 2 minutes.
4. Add the raisins and pecans. Add the remaining flour mixture to the bowl. Beat the mixture for 2 minutes more.

5. Replace the paddle with the dough hook. Turn the machine on medium and knead the dough for 8 minutes more.

6. Transfer the dough to a clean bowl. Cover tightly with plastic wrap. Allow the dough to rise until doubled in size, approximately 1 ½ hours.

7. Preheat the oven to 400°F.

8. Form the risen dough into a ball. Divide the ball into 12 pieces. Sprinkle a heavy baking sheet with cornmeal. Transfer each piece to the baking sheet. Cover the baking sheet with plastic. Allow the dough to rest for 30 minutes.

9. Dust the rolls with flour. Place the tray in the oven. Bake the rolls until golden and crisp, approximately 15 minutes.

10. Transfer to a wire rack to cool.

❧ Olive Rolls

Raisin-pecan rolls and olive rolls are two of our favorite goodies to purchase from bakeries. Without a steam-injected oven, it is difficult to create rolls like these at home. However, with careful attention to the consistency of the dough and a couple of simple techniques, you can produce great rolls in your kitchen. Although most bakeries don't add ground flaxseed to their rolls, it provides moistness, a pleasing earthy taste, and plenty of fiber and phytoestrogens.

Tip: *This dough should be wet and sticky. Add a minimal amount of flour when cutting and shaping the rolls.*

PREPARATION:
2 HOURS

COOKING:
15 MINUTES

YIELD:
12 ROLLS

1½ cups warm water (105–115°F)
2¼ teaspoons active dry yeast
½ cup flaxseed
3 cups unbleached, all-purpose flour, plus additional for dusting
2 teaspoons sea salt
1 tablespoon olive oil
1½ cups Kalamata olives, pitted and coarsely chopped

1. Place the water in the bowl of a standup mixer. Add the yeast and stir until dissolved. Allow the yeast to rest for 5 minutes.
2. Pulverize the flaxseed in a coffee grinder until it resembles flour. Transfer to a large mixing bowl. Add the flour and salt. Combine the ingredients thoroughly.
3. Stir the olive oil into the yeast mixture.
4. Attach the paddle to the mixer. Turn the machine on low. Add half of the flour mixture to the bowl. Beat the ingredients for 2 minutes.
5. Add the olives. Add the remaining flour mixture to the bowl. Beat the mixture for 2 minutes more.
6. Replace the paddle with the dough hook. Turn the machine on medium and knead the dough for 8 minutes more.
7. Transfer the dough to a clean bowl. Cover tightly with plastic wrap. Allow the dough to rise until doubled in size, approximately 1½ hours.
8. Preheat the oven to 400°F.

9. Form the risen dough into a ball. Divide the ball into 10 pieces. Sprinkle a heavy baking sheet with cornmeal. Transfer each piece to the baking sheet. Cover the baking sheet with plastic. Allow the dough to rest for 30 minutes. Remove the plastic.

10. Dust the rolls with flour. Place the tray in the oven. Bake the rolls until golden and crisp, approximately 15 minutes.

11. Transfer to a wire rack to cool.

🌿 Blueberry Granita

Blueberries are the fruit richest in antioxidants. We enjoy creating interesting ways to introduce this superfood into our diets. Besides the obvious quick breads and crumbles that can be prepared, we also enjoy them in frozen concoctions. Granitas are the easiest, most refreshing, and healthful of the frozen desserts. Prepared with little more than sugar, water, and fruit, they can be made in an ice-cream maker in 15 minutes. If you don't have an ice-cream maker, they can be made in a large bowl in your freezer. Simply place the bowl of granita in your freezer and stir it every 30 minutes to prevent large chunks of ice from forming. Remove the granita from the freezer and scoop it into bowls.

Tip: *Leftover granita can be refrozen. To return it to its original texture, first allow it to thaw slightly at room temperature. Then rake through it with a fork or pulse it in a food processor.*

PREPARATION:
20 MINUTES

FREEZING:
2 HOURS

YIELD:
6 SERVINGS

¾ cup sugar
½ cup water
5 cups fresh or frozen and defrosted wild or cultivated blueberries
1 tablespoon fresh lemon juice

1. Combine the sugar and water in a small saucepan over low heat. Heat the mixture until the sugar is dissolved, stirring occasionally, approximately 5 minutes. Refrigerate until cool.
2. Combine the blueberries and lemon juice in the work bowl of a food processor fitted with the metal blade and puree. Transfer to a large bowl.
3. Stir in the sugar water. Transfer the mixture to an ice-cream maker. Turn the machine on and process the granita until slushy, approximately 15 minutes.
4. Divide the granita among 6 dessert bowls and serve at once.

🐾 Rocky Road Ice "Cream"

PREPARATION:
15 MINUTES

PROCESSING:
30 MINUTES

FREEZING:
12 HOURS

YIELD:
1 QUART

This is the dessert to choose when you feel like indulging, but still want to enhance your diet with soy. Decadent and rich, this soy milk–based frozen treat will have you believing you are eating an ice cream loaded with cream and egg yolks. With 3 cups of soy milk, 12 ounces of soft tofu, and a cup of soy nuts, it is a great source of phytoestrogens. Try it next time you have a craving for something intensely chocolate.

*   **Tip:** The recipe can be prepared through step 6 a day in advance. Cover the bowl tightly and refrigerate it.*

6 ounces semisweet chocolate, finely chopped
3 cups plain soy milk
2 egg yolks
½ cup sugar
2 teaspoons vanilla extract
12 ounces soft tofu
2 cups small marshmallows
1 cup unsalted roasted soy nuts

1. Combine the chocolate and soy milk in a medium saucepan over medium-low heat. Cook the mixture until the chocolate melts, stirring often, approximately 6 minutes. Reduce the heat to low.
2. While the chocolate is melting, combine the egg yolks, sugar, and vanilla in a mixing bowl. Whisk the ingredients until pale yellow and smooth, approximately 2 minutes.
3. Add 5 tablespoons of the warm chocolate mixture to the egg yolk mixture and whisk thoroughly.
4. Gradually whisk the egg yolk mixture into the warm chocolate mixture. Thoroughly whisk the mixture.
5. Cook the mixture over low heat until it begins to thicken, whisking occasionally, approximately 6 minutes.
6. Transfer the mixture to a large bowl and allow to cool completely.
7. When the mixture is cool transfer to a blender or food processor fitted with the metal blade. Add the tofu and puree the ingredients.

8. Transfer the mixture to an ice-cream maker and follow the manufacturer's instructions.
9. During the last minute of processing, add the marshmallows and soy nuts.
10. Transfer the ice cream to an airtight container and freeze until firm, approximately 12 hours.

❧ Orange-Mango Ice "Cream"

Whether used in a smoothie, salsa, sauce, or ice cream, mangoes and oranges are a delightful flavor combination. The acidity of the orange tempers the sweetness of the mango. As with our Rocky Road Ice "Cream," this recipe is based on soy milk and soft tofu, making it creamy and rich in phytoestrogens. The mango and orange juice concentrate provide an abundance of antioxidants.

Tip: *Be certain that you puree the ingredients thoroughly. If the puree is at all chunky, the finished product will be granular.*

PREPARATION:
15 MINUTES

PROCESSING:
30 MINUTES

FREEZING:
12 HOURS

YIELD:
1 QUART

2½ cups soy milk
1 vanilla bean, split in half lengthwise
3 egg yolks
¾ cup sugar
1 tablespoon vanilla extract
12 ounces soft tofu
1 very ripe mango, peeled, pitted, and chopped
2 tablespoons orange juice concentrate

1. Place the soy milk and vanilla bean in a medium saucepan over medium-low heat. Heat the mixture until it almost boils, stirring occasionally, approximately 5 minutes. Reduce the heat to low.
2. While the soy milk is heating, combine the egg yolks, sugar, and vanilla in a mixing bowl. Whisk the ingredients until pale yellow and smooth, approximately 2 minutes.

3. Add 5 tablespoons of the warm soy milk mixture to the egg yolk mixture and whisk thoroughly.
4. Gradually whisk the egg yolk mixture into the warm soy milk mixture. Thoroughly whisk the mixture.
5. Cook the mixture over low heat until it begins to thicken, whisking occasionally, approximately 6 minutes.
6. Transfer the mixture to a large bowl and allow to cool completely.
7. When the mixture is cool transfer to a blender or food processor fitted with the metal blade. Add the tofu, mango, and orange juice concentrate and puree. Transfer the mixture to an ice-cream maker and follow the manufacturer's instructions.
8. Transfer the ice "cream" to an airtight container and freeze until firm, approximately 12 hours.

Index

Page numbers in **bold type** refer to recipes.